Fine Homebuilding®
on
Baths and Kitchens

Fine Homebuilding®
on
Baths and Kitchens

The Taunton Press

Cover photo by Sandor Nagyszalanczy

First printing: August 1990
International Standard Book Number: 0-942391-58-6
Library of Congress Catalog Card Number: 89-40581
Printed in the United States of America

A FINE HOMEBUILDING Book

FINE HOMEBUILDING is a trademark of The Taunton Press, Inc.,
registered in the U.S. Patent and Trademark Office.

The Taunton Press, Inc.
63 South Main Street
Box 5506
Newtown, Connecticut 06470-5506
U.S.A.

CONTENTS

I N T R O D U C T I O N

Of all the rooms in a house that are remodeled, kitchens and baths get the most attention. One reason is that these two rooms get the most wear and can look dingy, even when the rest of the house appears to be in good shape. Another reason is that cooking and washing are intimate activities, and people feel better when they create personalized spaces for doing these things.

This book contains 30 articles from back issues of *Fine Homebuilding** magazine. Many of the articles focus on design ideas, while others provide detailed information on such topics as the fundamentals of setting tile, installing supply and drain lines, building kitchen cabinets, making countertops and laying sheet-vinyl flooring, to name a few. So if you're looking for inspiration or if you need practical, hands-on instruction, you'll like this book.

—John Lively, editor

*The six volumes in the *Fine Homebuilding* on... series are taken from *Fine Homebuilding* magazine numbers 1 through 55, 1981 through mid-1989. A footnote with each article tells when it was originally published. Product availability, suppliers' addresses, and prices may have changed since then.

The other five titles in the *Fine Homebuilding* on... series are *Builder's Tools; Frame Carpentry; Floors, Walls and Stairs; Foundations and Masonry;* and *Doors and Windows*. These books are abridgements of the hardcover *Fine Homebuilding* Builder's Library.

Designing a Functional Kitchen

Planning around your family's lifestyle and work habits will get you beyond standard solutions

by Sam Clark

The key to kitchen design is movement—how people move through the house; how supplies, tools and foods are moved in the kitchen itself; and how people use their arms, legs, eyes and hands as they prepare meals and clean up afterwards. A small, simple kitchen designed in harmony with this movement will be a more inviting and efficient place to work in than the most lavishly equipped showplace laid out with standard formulas and stock cabinets.

Siting—Begin with how the cooking area will fit into the house. Siting the kitchen in the house is as important as siting a house on the land. No interior design can compensate for a lack of light and air; so the first step is often to take down walls, add windows or move the kitchen to a brighter part of the house.

Remodeling a kitchen often means reorganizing the house plan (drawing facing page, bottom). Consider the chief activities of your home, such as cooking, eating, visiting, entertaining, sleeping, studying, playing, listening to music, cleaning, reading, coming in and going out. Your kitchen design to a large extent will determine how these activities mesh.

In some cases the best relationship between two activities or spaces is the same for most households. A kitchen entry near the garage, for example, is always ideal. Indoors, the dining table should be near the cooking area.

But on many questions, family needs will differ. The dining area is a good example. If your entertaining tends to be informal, you might want the dining table to be in the kitchen or open to it. Guests can help cook, and the cleanup crew need not be excluded from after-dinner conversation. On the other hand, you may prefer a separate and more formal dining room. It isolates the cook, but it also isolates kitchen mess. The same considerations apply when you decide whether to include a conversational sitting area in the kitchen.

Decorating magazines often recommend a kitchen play area for families with small children, but segregating the play area would be much better for many families. Similarly, the stereo, the laundry, a homework and hobby area, or a TV might either fit well in your kitchen or disrupt it. In general, a more open and inclusive layout works best when the family is small or relatively well disciplined, and when there is a quiet den to retreat to.

Siting and layout have a more telling effect on how pleasant and functional the kitchen will be than any decorating you might do. If your funds are short, spend first on the layout, and be stingy with the cabinets, appliances and fixtures. You can always upgrade the equipment later.

Three principles regulate the internal design of the kitchen work area, or indeed any work place: storage at the point of first use, grouping counter space and equipment into work centers, and ordering these centers according to work sequences.

Storage—Most people store things by category. The beans are stored with the flour because both go in canisters. Corned-beef hash and chicken noodle soup go together in a larder because they come in cans. In an efficient plan, though, foods and equipment should be stored where they will be used first. You rinse dried beans and dilute canned soup, so both should be stored near the sink. Flour is usually scooped dry right into a large mixing bowl, so it should be kept near the bowls. The canned hash goes straight into a skillet—store it at the stove. Think the same way about utensils. Saucepans are usually filled with water first, so they might well be stored at the sink. Griddles belong near the stove.

Many items, such as knives, can openers, mixing bowls, cooking oil, and salt and pepper, are used at two or three different stations. It makes sense to store them in several small stashes rather than in one central spot.

Work centers—Since different kinds of kitchen work call for different tools, supplies and work surfaces, the kitchen should be divided into distinct work centers, set up to make the basic jobs as convenient as possible. Though the centers have been defined many ways, I find it most useful to picture three basic centers: the *cleanup center* at the sink, the *mix center,* and the *cooking center* at the stove.

The *cleanup center* ( ) is for dishwashing and for cooking tasks that require water. Its focus is the sink, which should have about 2 ft. of counter on the dirty-dish side (a good place for this is an inside corner where two counters meet) and at least 20 in. of counter on the clean-dish side. It also needs either a built-in dishwasher (24 in. wide and 34½ in. high) under the counter, or a large dish drainer, which can be built in above the sink. A trash can should be nearby. All the soaps, pot-scrubbers and sponges you use for washing dishes are kept here. A set of drawers or wire bins for potatoes, onions and other non-refrigerated produce is nice if there's room.

Though tableware is often stored in a separate serving center, dishes you use every day really belong near the sink. The chore of putting clean dishes and pots away in cupboards and drawers all over the kitchen is archaic and unnecessary. If you have a dishwasher, build racks or shelves for clean dishes within arm's reach. If you wash by hand, a draining dishrack built above or to one side of the sink can be designed to hold most of the daily dishes and basic bowls and saucepans. This will give you a place to put rinsed dishes away wet, eliminating the need to dry or drain them first. Given this arrangement, washing dishes by hand will take about the same effort as loading and unloading the dishwasher, so you may decide to do without a dishwasher and use its space beneath for storage.

The *mix center* (B) is the place where ingredients are combined. Think of the mix center as your main work surface. It should be roughly 3 ft. to 5 ft. long. Bowls, whips and whisks, electric mixers and blenders, measuring tools, baking dishes, spices, shortening, oil, baking powder and grains are among the items properly stored here.

The *cooking center* (C) is the third major work area. It encompasses the stove, and attendent utensils—griddles, skillets, spatulas, hot pads. The cooking center also needs a work surface and a heatproof area to set down hot dishes. It's the place to store oil, some spices and the foods that go straight onto the burners or into the oven. You will probably need additional counter space here, either all on one side of the stove or in sections on each side. Often the cooking center is expanded to create a second large work area for preparing big meals and to make space for a second cook to work. I like a large butcher block here, and perhaps a compost drawer (photo p. 11, top) for easy cleanup.

Sometimes a large counter between the sink and stove, equipped with portable trivets and cutting boards, can serve as a combined mix and cooking center. This is an excellent plan for one orderly cook or for tight layouts, as long as a kitchen table or sink counter can be requisitioned when you need extra space.

Many books and magazine articles assign the refrigerator to the mix center. This gives

From *Fine Homebuilding* magazine (April 1983) 14:54-57

A

Three work centers. The cleanup center (A) is at the sink. It includes either a dishwasher or a large dish drainer over the sink, as shown. Foods and tools used first at the sink are stored in the cleanup center. The mix center (B) is a counter where recipes are usually put together. Often it is next to the refrigerator. Mixing utensils and staple ingredients belong here. Open shelving makes it easy to locate what you need. The mainstay of the cooking center (C) is the stove. Frying pans are kept here, along with the food that goes directly into them. In the photo below, the pots and pans hang from an overhead rack. All of the kitchen centers have accessible storage areas.

C

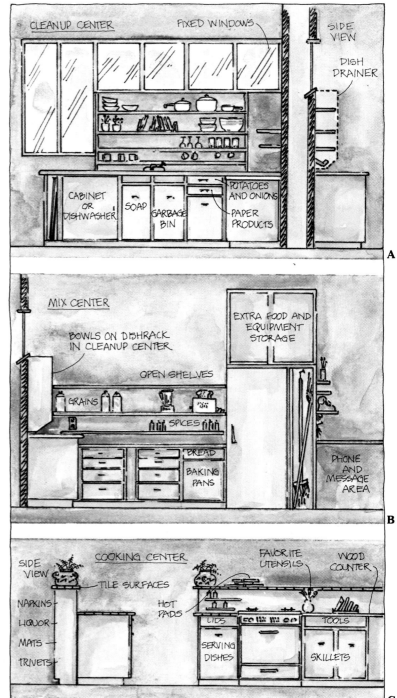

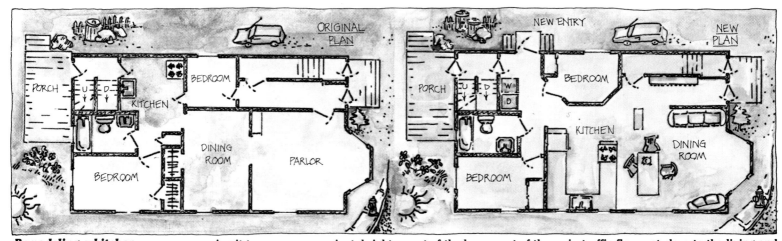

Remodeling a kitchen may mean moving it to a more convenient, brighter part of the house, out of the main traffic flow, yet close to the living and dining areas. In the original plan, left, the kitchen is far from the dining room, in a dark, cramped corridor between the entry and the rest of the house. In the new plan, right, a well-lit kitchen with ample counters is open to the dining and living spaces; and a new entry simplifies the path in and out.

Photos: Wendy Page; Illustrations: Barbara Smolover

the kitchen layout a nice symmetry: three centers, each with its own major appliance. But functionally, the refrigerator—along with a 12-in. or 18-in. counter on its handle side to make loading and unloading convenient—can be separate as long as it is not too far from the work stations. Treating the refrigerator as a fourth layout component gives you much greater flexibility because it multiplies the possible configurations.

If space allows, two small additional centers may be useful. A *serving center*, located on the table side of the stove, can hold serving bowls and spoons, napkins, tablecloths, or place-mats, trivets and the like. Heatproof counters are handy here. Mounted on casters, a serving center can double as a serving cart. A *planning center* with a desk, cookbooks, a phone, a message board, pencils and mail slots is also nice to have if a small spot at the edge of the work area is available.

You'll also need spaces at the work centers for small appliances, bread, snacks, a radio, coffee and tea, and liquor. Sometimes subcategories of this kind are elaborated into additional centers such as a bar, a hobby center, a canning center, a recycling center, a snack center and so on, making the kitchen needlessly large and destroying its efficiency. I think it's best to keep things simple. Stick with the basic centers, and use special drawers, shelves or racks as subcenters.

Work sequences—When possible, arrange the work centers to correspond to logical work sequences. The drawings below show the travel path for preparing a cooked vegetable in two different layouts. In the one on the left, the path is short and logical from the back door to the table. In the one on the right, it is not. No sequence will work perfectly for all types of kitchen work, but a good order to strive for might go thus: from back door to refrigerator to sink center to mix center to cooking center to table.

Layout methods—Many books and articles on kitchen planning suggest arriving at a design by collecting "kitchen ideas" the way kids collect baseball cards; eventually you have a complete set. I like a different approach. Get a notebook, put a comfortable

chair in a corner of your current kitchen, and watch what happens. Observe who does which jobs. Identify which tasks seem simple and straightforward, and which clumsy and time-consuming. Notice when people rub their backs in pain, when they reach comfortably, where collisions occur. Determine which jobs now require extra steps, and which can be completed with just a few. Kitchen researchers used to compare layouts by listing or photographing every reach, bend, search and step. Without going to the lengths they did, you can use careful observation to evolve your new or improved kitchen.

Based on these observations and your other ideas, write a program—a list of your design goals. It should include the ways you want your new kitchen to be different from your present one. Here's an example.

Cooking area: more storage; space for two cooks at once; space for freezer; direct access to yard and car.

Desired special features: very sunny; spacious feeling; family encouraged to help out; guest and cooks not isolated—guests help out.

Activities to be included in kitchen: phone; meal planning; laundry; canning; desk.

Things to be excluded: street noise; TV noise; formal visiting (separate parlor desired); older children's noisy play.

Dining: all meals in kitchen; seating for five daily, up to ten maximum with guests; dine on south wall, overlooking garden; no view of street from table.

Cost: money, $6,500 max.; time, ten weekends at ten hours of work each, or 100 hours.

Disruption: No more than a month of living in dust, but up to three months with some details incomplete.

Next, begin drawing possible layouts, locating the kitchen within the home, and the work centers within the kitchen. Include all areas inside and out that may be involved or related to the design. Beware of the standard U, L, galley, island, and peninsular layouts you see in all the kitchen books and decorating magazines. These conventions were devised over 30 years ago as guidelines for evaluating kitchens in mass-produced housing. They usually result in decent, general-purpose designs, and you can learn from them. Just don't be bound by them. In remodeling, for ex-

ample, trying to achieve a standard U or L could force you to move walls, stairs, doorways or plumbing that could just as well stay in place.

Beware also of the well-known triangle rule. The work triangle was developed around 1950 at the University of Illinois as a test for layouts in tract housing. According to the studies done there, the distances between the three

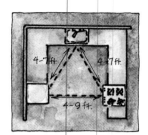

major appliances (the sink, stove and refrigerator) should be within the limits shown at left. If they are longer, the cook will take unnecessary steps. If they are shorter, the kitchen will be congested, and the work areas too small. Many people base their kitchen layout entirely on this idea. I think that intelligent storage and well-thought-out work centers are much more important.

Although standard design conventions are helpful rules of thumb, they shouldn't be followed slavishly. Draw your possible layouts as freely, playfully and loosely as you can.

Evaluating layouts—Evaluate your plans by comparing each with your design program and with the notes you made during observation. Fasten push-pins at the main stations of your plans, then wind yarn from point to point as you imagine performing various cooking and cleanup sequences. The length of yarn you use gives you a scaled measurement of the hypothetical distances traveled, so you can check the efficiency of each design for a given task.

Designing work centers—Design the work centers by making a series of elevation drawings in the same scale you used for the plans. Refer again to your initial program and to the notes you made during your observations. This is where the principle of storage at the point of first use comes into play. The design of the centers should reflect the specific ways in which each will be used. First plan the work surface itself. Most kitchen designs force us to work standing up, assembly-line style. If there's room, plan one or two places where a tired or meditative cook can work sitting down. An old-fashioned kitchen table, for example, isn't just a spot for informal meals. It also lets two or three people work sitting down and facing each other instead of staring at the wall.

In each area, find the counter height that leaves your back straight and your arms comfortable while you work. Have someone measure from your elbow to the floor while you stand straight with your upper arm vertical and forearm horizontal. For most people, a counter two or three inches below this point will be just about right for washing dishes, making sandwiches, and for most cooking activities. For kneading bread, rolling out dough, mixing heavy batters, or working with

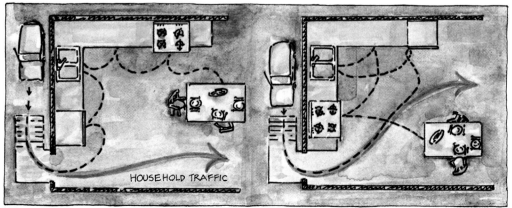

Planning for efficiency. **Both of these layouts look fine until you trace the travel paths for a typical kitchen task. Then the superiority of the arrangement on the left becomes evident.**

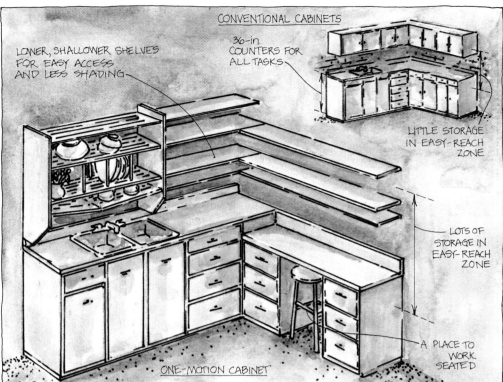

CONVENTIONAL CABINETS

LOWER, SHALLOWER SHELVES FOR EASY ACCESS AND LESS SHADING

36-in. COUNTERS FOR ALL TASKS

LITTLE STORAGE IN EASY-REACH ZONE

LOTS OF STORAGE IN EASY-REACH ZONE

A PLACE TO WORK SEATED

ONE-MOTION CABINET

Sensible counters and cabinets are built for convenience. Storage is designed for specific contents, counter height is tailored to the task, and drawers make it easy to retrieve things. Most of the storage space in standard cabinets is hard to reach. All counters are the same height, and there are no special accessories like the composting drawer and the knife slot in the photos at left.

long-handled tools, the counter should probably be 6 in. to 7 in. below the elbow, especially if you bake regularly. This will leave the stove and sink counters a few inches higher than the mix-center counter.

Consider your counter surfaces carefully. Raw or oiled wood is good for chopping vegetables, but not for chopping raw meats (because of potential bacterial contamination). Tile will resist heat at the stove. Plastic laminate, polyurethaned wood and other non-porous surfaces are convenient at the mix and sink centers. Remember that you can always use trivets or cutting boards on top of a counter that won't stand up to heat or chopping. Just make sure that the sink counter won't be damaged by water.

Next, plan storage. If the first rule of work-center design is storage at the point of first use, the second is to give prime locations to items used most often. While it's nice to have all your bowls handy, it is essential to have your favorite one or two immediately at hand. Arrange things so that these everyday items can be put away and retrieved without wasted movement. Items you use constantly should be available with a single motion if possible.

A knife slot at the back of the counter (photo above left) is a good example of one-motion storage. The reach is short, there are no doors or drawers to open, and the knives, at hand height, are accessible without your having to stoop or stretch. The rack is fully visible, and selection is easy. The knives are handle up, so that you can grasp the one you want with the grip required for its use.

Remember that all storage isn't equal. Some spots are harder to get at than others. Any-

thing above 20 in. and below 60 in. (roughly between the knees and the shoulders) can be reached comfortably. The drainer, the knife rack, open shelves at or a little below eye level, and other racks just above counter height are one-motion locations. The bottom shelves of enclosed overhead cabinets and the top one or two drawers below the counter are almost as handy. You have to open something, but there's no bending or stretching. Lower drawers and higher shelves are accessible, but you have to stoop or reach to get at them. The top shelf and bottom drawers, which are outside the 20-in. to 60-in. field, are quite inconvenient. The worst spot of all is on fixed shelves behind doors in base cabinets, because finding something there inevitably requires a lot of shifting of the stored items and fumbling in the dark.

The drawing above contrasts standard and functional kitchen storage. In conventional kitchens, the best storage spot—the back of the counter—is the one place no storage is provided. Overhead cabinets usually start about 54 in. above the floor, which is at the top of the area easily reached by the average person. A typical base cabinet has one good storage spot, the top drawer. Most of its contents are buried in the deep fixed shelves.

A more functional model might look something like the one-motion cabinet in the drawing above. It would have narrow open shelves at the back of the counter, perhaps up to head height, or racks designed for specific contents. Almost everything below counter height would be in drawers, on rolling shelves, or on racks mounted to the inside of cabinet doors. This was the model developed by the Cornell

Kitchen, the most advanced and also the most ignored of the 1950s research kitchens.

Locate the most used items first. Then find storage for the items used regularly but not constantly. Finally, deal with the turkey pan, waffle iron and other infrequently used items.

A good test of the designs you draw in elevation is to imagine performing work sequences, movement by movement. Picture each reach, step or grasp, each opening or closing of a door or drawer. Think where your hand will be at the exact moment you need a tool—this is the ideal storage location. These imaginary movies are analogous to the string diagrams you performed on your layouts.

A kitchen designed in this way does not just save time; it changes what it feels like to work in the kitchen. Your movements as you cook become more economical, deft and sure. Work bounces and jerks less, and flows more. Because cooking becomes more artful and graceful, the work becomes a pleasure in itself.

The kitchen you design this way may look odd. It will probably have fewer doors than other kitchens, and more drawers. It will have more racks, bins, and other special storage setups. The various counter heights may give it a less streamlined look. However, it will cost less, because it will have been designed for function, not show. Perhaps most important, it will have been designed for the way people move through your house, and the way you and your family cook and clean up, so it will work better for you. □

Sam Clark is a carpenter and author. His book, Rethinking the Kitchen, *will be published in the fall of 1983 by Houghton Mifflin.*

Custom Kitchen Planning

A designer's thoughts on renovating the home's most complex room

by Matthew Kaplan

The kitchen is the most difficult room to design. No other area contains such a crush of objects—from cereal boxes to sinks—and such a stew of human activities. Deciding which objects must be accommodated is one of the first steps in kitchen planning. At the same time, refrigerators, ovens and other mechanical helpers should not encroach on the largest and most important spaces, which belong to the people who cook, work and dine there. Planning a kitchen renovation to meet their needs means that both construction options and personal preferences must be recorded, organized and integrated.

Before I begin designing a kitchen, I interview the owners to find out what they will need. Their old kitchen is thoroughly analyzed and often reveals characteristics that can be useful in the new design, such as hobbies, collections of plants, or small dining areas. The most important element in developing a custom-tailored room is a detailed, written description of the owner's ideal kitchen. Obviously, later on compromises will be made for lack of money or lack of space, but I have found it better to modify, revise or even eliminate features than to add on in the latter stages of planning.

The kitchen form—As an aid in developing a written description, I ask my clients to fill out a kitchen form similar to the one shown on the right. It is organized from the general to the par-

---

THE KITCHEN FORM

Use of space—Describe in detail all functions.

Sewing/ironing/	Desk
laundry	Play area
Bar/dining-room	Other

Major appliances—Makes and models to be chosen during preliminary design phase. Underline those you would include.

Range	Dishwasher
commercial-features	trim panel
residential-features	Sink
Ovens	number of
double or single	compartments
gas or electric	faucet action
venting required	spray, pop-up drain
self-cleaning	soap dispenser
color, size	chopping board
doors - glass vs. solid	garbage disposal
Cooktop	Grill
gas	Freezer
electric	Compactor
commercial	Washing machine
residential	location
Refrigerator/freezer	front or top loading
ice maker	Dryer
color, size	gas
side by side	electric
top or bottom freezer	
trim kit	

Small appliances—Those you own or plan to purchase. Will they be displayed or concealed?

Toaster	Electric knife
built-in	chargeable
portable	nonchargeable
Toaster oven	Can opener
Coffee maker	electric
Coffee grinder	manual
Mixer	drawer-mounted
Food grinder	wall-mounted
Blender	T.V.
Ice crusher	Radio
Yogurt maker	In-counter motor for
Scale	combination
Ice-cream maker	appliances
Deep fryer	Other

Storage types—Concealed or displayed.

Foods	Canisters for staples
stored in quantity	Spices
and used daily	location
packaged, canned,	Paper goods
jars, bottles	Tea, coffee
Bread	Wine, liquor, aperitif
storage location-	Pots, pans
special drawer	Fondue set
Potatoes and onions	Glassware and dishes
type of storage	

Decorative

Wall	Stained glass
applied fabric	Plants
graphics	

Other considerations

Intercom	New doors and
Smoke detector	windows
Burglar alarm	Air conditioning
Fire extinguisher	Lighting

---

ticular, from the description of functions to the housing of kitchen equipment and supplies.

Use of space. If the kitchen is complex, it is also the most versatile space in the house, and you can't spend too much time discussing use. It is used for cooking and dining in traditional ways, for kibitzing over coffee with neighbors, and even for paying bills and doing homework. If there are young children, incidentally, now is the time to take their presence into account so that you can design tamper-proof storage areas and safe play areas.

Major appliances. Consider large appliances next because, after spaces for people, these take up the most room. Many people decide to buy new appliances when renovating kitchens. Although the information about types, sizes and special features is not crucial in the early stages of planning, it's important to order appliances as soon as possible. By setting up delivery dates about two months before the anticipated completion of the project, you may avoid price increases and you'll expedite construction. If an incorrect model is sent, it can be returned at once and little harm will be done. If you are planning to include custom cabinet work, the cabinetmaker can ascertain exact sizes and note the location of appliance seams that might affect cabinet detailing. Electricians and plumbers can determine in advance what connections will be necessary. The disadvantages of ordering appli-

Within this 15-ft. by 15-ft. kitchen there is an informal dining area, an island counter, the usual battery of appliances, a pastry counter and a wine vault housing 1,000 bottles.

This kitchen was designed so that two cooks could work there simultaneously. All the details—from appliance choices to activities—were discussed before plans were drawn.

Photos: Mark Jenkinson

Above, cleft slate was used for the countertop (left) because of its beauty and durability. Although it is expensive and heavy, hot pots cannot damage it. Two maple cutting boards were recessed in the slate. Under-counter drawer space was designed to accommodate the owners' needs. Floor-to-ceiling pantry and cabinet (right) was designed to accommodate all sizes of pots and pans.

Cabinets and Countertops

Cabinet design requires a bit of head-scratching. For the kitchen shown on these pages the clients wanted a tone of warmth and elegance. The cherry gave the warmth; the molding, the elegance.

Once we had decided upon the molding profile shown below, I thought about joinery. I had intended to mill the profile into the rails and stiles, joining the corners with a mortise-and-tenon joint and coping the ends of the rails to the profile of the stiles, giving a good fit with lots of gluing surface. But a molding so ornate made coping impossible. I decided to join the stile and rail with a spline joint, and add the door molding afterwards.

After several hundred feet of cherry molding

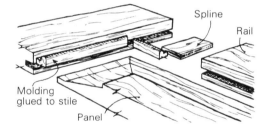

Spline

Rail

Molding glued to stile

Panel

had been milled to my specifications, I realized that it would dwarf the panels. After many experiments, I decided to cut down the molding, using just the curl. I think it works—a little spicy, but light-handed.

The slate countertops are held in place by gravity. I ran a bead of silicone on the top of the ¾-in. plywood frame and used black silicone between slate edges, but otherwise used no hardware—no L-braces or joining plates—to attach slate to wood. Although the top of the slate is cleft and quite irregular, the bottom is finely cut and perfectly flat.

Cooking surfaces built into wooden cabinets can be problematic and dangerous because extreme changes in temperature or moisture are hard on wood. To isolate the cooktop's intense heat, I lined its opening in the cabinet with Transite insulation board and then fitted a specially fabricated stainless-steel liner. Because this insulation board has asbestos fibers, cutting it with a saw will put these fibers into the air and your lungs. Instead of cutting, I suggest wetting and scoring it repeatedly with a utility knife until you can snap it easily. □

—Peter Dechar, a cabinetmaker in Brooklyn, N.Y.

ances early are the possibility of theft if no one lives in the building, or that they'll be in the way during construction.

Selections of major appliances are influenced by how the owner will use the appliance, performance of the appliance, size and capacities needed, gas or electric hookups, optional accessories wanted and durability. The choices are narrowed down until they coincide with the space available, the location of utility lines and the kinds of finished surfaces planned for the completed kitchen. Here are some points to consider in deciding on appliances:

Commercial ranges are expensive and take up too much space; their purchase is unjustified for most households. Domestic ranges are the best bet, especially easy-to-clean models with trim that overlaps the countertop.

Double ovens allow for simultaneous preparation of dishes that require different cooking temperatures. The height of the double ovens is flexible; I like to position the top one so that its open door will align with the countertop. This allows for the easy transfer of hot dishes.

Cooktops are often used in conjunction with double ovens. I recommend cooktops 30 in. long because they consume little counter space and their shallow depth allows more drawer space underneath. The standard height of cooktops is about 36 in., but I place them slightly lower, from 32 in. to 34 in. This height allows easier stirring and a better view into deep pots. Because many cooktop dishes need short cooking times and high temperatures, I favor gas cooktops over electric. Either type should have removable trays under each burner and removable tops for easier cleaning.

A dishwasher with the fewest buttons is the best choice. Not only will it be less expensive, but most of the buttons on complex models are seldom used anyway.

Sink styles are nearly infinite, and selection depends upon the cook's preferences. Heavy-duty sinks are worth the extra money. Stainless-steel sinks pair nicely with plastic laminate counters, and synthetic stone sinks work well with slate, granite or marble counters. Sink height depends on the height of the principal cook; best in general is the 32-in. to 34-in. height I recommend for cooktops. A lever-type faucet is

handy because you can turn it with your wrist if your hands are dirty. Pop-up drains obviate having to fish in hot, greasy water for drain plugs.

Washers and dryers stacked vertically conserve space, an advantage in small rooms; side-by-side machines under counters also create unobtrusive laundry areas.

Small appliances and storage. After locating major appliances and cabinets, think about any special equipment you'd like to have close at hand. It's useful to know if an extensive collection of small appliances will require additional outlets or if a blender needs an in-counter motor. Some people are crazy about their spices and like to display them in special racks. Others want to have such staples as potatoes and onions close at hand. These specifics are important once work begins on preliminary drawings, because the counter space must accommodate all the equipment and supplies that will be used there.

Lighting. Make sure that working surfaces are broadly illuminated. Although I prefer the warm light of incandescent bulbs, newly developed warm-white fluorescent tubes are worth considering. They use less electricity, burn cooler and

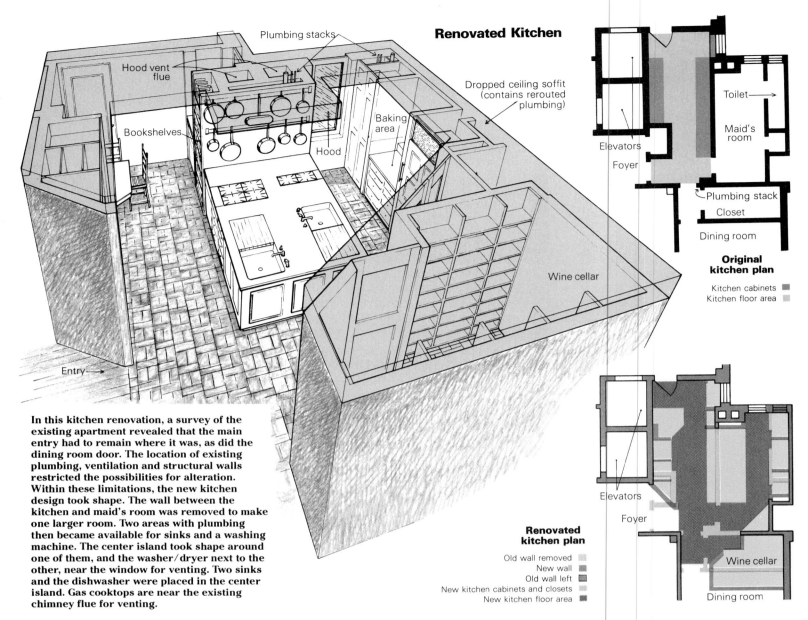

Renovated Kitchen

Plumbing stacks
Hood vent flue
Bookshelves
Hood
Baking area
Dropped ceiling soffit (contains rerouted plumbing)
Wine cellar
Entry →

Original kitchen plan

Elevators
Foyer
Toilet →
Maid's room
Plumbing stack
Closet
Dining room

Kitchen cabinets ■
Kitchen floor area ▨

Renovated kitchen plan

Old wall removed ▨
New wall ▨
Old wall left ■
New kitchen cabinets and closets ▨
New kitchen floor area ▨

Elevators
Foyer
Wine cellar
Dining room

In this kitchen renovation, a survey of the existing apartment revealed that the main entry had to remain where it was, as did the dining room door. The location of existing plumbing, ventilation and structural walls restricted the possibilities for alteration. Within these limitations, the new kitchen design took shape. The wall between the kitchen and maid's room was removed to make one larger room. Two areas with plumbing then became available for sinks and a washing machine. The center island took shape around one of them, and the washer/dryer next to the other, near the window for venting. Two sinks and the dishwasher were placed in the center island. Gas cooktops are near the existing chimney flue for venting.

provide more diffuse light. If you want light fixtures inside vent hoods, use commercial housings to seal out moisture and to contain the glass bulb should it break.

Surveying the space—Photos of the existing kitchen layout are helpful during schematic drawing stages, so take them as early as possible. Photos record stylistic elements such as intricate plaster work, wood moldings or paneling that may affect the final design, if you are trying to preserve the style.

After measuring the kitchen, document the composition and condition of existing surfaces and the locations of existing mechanicals, such as plumbing, electrical wiring and vents. Information about these systems is easy to get: Where were the old appliances, fixtures and the lines that served them? To be sure I remember the location of mechanicals, I'll often sketch in the systems on Polaroid photos while I'm on the site. But to know for sure what is behind the walls, it's sometimes necessary to cut into them. By determining the routes of mechanical systems early, you know the parameters of dif-

ferent design solutions. For example, you may not want to move sinks and dishwashers across a room if it means installing a new system of drain pipes to accommodate them. Although pipes and wiring are flexible to a degree, some choices are prohibitively expensive. Cutting into walls for a look can be crucial, for surprises uncovered after construction begins can make meticulously drawn plans useless.

Schematic drawings—From the filled-in kitchen forms and the survey you'll have enough information to begin drawing a number of kitchen schematics. There are as many methods of depicting kitchen space as there are books on the subject, but I prefer to draw a basic floor plan from the survey and to sketch various alternatives on tissue-paper overlays. I prefer a scale of $\frac{1}{2}$ in. to 1 ft. Any larger size requires an inordinate amount of drawing, and anything smaller produces drawings without much detail.

The order of allocating space roughly follows that of the kitchen form, beginning with the movement of people. Main corridors must always be wide—3 ft. to 3½ ft. is minimum—so

that people returning home with groceries or passing while cooking have enough room. If several cooks will be working together, all the corridors should be at least 3 ft. wide.

Venting and waste line requirements have a lot to do with appliance location. Sinks, washing machines, gas cooktops and electric ovens require venting to the outside and should be placed as close as possible to a wall or a chimney vent (shown in the drawing above). Gas ovens and refrigerators are the most flexible to place.

Counter space is always a battle at the end, for each major appliance must have a counter next to it. Calculate drawer and shelf space when you sketch what each wall of cabinets and appliances will look like. Pantries and floor-to-ceiling storage cabinets save space and are more convenient to use than conventional cabinets.

Where confusion about the drawings persists, chalk final plans on walls or floors. This way you can walk around in the space and live with it awhile before beginning construction. □

Mathew Kaplan is an architect who practices in Brooklyn, N.Y.

Expanding a Kitchen, Step by Step

In renovation, one thing always leads to another

by Eric K. Rekdahl

Renovation work is full of surprises. Even in simple-looking jobs, digging into one area will invariably expose unanticipated problems in another, which in turn will force you to rearrange something else. Good renovators are clever enough both to anticipate some of the trouble they're likely to run into and to know that lots more will show up. They are flexible enough to improvise when plans go awry, and imaginative enough to take advantage of situations as they arise. Technical skills are also important to minimize tedium and frustration.

When Dick and Renie Riemann acquired their 1928 Tudor Revival house, designed by the architect John Hudson Thomas, they also inherited a kitchen with 48 sq. ft. of floor space and 5½ ft. of

countertop, separated from the dining room by two doors and a pantry (drawing, below). The refrigerator was in the laundry, a sagging foundation was causing the floor to droop, and inadequate framing had cracked the plaster.

The Riemanns wanted a modern, functional kitchen with a family eating area and a desk for planning. They wanted an open, informal space, with enough room for guests to chat with the cook. The obvious solution was to eliminate as many walls as possible, streamlining the maze-like circulation created by the pantry, kitchen and laundry room. They also wanted to enlarge the kitchen by enclosing an area north of the laundry wall that was covered by an overhanging second-story bedroom floor.

Laundry wall—The area was broken up into so many small rooms that we hardly had space to set up our equipment and move around. By removing the non load-bearing walls (D, G and E in the drawing), we created a good-sized working area. This was straightforward work, except for a problem we had anticipated: The cast-iron drain from an upstairs toilet ran through wall D. We disconnected the plumbing and removed the pipe. It would have to be relocated later.

Then we tackled wall B, the laundry's north wall. It was framed with a 2x4 stud wall, which carried 4x6 floor joists for the bedroom above. Instead of removing the wall and replacing the top plate with an 8x10, we kept the double 2x4 top plate and sandwiched it between two rough-

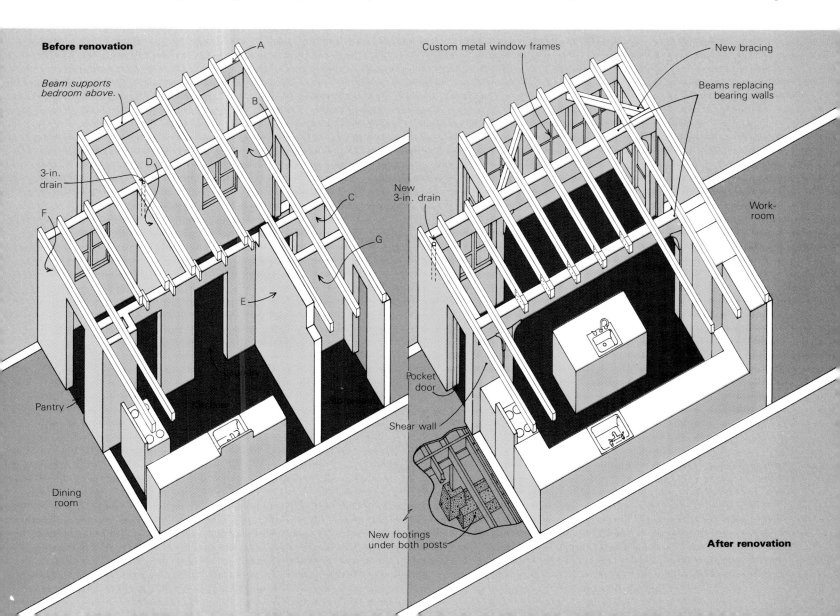

Before renovation

Beam supports bedroom above.

3-in. drain

F

D

E

Pantry

Dining room

A

B

C

G

Custom metal window frames

New bracing

Beams replacing bearing walls

New 3-in. drain

Work-room

Pocket door

Shear wall

New footings under both posts

After renovation

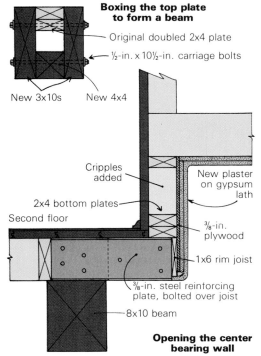

Original doubled 2x4 plate

½-in. x 10½-in. carriage bolts

New 3x10s   New 4x4

Cripples added

New plaster on gypsum lath

2x4 bottom plates

Second floor

⅜-in. plywood

1x6 rim joist

⅜-in. steel reinforcing plate, bolted over joist

8x10 beam

Opening the center bearing wall

Opening up the north wall of the kitchen revealed 10-in. long 2x6s supporting an upstairs wall (below). These were replaced with steel plates and 4x6s, as shown above. At the south side of the kitchen (bottom), joists were attached without cripples or blocking.

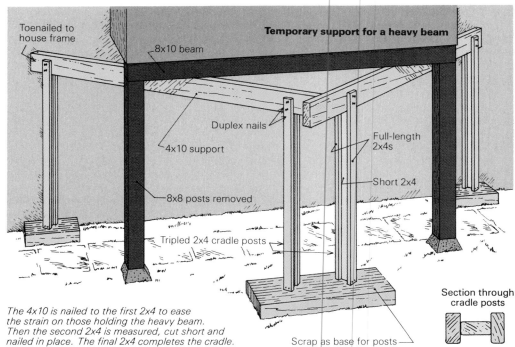

Toenailed to house frame

Temporary support for a heavy beam

8x10 beam

Duplex nails

4x10 support

Full-length 2x4s

Short 2x4

8x8 posts removed

Tripled 2x4 cradle posts

Section through cradle posts

Scrap as base for posts

The 4x10 is nailed to the first 2x4 to ease the strain on those holding the heavy beam. Then the second 2x4 is measured, cut short and nailed in place. The final 2x4 completes the cradle.

sawn 3x10s. This way we could use the old framing as bracing while using the same sandwich approach to beef up the posts at the beam ends. After the 3x10s were bolted in place, we removed the stud frame. To complete the beam we bolted a 4x4 between the 3x10s, flush with their bottom edges (drawing, above left).

The upstairs bedroom floor joists extended 4½ ft. beyond the laundry wall to rest on an 8x10 beam (A in the drawing on the previous page), supported by 8x8 posts just beyond a concrete path. Extending the exterior wall to include these posts and beams would gain about 50 sq. ft. of kitchen space without affecting the house's original roofline or proportions—an opportunity we couldn't resist. But we would need to remove the 8x8s temporarily so we could pour a stem-wall foundation and a slab floor.

To support the 8x10, we used two 4x10s extending from the side of the house and meeting at a point beyond the beam (drawing, above right). We supported the 4x10s on four posts, each built up out of three 2x4s. We first nailed one 2x4 to the side of a 4x10. This took most of the weight off whoever was holding the heavy beam, so measuring and cutting the second 2x4, which would sit at right angles to the first to form a saddle for the heavy timber, was easy. The third 2x4 was nailed up full length and parallel to the first to cradle the 4x10.

Once the foundation work was done and the slab poured, we replaced the 8x8 posts, removed the temporary supports, and fitted custom metal window frames in the new wall.

Central wall—Once we finished the north wall of the laundry, we moved on to the area's central bearing wall (C), just north of the small original kitchen wall (E). Removing the plaster ceiling, we were astonished to find cantilevered 2x6 joists only 10 in. long carrying the load of an upstairs bearing wall (photo, center left). Had the 4x6 joists for the bedroom over the laundry been 8 in. longer, they could have carried the

offset upstairs wall without a problem. We could only surmise that some change in plans had produced this structural anomaly. As it was, the 2x6 rim joist was carrying most of the load. Since we were changing the rim joist's end bearing, we needed to extend the 4x6s the extra 8 in. to carry the upstairs wall.

To do this, we bolted half the length of ⅜-in. steel plates, 5½ in. wide by 15 in. long, to each face of the 4x6s. We then bolted 8-in. 4x6s between each set of plates, and nailed a 1x6 rim joist to the ends of these extended beams (drawing, above left). The floor joists over the kitchen had been face-nailed to the studs of the upstairs wall without blocking or cripples beneath them, which we added before nailing up a skin of ⅜-in. plywood to tie everything together.

At the south wall of the kitchen, the same floor joists had been face-nailed to the roof rafters with no bracing (photo, bottom left). Where the joists didn't line up with the rafters, cripples had been inserted at the angle of the roof. I think it was just the lath and plaster that held them in place. We added blocking under each joist to form a new soffit, and nailed a ⅜-in. plywood gusset to the blocking, cripple and joist for rigidity. Then we could get back to the storeroom/kitchen wall (C in the drawing).

The wall's load had been evenly distributed, requiring only modest footings. Our plan to replace the framing with an 8x10 beam spanning 12 ft. meant larger footings to take the two concentrated loads.

A 4x6 carried the 2x8 floor joists under the wall. It was supported in turn by 4x4 posts on isolated piers about 4 ft. on center. The crawl space was barely a foot high at its east end, and the whole thing was clogged with heating ducts, so the easiest approach was to take up the flooring and excavate from above. We undermined about half the bearing of the pier closest to each point of concentration, poured concrete under both, and incorporated them into new footings about 2½ ft. wide by 4½ ft. long and 10 in. deep

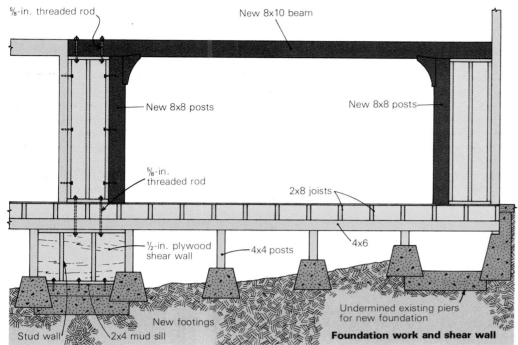

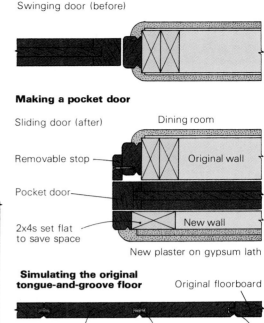

5⁄8-in. threaded rod

New 8x10 beam

New 8x8 posts

New 8x8 posts

5⁄8-in. threaded rod

2x8 joists

1⁄2-in. plywood shear wall

4x4 posts

4x6

Undermined existing piers for new foundation

Stud wall

2x4 mud sill

New footings

Foundation work and shear wall

Swinging door (before)

Making a pocket door

Sliding door (after)

Dining room

Removable stop

Original wall

Pocket door

2x4s set flat to save space

New wall

New plaster on gypsum lath

Simulating the original tongue-and-groove floor

Original floorboard

New boards grooved

Spline

Tongue

(drawing, above). We realized we now had an opportunity to add a shear wall tied directly to the ground to keep the house from racking, so we formed a stem wall on the new west footing directly below the 4x6 beam with anchor bolts and a 2x4 mud sill. We then incorporated adjacent 4x4 posts in a short 2x4 stud wall 12 in. o.c. under the 4x6. Before sheathing it with ½-in. plywood, we ran two ⅝-in. threaded steel rods to the bottom plate of the new west shear wall on the kitchen floor level, binding the new 8x8 post and the 8x10 beam together into a racking panel that carried right down to the new footing.

Pocket door—Fixing our last nagging problem brought our structural work full circle. The house had settled so much that the swinging door between the pantry and the dining room wouldn't pivot more than 90° before it hit the floor and jammed. When it opened into the pantry it was in the way of the stuff stored there. We decided that the best solution was to build a pocket sliding door. So we framed up a new wall in the former pantry out of 2x4s, face side out, covered with gypsum lath and new plaster (drawing, top right). This left us plenty of room to install the original door on its new sliding track, and enough space in the corner to tie up another loose end, the waste line from upstairs.

Re-routing the drain produced three new problems. First, because the upstairs flooring and 4x6 floor joists were to be the finished downstairs ceiling, we had to run the drain line above the upstairs floor. Thus the use of a back-flush toilet, which flushes back rather than down. Its 3-in. drain is about 2½ in. above the floor, and allowed us a 10-ft. horizontal run (at a fall of ¼ in. per ft.) before we would have to penetrate the floor. Our pocket-door corner was 7 ft. away from the toilet, well within range.

Second, some of the flooring under the old toilet needed to be replaced, and numerous calls to lumberyards revealed that 1x6 roughsawn V-joint, tongue-and-groove fir was not a stock

item. We decided to simulate the original material as best we could by using 1x6 rough fir. We would chamfer the edges on a table saw and groove them for splines with a router (drawing, above right). It turned out that 1x6 rough fir wasn't stock either. So I found myself standing at the lumberyard in front of a bandsaw where they were resawing 8x16 fir beams. All I wanted was two 1x6s, 12 ft. long. The operator sent one of his helpers to locate a 2x6, which he brought back on a forklift, and within minutes I drove away with my custom-milled, roughsawn fir planks.

Third, we had to patch the 4x6 beam that had been hacked away by the plumber installing the original drain. This beam would be visible in the new ceiling, so we carefully chiseled and planed a square recess around the damage, then let in a

patch of rough 2x6 with similar grain. This we secured with glue and finish nails.

Our simple-sounding assignment to open up the room for more space led us inexorably to everything from foundation work under the house to installing plumbing on the next floor. We found serious structural flaws that had to be remedied, and had ourselves created conditions that would have been unsafe if we hadn't followed through properly. We'd worked around the unavailability of materials, and had taken advantage of opportunities to improve the structure of the house as we went along. Most renovation work is like that.   □

Eric Rekdahl is a partner in the design/build firm of Rekdahl & Tellefsen in Berkeley, Calif.

In the expanded kitchen, the new carved beams and brackets echo details found throughout the house. Red oak cabinets by Robert Zummwalt harmonize with the oak flooring and trim.

Kitchen Overhaul

Easy maintenance, abundant storage and plenty of workspace in 100 sq. ft.

by Gillian Servais

Shortly before Christmas a few years ago, I received a frantic call from a couple in Berkeley. They had just bought a lovely old house that had been built in the 1920s. Other than a few minor repairs and the usual repainting, it was ready to occupy—except, that is, for the kitchen. It needed a total transformation, and they were expecting their first child in two months.

The existing kitchen was cramped and inefficient. In addition to lacking adequate storage space, light and charm of any sort, its counter peninsula projected awkwardly into the center of the room (drawing, p. 20). The stove was at the other end of the counter, crammed into a corner that left no work room to the left of the burners (photo right). As a gesture to ventilation, a small fan had been stuck in the wall behind the stove. Unfortunately, there was no hood to collect the cooking vapors. A 2-ft. dia. table and two chairs took up the remaining space. They were in a small bay with three windows overlooking the backyard garden to the south. The view from the east-side window was into the neighbors' kitchen, just beyond a nearby fence.

Priorities—Before I meet with my clients to begin design work, I ask them to prepare a wish list that includes the most important features in the new room. The list gives us a starting point, and once we get into discussing the project a hierarchy of priorities usually emerges.

In this case, speed was on my clients' minds. They didn't want a construction project and a new baby, so the kitchen had to be completed in two months. Next, the kitchen had to be an efficient workspace for people who enjoy preparing meals, with durable, easy-to-clean surfaces and high-quality cooking equipment. They wanted the new kitchen to have a modern appearance, but without clashing with the 1920s decor in the rest of the house. Also, it had to have plenty of light and storage space. The clients had a lot of

Inadequate storage and a cramped workspace made the original kitchen (above) unsuitable for people who like to cook a lot. A view in the same direction of the remodeled kitchen (facing page) shows the extent of the changes made in this room. White painted surfaces and cabinets get the most from the available light, while track lighting illuminates the work areas. The floor is covered with 12-in. square tiles of heavy-duty vinyl flooring. Drawer pulls of brushed stainless steel complement the stainless hood and sink. To the left of the oven, a marble countertop serves as a pastry surface.

small appliances and specialized gadgets for exotic cooking. While they don't use them very often, they needed places to keep them out of sight. Finally, the kitchen needed a corner to do pastry work.

A tight budget wasn't an issue in this project, so we could have added onto the house to expand the size of the kitchen. But that would have taken the completion date well beyond our deadline. Consequently, our first decision was to avoid any structural changes by staying within the existing space. To gain a little more room, we decided to annex the bay window area occupied by the round table. This still left us with only about 100 sq. ft.—not a very large kitchen for people who cook a lot. Clearly, we had to exploit all the available space.

Because light was a precious commodity in this room, white walls and cabinets were a must. To make it easy to clean the tiny handprints to come, we all agreed that plastic laminate cabinets were the right choice. Their stark simplicity would also lend a feeling of open space. The adjacent dining room has wood trim painted pale grey, so we repeated the grey trim in the kitchen to relate the two rooms. This palette, while durable and bright, borders on the antiseptic. For some highlights and warmth we added stainless steel and natural wood (photo facing page).

A deep wood counter—First we took out all the existing cabinets and the appliances that we wouldn't be reusing in the new kitchen. Then we removed the angled counter and put the sink under the windows that overlook the garden (drawing, p. 21). Because the other window provided some light but no aesthetic value, we made it fade away by covering it with a grey Levelor blind.

The new cooktop and oven are below this window, installed in a 30-in. deep, butcher-block counter. Some of my clients who request butcher-block counters want them only for their

From *Fine Homebuilding* magazine (June 1987) 40:64-67
Photo this page: Gillian Servais

The cleanup center now occupies the bay window, giving the person at the sink a view of the backyard garden. A hinged shelf below the sink hides pot scrubbers and sponges, and the drawer below provides easy access to kitchen cleanup items and the trash bin.

A 30-in. deep counter allows enough room for extra-long drawers. This one was sized to hold pot lids, and divided to make them easy to find. Cookie sheets and pizza pans are stored under the oven.

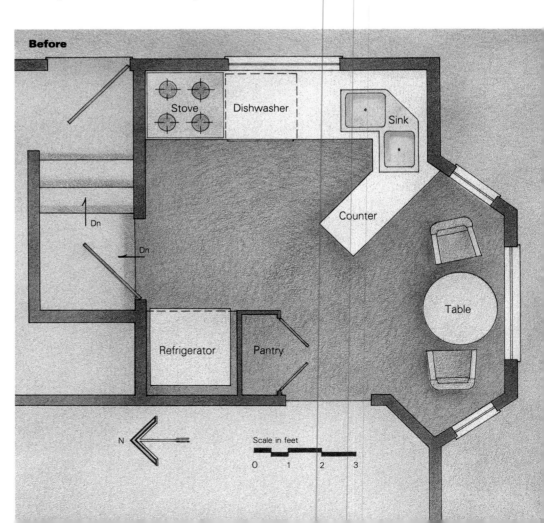

Before

Stove

Dishwasher

Sink

Counter

Dn

Dn

Refrigerator

Pantry

Table

N

Scale in feet

0   1   2   3

looks, rather than their intended use—a chopping surface. Sometimes a client will want to put a sink in a butcher-block counter, which is inviting trouble because the wood will inevitably rot and delaminate around the sink rim. I think this installation strikes the right note between utility and style when it comes to wood counters. This one is separate from the the sink counter, so moisture isn't an issue. It is also used as a chopping surface, taking on the textures and colors that come with using a work surface that is built to be used for a long time.

Evidently some of the companies that make wood counters assume that their products will never feel the sharp edge of a knife, because countertops are often finished with polyurethane varnish or lacquer. In this situation, I have the finish removed with a thickness planer or a belt sander. Then I have the counter refinished with a few coats of mineral oil. I've got a wood counter in my own kitchen, and I touch up the spots that get chopped on about once a week. I just soak a paper towel with some mineral oil, and mush it around on the areas that need it.

Wood counters can get stained. Sometimes a cast-iron pot will leave an ugly black ring on the wood. When this happens, I cut open a lemon and squeeze its juice on the stain. The juice will remove the mark, leaving the wood a little lighter than the surrounding surface and ready for a mineral-oil touchup.

Although a 30-in. deep counter doesn't sound like a big improvement over the traditional 24-in. counter, it is. For one thing, the extra depth provides enough space at the back of the counter to keep appliances and foodstuffs that are in constant use, while still allowing workspace

along the front of the counter. The extra 6 in. also allows added drawer space. For this kitchen, we asked cabinetmaker John Banks to make the drawers the full depth of the counter. Mounted on full-extension drawer glides, the drawers are divided in halves. Frequently used items are in the front sections—seldom needed utensils are stored in the back.

To supply power to the appliances along the back of the counter, we installed a strip of Plugmold (Wiremold Co., 60 Woodlawn St., West Hartford, Conn. 06110). Plugmold is a linear housing that has electric outlets every 6 in. or 12 in. The strips come in 5-ft. lengths, and they are designed to carry 20 amps for every six outlets. I like to use these strips for groups of plug-in appliances because they cut down on power cords draped across the counters.

A stove and a hood—Both the cooktop and the oven were made by Gaggenau, a West German company that makes high-quality appliances (Gaggenau USA, 5 Commonwealth Ave., Woburn, Mass. O1801). While the two are separate pieces, they are made to be used in tandem as built-ins. These are expensive appliances. The cooktop lists for about $550, and the oven costs a bit over $1,200. But for people who love to cook, the capabilities of these appliances may outweigh their expense.

The cooktop burners are sized according to the tasks they most often perform. The front right burner is rated at 12,700 Btus—hot enough to do a real stir fry or sauté. The back left burner performs at 9,520 Btus for boiling water in a hurry. The other two burners are rated at 6,350 Btus, which is the size of the typical burner on a

residential stove. To turn them on one must push in the knob and turn it at the same time to engage the electronic ignition and open the gas valve. This makes it virtually childproof.

The oven is the convection type, which uses a fan to circulate the heat. This kind of oven is especially good for cooking breads and pastries, and it makes for crispy skins on chickens and roasts. The oven door swings to the side instead of down so that you can really see into the oven without hitting your knees on the door. On the other hand, the feature called ''continuous cleaning'' doesn't really clean very well. Fortunately, the interior walls are easily disassembled, and they will fit into a dishwasher for cleaning.

The stainless-steel hood was custom built to overlap part of the window without overwhelming the space. It houses a Trade-Wind 1501 Ventilator by Thermador, which is rated at 290 cfm.

A good vent is important in a kitchen for two reasons: not only will it cut down on grease and odors, but it will also carry away potentially dangerous combustion by-products from gas cooktops. As a rule of thumb, the vent should move 100 cubic feet of air per minute, per square foot of cooktop. The hood is most often installed 30 in. above the cooktop. Tall people need hoods a bit higher to keep from banging their foreheads when they peek in the soup pot. Thermador (5119 District Blvd., Los Angeles, Calif. 90040) publishes a useful brochure for people who are interested in kitchen ventilation. It's called ''Basic Concepts of Residential Kitchen Ventilation,'' and it's free for the asking.

A place for everything—Before I drew up cabinet details, we took an inventory of everything the clients planned to keep in the kitchen. We measured oversize pans, decided what could be stored vertically and measured lineal feet of cookbooks. Big cookie sheets and pizza pans fit in a short but wide space under the oven (bottom photo, facing page). To its right, a tall drawer with dividers contains pot lids.

The upper cabinets run all the way to the ceiling, where they house infrequently needed pots and pans. At the intersection between the cabinets on the north and east walls, two-piece doors joined with piano hinges allow full access to this otherwise awkward hollow.

The cleanup center now occupies the bay window (top photo, facing page). Banks built this complicated cabinet knowing that he would have to fit it into a three-sided space that was neither plumb nor square, and it was still an installation nightmare for him. To make the necessary scribe cuts in the laminate edges, he first made plywood templates of the wall contours, then used his router along with the templates.

A big drawer fits into the space under the sink, making it easier for grownups to get at the trash bag but harder for toddlers. To its left, an angled drawer ekes out a bit more storage room. Since there was still a little room remaining to the right of the dishwasher, Banks built a special cabinet to house a stepstool for reaching the things in the upper cabinets. □

Gillian Servais is a custom kitchen designer based in Berkeley, Calif.

After

Cooktop
Wood counter
Double-hinged cabinet door
Marble pastry counter
Dn
Dn
Sink
Refrigerator
Pantry
Dishwasher

In the remodeled kitchen, the sink has been moved to occupy the sunny bay window along the south wall, and the awkward counter in the center of the original kitchen has been removed. An extra-deep counter on the east wall makes it possible to keep appliances along the back of the counter without eliminating valuable workspace.

Gourmet Kitchen Remodel

Problem-solving on a tight schedule brings light,
style and order to an outdated kitchen

by Valerie Walsh

I like to work under pressure, so the kitchen remodel I did for Wally Sargent last year really held my interest. Sargent lives in an adobe-style house in Tesuque, a community just north of Santa Fe, N. Mex. He is a connoisseur of Western art, classic cars and gourmet cooking, and while his art and car collection are first rate, his kitchen was a cramped, outdated jumble of plastic laminates in garish colors (photo right). When he asked me to design and build a new kitchen and breakfast room for him, I knew it had to be special. To complicate matters, I was offered the contract on the condition that I have Sargent in his new kitchen cooking Christmas dinner for 40 relatives. This gave me just nine weeks to design and build his kitchen.

The goals—Sargent gave me some general guidelines to follow as I began preliminary drawings. He wanted plenty of well-lit work space, and he wanted to move the informal dining area out of the kitchen proper (drawing, below). The new kitchen had to have the appeal of a commercial kitchen, with durable, rugged appliances. It was to be light, airy and showy. He wanted to make as big a change as possible from his 1950s-style kitchen, and he insisted that I "get rid of the clutter."

We agreed that a new room had to be added off the kitchen for the informal dining area. It had to be spacious enough to accommodate a

Wally Sargent's old kitchen was an orange and yellow relic from the 1950s that didn't have enough storage and counter space for his burgeoning collection of utensils and appliances.

table for a family of six, plus a breakfast bar and space to lounge around a kiva fireplace in the corner. Sargent also wanted to incorporate a south-facing clerestory into this new north-side breakfast room.

After our first meeting, Sargent was so anxious and full of enthusiasm that he wanted to see some immediate action. I could see he was a bit deflated when I told him that a kitchen was a very detailed and personal room, and that I had to design it before we could start construction. What turned out to be three intensive weeks of drawing and organizing for me was an eternity for this home owner.

The plan that I came up with placed the room addition adjacent to the kitchen, in a trapezoidal space that was at one time a dog run between the original building and a retaining wall. A peninsula composed of a breakfast bar and a sink counter separates the kitchen from the new space (photo below). In the center of the new kitchen, a 3-ft. by 6-ft. island counter lies under a new 11-ft. by 3-ft. skylight (photo facing page). This plan maintained the original circulation patterns, which kept modifications to the adjacent rooms to a minimum. Many of the interior walls are massive stacks of masonry, so one does not move these walls around without serious consideration.

For the primary finish materials, we decided on cabinet doors made of horizontal oak strips,

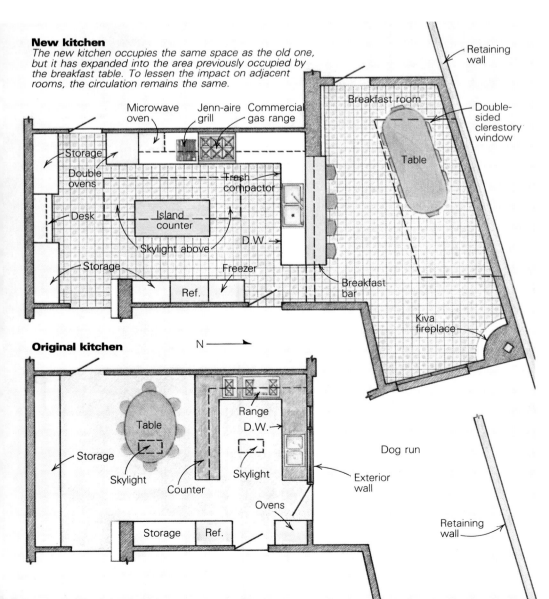

New kitchen
The new kitchen occupies the same space as the old one, but it has expanded into the area previously occupied by the breakfast table. To lessen the impact on adjacent rooms, the circulation remains the same.

Microwave oven · Jenn-aire grill · Commercial gas range · Retaining wall · Breakfast room · Double-sided clerestory window · Table · Storage · Double ovens · Trash compactor · Desk · Island counter · Skylight above · D.W. · Storage · Freezer · Breakfast bar · Ref. · Kiva fireplace

N ——▶

Original kitchen

Range · D.W. · Table · Skylight · Storage · Skylight · Counter · Exterior wall · Dog run · Ovens · Storage · Ref. · Retaining wall

A peninsula separates the new kitchen from the breakfast room, and provides a counter for informal meals. The wall beneath the counter is covered with tile, which resists scuff marks and is easy to clean. Above the counter, a built-up header of three 2x12s carries the 6x10 timbers that support the roof.

a floor of Italian tile in terra-cotta and slate blue, white Corian counters (Du Pont, Corian Building Products Div., Wilmington, Del. 19898) and slate-blue tile backsplashes. These earthy colors are in keeping with the rest of the house, and they provide a harmonious backdrop for Sargent's copper pots and pans and the copper hood over the range.

On the fast track—Once the drawings were complete, every day was a countdown to December 24. We had no time cushion to make up for the usual delays and setbacks caused by suppliers, subcontractors, the weather, and of course, the unexpected.

Although the north retaining wall is sturdy enough to carry a roof load, I chose not to build the new structure atop this wall because it would be next to impossible to waterproof it adequately without extensive excavation. Consequently, we had to build a new block wall on a footing just inside of the retaining wall, where there was less soil to remove (drawing, facing page). As we dug for the new footing, we discovered the gas line to the barbeque—it perfectly bisected our foundation trench, and it had to be moved before anything else could be done. Soon after, we were hit with our first brutal snowstorm of the season. Despite the uncooperative weather (and a strong urge to take off and go skiing), we moved the gas line and completed the foundation, stem walls, and slab in the first week.

Before I began tearing out the old kitchen on November 12, I had to fashion some temporary kitchen facilities for Sargent's four teenage boys. They weren't about to put up with limited food access for five weeks. I stuck the refrigerator, fully loaded for after-school food raids, in the carport, and the microwave in the family room. All of the pantry foods were strewn out like a permanent buffet in the once formal dining room. It was paper plates, snack food and frozen pizzas until Christmas.

While the mason began work on the kiva fireplace in the new room, the sandblaster removed the old white paint covering the kitchen ceiling and beams. This was the most unpleasant chapter in the entire project. Sandblasting the wood created blinding clouds of dust and unbearable noise. Despite our efforts to keep the dust out of the rest of the house (which included sealing the three doorways with multiple layers of Visqueen), we found ourselves fighting a losing battle. Fortunately, it was over in a day.

Sargent was planning to give away the old appliances and cabinets, so we removed them with great care. By this time the entire kitchen was stripped to the studs. Every subcontractor imaginable was crowded into this kitchen while the walls were open. I allowed two weeks for stripping the old kitchen down, running new electric service, water lines, heating ducts, building soffits, sheathing walls and plastering. The pressure was on.

Simultaneously, laborers had the tedious job of scraping off the old linoleum flooring, which had become one with the slab. It had to be scraped off inch by inch with sharpened floor scrapers. At one point, I considered setting the

To take advantage of a view of a tree-covered hill to the north, Walsh extended the north wall of the breakfast room above the plate height with windows in the bays between the beams.

floor tile right on the old linoleum since it was so well bonded, but decided against it. I had visions of the tile pulling up somewhere down the line, so I played it the hard and safe way.

The slab required some leveling work before setting the tiles. To this end, I troweled on some POR-ROK, which is a concrete material made by Minwax (Minwax, Construction Products Div., 102 Chestnut Ridge Plaza, Montvale, N. J. 07645). I applied it to the low spots and feathered it in to create a level surface.

The plasterers put us one day behind schedule when they didn't show up because of a little snow and ice on the dirt road leading to the house. Because of the time crunch, I decided to use Keene's plaster rather than Structo-Lite (both are made by U. S. Gypsum, 101 S. Wacker Drive, Chicago, Ill. 60606). Keene's is an extra-hard finish plaster that sets up almost immediately. As a consequence, you can get two coats on a surface in one day instead of two. You have to mix Keene's plaster in very small batches because it dries out almost as soon as it's troweled onto the wall. Our cabinet man was scheduled to begin his installation the next day, so the quick-setting plaster kept us from falling behind.

From *Fine Homebuilding* magazine (August 1986) 34:62-66

As the builders opened up the roof to cut a hole for the kitchen skylight, they first discovered a layer of urethane insulation. Under it they found another layer of poured pumice that had to be removed with a jack-hammer, and an electric cable traversing the well.

The addition occupies a space between the original house and a retaining wall to the north. To bring light into the new space, Walsh added this shed-roofed clerestory. A fan mounted on its roof evacuates hot air if temperatures inside become uncomfortable.

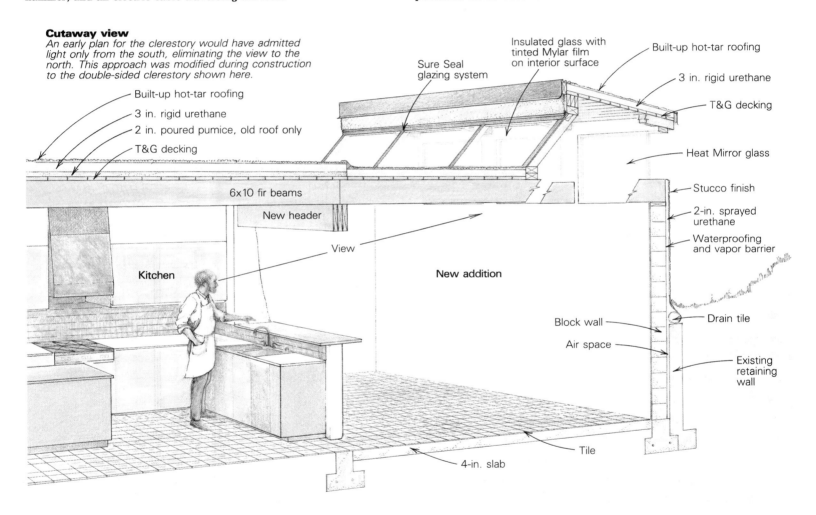

Cutaway view
An early plan for the clerestory would have admitted light only from the south, eliminating the view to the north. This approach was modified during construction to the double-sided clerestory shown here.

Built-up hot-tar roofing
3 in. rigid urethane
2 in. poured pumice, old roof only
T&G decking
6x10 fir beams
New header
View
Kitchen
New addition

Insulated glass with tinted Mylar film on interior surface
Sure Seal glazing system
Built-up hot-tar roofing
3 in. rigid urethane
T&G decking
Heat Mirror glass
Stucco finish
2-in. sprayed urethane
Waterproofing and vapor barrier
Block wall
Air space
Drain tile
Existing retaining wall
Tile
4-in. slab

Clerestory—Meanwhile, the breakfast addition was progressing. On November 15 we placed a header where the exterior wall used to be, and positioned the new ceiling beams. When we began decking the roof with 2-in. T&G pine, I realized that the placement of the clerestory needed adjusting. As the roof closed in, board by board, I could see that beautiful hill of trees to the north begin to fade out of view. The roofers were scheduled in two days and this was no time to be experimenting, but I was suddenly struck with an idea for an unusual structure for the clerestory. Instead of a sawtooth clerestory,

I thought a better solution would be to extend the north wall with glass above the plate line, and place south-facing glass over the center of the room (photo above right). This strategy would allow some solar gain, and also preserve the view of the trees for diners at the table and for the cook at the sink (photo facing page).

I drew my idea, but nobody, including Sargent, could envision it. So we built a full-scale mockup of this unusual double-sided skylight and set it in place to get Sargent's opinion. The mockup was rough, but he agreed to the idea.

Fortunately, the double-sided skylight was a

success, but not without a shattering experience in the process. Being a passive-solar purist of sorts, my suggestion to use north-facing glass reflected a compromise. To reduce the heat loss and assuage my guilt, I installed Heat Mirror insulating glass on the north side of the skylight. Heat Mirror (Southwall Technology,1029 Corporation Way, Palo Alto, Calif. 94303) is a clear polyester film suspended between two panes of glass. It insulates by reflecting far infrared (heat) rays back into the living space.

I ran into trouble when my sloping, south-facing clerestory glass cast an annoying glare on

Drawings: Elizabeth Eaton

the north-facing glass, obscuring the terrific view. My first "fix" was to install bronze glass on the outside of the north windows (there was no room on the inside jamb). This cut down on the glare considerably, but within a week, one of the Heat Mirror units blew out. In hindsight, I could easily have checked with the manufacturer about my wild scheme. I would have been told that the Heat Mirror units must be allowed to "breathe," and that an outer pane would create an undesirable build-up of heat.

I quickly removed the other two bronze panes, and considered the south-facing glass for a solution. I ended up sticking tinted Mylar film to the inside surface of the angled glass. The stuff was tricky to apply. It is a lot like hanging wallpaper—you wet the window, press on the Mylar and squeegee out the air bubbles—only the film is so flimsy that it tends to wrinkle and tear easily. The Mylar eliminated most of the glare, and Sargent was pleased with the way the windows looked. Mylar is available at building-supply stores.

I have successfully used the Sure Seal Glazing System (U. S. Sky, Div. of Brother Sun, 2907 Agua Fria, Santa Fe, N. Mex. 87501) for glass installation, so I chose it again for the south-sloping clerestory glass. This system uses aluminum glazing bars and neoprene gaskets to seal out the weather. The parts cost about $5/lin. ft., which includes bars and gaskets, and the screws needed to attach them. It comes in either a bronze anodized or white enamel finish, and it has a clean look. The gasket material must be inserted by the contractor, so keep it in a clean place until you are ready to use it. The least bit of job-site sand, dirt or grit in your gasket could mean leaks later. The Sure Seal solves all of the common problems of warped or split wood battens and of caulks failing when they dry out.

Opening up the roof—Late November in New Mexico is a risky time to cut a hole in a roof. It rained or snowed practically every week from the time we began in October, but that didn't stop us from cutting a 3-ft. by 11-ft. hole in the center of the kitchen ceiling for the new skylight (top left photo, previous page). This was another exercise in discovering the unexpected. First, we found several inches of poured pumice under the tar and gravel roof. In this part of the country, roofers sometimes establish drainage on flat roofs by sloping a layer of this material toward the *canales* (scuppers). Usually it is a granular substance, like sand, and it is easily moved around with a shovel. But not on Sargent's roof. Here we found a slab of pumice that had to be removed with a jackhammer. Then an unwelcome electric conduit line appeared running right across the skylight opening. The 2x12 curb could not be set or enclosed until this line was re-routed. Yet another scramble.

I kept hoping that the roofer would be able to hot-tar a skylight curb one day soon, just as I hoped my supplier would deliver the skylight on time. No such luck. We installed the curb and sealed its junction with the roof with a temporary layer of cold tar, then we covered it with plywood and plastic.

The low winter sun couldn't dry out the flat roof enough to allow the hot-mop crew to do their job, so every day we shoveled the new snow and slush off the roof and cast shovel-loads of Bentonite on the persistently wet areas. Bentonite is a powdery clay that can be a savior when you need temporary leak-stopping help. When you dust it on a puddled area, it becomes a gooey substance that clogs leaky holes. I have used it on flat tar-and-gravel roofs with great success. It eventually dries out and blows away as dust, although some traces of it remain embedded in the gravel. We buy Bentonite in 50-lb. sacks for about $12, from American Colloid Company (5100 Suffield Ct., Skokie, Ill. 60077).

Appliances and counters—On November 28, the cabinetmaker began installing the carcases, and we were right behind him putting in the appliances. The heavy-duty commercial Wolf range dropped into place beautifully. The perplexing part was figuring out the magical pattern necessary to have the six heavy cast-iron grates sit level. All six were rocking, and we finally decided that they never did sit in a level pattern. The Wolf rep promptly sent a serviceman who measured, marked and ground the corners to fit. I immediately marked the range-base with symbols that correspond to marks scribed into each burner grate.

The Jenn-Air grill exhausts very simply through a wall vent as a rule—that is, when the cabinet is on an outside wall. That was not the situation on this job—there were no outside walls anywhere in this kitchen. So the alternative was to run a rectangular 4¼-in. by 10-in. duct in the toe-space under the cabinets or in the stud wall behind the grill. Finally, we ran it in the stud wall because the toe-space option would require too many bends to allow an unimpeded flow of air.

Because this was my first Corian countertop job, I decided to subcontract the installation. I had heard that a proper Corian installation is a delicate and painstaking task, and I didn't have enough time to allow myself the luxury of figuring out the material on my own. Corian is a durable marble-like material that resists stains and scratches. It can be drilled, cut or routed with carbide edge tools. Carefully made seams are nearly invisible when you use Du Pont Joint Adhesive. Du Pont Silicone for Corian is used to fasten the Corian to the cabinets or wooden support strips, and is color coordinated to the different shades of Corian. Full underlayment should not be used, as it can cause warping or cracking. For more on working with Corian, see the article on pp. 52-55.

Corian is also relatively expensive at $15 per sq. ft. for the ¾-in. material, but considering its sleek, stylish look, durable nature and workability, I think it's a good long-term value, though it is extremely heavy to transport and move about. It comes in lengths of 98 in., 121 in. and 145 in., with widths of 25 in. to 30 in. The 5-in. cutoff from the 30 in. serves as backsplash and is available in three colors.

I have since attended a Corian fabricators' workshop and recommend following the "Installers Guide" Du Pont will provide you with. The guidebook isn't long on why's, but if you

ignore the instructions, you'll be sorry. For instance, screwing into the Corian can crack it. The guide instead suggests securing some appliances with silicone.

For hold-down screws (needed for dishwashers and cooktops) a wooden block or dowel is inserted with a bore to hold the screw. Even then, only two of the four screws are used so that the appliance can contract and expand. Our local installer charges $25 to secure the dishwasher properly, which could save as much as $1,000 in pulling out and replacing a finished sink top later.

Urethane insulation—Sargent wanted the entire north side of his house insulated, as it was all just stuccoed block. This was a spray urethane job so I had the new north addition foamed at the same time. The irregular contour of a spray insulation job is often desirable for a sculpted adobe look here. We chose to cover the house with 2 in. of urethane for an R-factor of 15. A 2-in. thick layer costs about $1 per sq. ft. The walls must be clean, dry and not cold to the touch. Before the spraying, I attached 4-in. and 6-in. stick pins to the raw block walls. These pins are joined to a 1-in. square plate that you can stick to the wall with a dab of caulk. When you're ready for the foam, the building looks like a porcupine, and you don't want to lose your balance and fall toward it. The pins protrude through the finished layer of foam, and are bent over the stucco mesh to provide a secure anchorage for the stucco. I space them about every 12 in.

The urethane is tricky to control, so all nearby areas must be masked off, including shrubbery and trees. It is then sprayed onto the wall by means of a large compressor, a hose and a fine nozzle. The air must be still or the winds will place the sticky, yellow foam everywhere but where you want it.

On this job, by the time the building was warm and dry enough, with pins in place, surrounding areas masked and equipment ready to go, the wind came up for four days consecutively, making it impossible to spray. If the conditions are not right (too cold or too wet), it will probably be evident right away, as the material will pull away from the wall in sheets.

Finishing up—The Italian floor tile was left for the end so it would not be scratched or chipped. Finally, on December 21, I let Sargent into the kitchen to begin stocking his luxurious new oak cabinets and pantries. Of course he had to fight his way through the touch-up crew simultaneously attending to final details. This gave him only the weekend to stock the kitchen with food and familiarize himself with the spacious new work area.

But he adapted quickly to his nearly $90,000 kitchen/breakfast room, and his Christmas dinner for 40 was a smashing success. I, in turn, went to Taos to enjoy the snow on skis, and put the memories of fighting it behind me. □

Valerie Walsh owns and operates Solar Horizon, a general-contracting and design firm in Santa Fe, N. Mex.

Accessible Kitchen Remodel

Creative design makes a cozy and practical kitchen for a client with severe arthritis

by Sam Clark

For many people with mobility impairments, transitions from level to level, room to room, and activity to activity are a challenge, and sometimes an ordeal. For designers and builders, each of these transition points requires special study. Minor adjustments in dimensions, hardware and other details can make both new and existing buildings accessible and comfortable for more people, without necessarily compromising other design goals. I want to use this kitchen remodel (photo above), which I designed and built for a disabled client, to show that barrier-free design can be cozy and inviting, and to suggest the general approach needed to make spaces accessible for disabled people.

The first job is to study in detail the client's physical abilities and limitations, with emphasis on what resources he or she can bring to bear on ordinary household activities. My client, Karen

Fiser, has a knee condition called patello-femoral arthritis. She can walk and stand with some difficulty and discomfort, but she often uses a cane, crutches or a wheelchair. At the present time, the wheelchair is used mainly inside her apartment. The more she walks in any given period, the more her knees weaken and hurt. But her upper body is strong and she has a long reach.

Any disabled person knows infinitely more about his or her situation than the designer can

Well-organized work centers and convenient storage are important to any kitchen, but they're essential when the client is a disabled person. Knee space at the work centers, a variety of counter heights and open shelving are among the details that keep this kitchen (top) accessible. The wall-mounted dishrack has gutters and slots that drain into the sink, allowing dishes to be put away wet.

ever know, and so should be fully involved in the whole planning process. A designer's job may not be to find the solutions, but to help and encourage the client to do so. Fiser and I designed her kitchen together. She defined our primary goals: a kitchen that was comfortable to work in whether she was standing, seated or in a wheelchair; and a kitchen designed to minimize the stress on her knees.

There were other requirements as well. The room was small (bottom drawing, next page) and was to be used for both eating and cooking. We had a deadline that made moving walls and windows impractical. And three off-the-shelf cabinets (34½ in. high) and a Formica countertop had already been purchased. These constraints, along with the proverbial shoestring budget, meant that we weren't able to do everything that we'd have liked. For instance, we

The draining dishrack allows dishes to be washed, rinsed and put away wet. Slots cut into the upper shelves drain the water down into the bottom shelf. The shape and 20° pitch of the bottom shelf, along with its routed channels and the curb across the front, lead the water to a hole near the front edge that drains down into the sink. All the wood is protected with three coats of polyurethane.

couldn't get a new refrigerator that would open the right way for this layout. Working within such limitations is tough, but often results in the most creative solutions.

The chair—It was hard to imagine work centers comfortable for a cook who might be standing or in a wheelchair. Fiser decided to buy an office chair on casters, the type used for drafting. In this chair, she could work comfortably whatever the current state of her knees. It offered a nice intermediate perch, somewhere between standing and sitting. The chair's swivel seat provided better mobility than would have been possible in a conventional wheelchair, which is awkward in tight spaces. This chair became the pivot of our design.

Accessible kitchens are usually large, to allow for wheelchair maneuvers. We went in the opposite direction. Our U-shaped layout, including the table, was as small as possible, like an office work center that has a desk, typewriter and computer grouped around the swivel chair. I felt it should be possible to cook, serve, eat and clean up with the chair moving only a few feet.

Proposed storage locations, counter and chair heights and other details should be tested empirically whenever possible. We propped up plywood at various heights, and piled phone books on a stool to try to find the best working heights to use. Working under time and cost pressures, we relied too much on intuition and guesswork, and on the fact that the proposed drafting chair would be adjustable. At this stage of the planning, it would have been very useful to have had access to a training facility with a formal system for mocking up proposed arrangements.

Kitchen layout—When you build for people with limited mobility, labor-efficient design is vital. In this kitchen, the equipment is arranged in the classic sequence: refrigerator, sink counter, main work counter, stove, serving area and table. This minimizes travel distance, since it's the order in which most work progresses.

The sink counter, or cleanup center, is at the normal 36-in. height because we needed to use the two drawer units that had already been purchased. This height is comfortable with the drafting chair adjusted 27 in. from the floor, but a wheelchair can be used if necessary. (The usual sink height for wheelchair use is 32 in. to 33 in., with about 29 in. clearance below.)

In base cabinets, drawers with full-extension hardware are much better for disabled users than conventional units with doors and shelves, because they hold more, and because their contents can be seen and retrieved from above. The unit to the left of the sink was already purchased, so it did not have full-extension drawers. Since the drawers on the other side of the sink are very deep and open under the counter of the mix center, we cut down the drawer sides facing the sink to allow easier access once they're opened. This is the kind of ad-hoc arrangement that resulted from our time and budget constraints. Both units got new drawer fronts to match the rest of the new work.

A dishwasher might seem essential in such a kitchen. But dishwashers require extra space,

Drawings: Chuck Lockhart

and we had none. They also require a lot of up-and-down movement to load and unload, and this is the most difficult kind of movement for a person with knee problems. In this kitchen, dishes, utensils, silver, and some pots and pans are stored on shelves above the sink. These shelves are slotted and drain down into the sink (top drawing, facing page). Dishes can be washed, rinsed and put away wet with a few simple motions. The racks are also very low on the wall for easy reach without standing. In general, open shelves above the counter provide better storage for an accessible kitchen than traditional wall cabinets, especially if they're kept as low as possible.

In any kitchen, putting the main work counter, or mix center, between the sink and the range is the key to an efficient layout. Here the open counter under the window is the main food preparation area. At a height of about 33 in., it's fine for wheelchair use, but comfortable also for the drafting chair. From this position Fiser can reach the two-burner hot plate to the right, pots and pans in the drawers under the burners, and most of the dishes and utensils above the sink. A slot at the back of the counter keeps knives close by.

We used a simple two-burner hot plate for the cooking center because it would handle most cooking needs and take up less space than a full-size cooktop. But there is also a conventional range on the opposite wall for more extensive cooking. Shelves above the hot plate hold spices and foods that are used most often. Consider-able additional storage is provided on the wall opposite the work centers and in the pantry.

The table completes the U-shape of the kitchen layout. This makes it more convenient for Fiser to serve meals, and also provides extra counter space for the cooking center. A tile inset at one end of the table is a handy place for hot pans and dishes. At 31 in., the table has wheelchair clearance below.

This kitchen is small, but all the dishes, cookware and food for a small household can be stored here, if unnecessary items are weeded out. And it is this smallness that helps make the kitchen accessible by saving steps and making it less tiring to use. □

Sam Clark is a builder in Cambridge, Mass.

Further reading on barrier-free design

Here's a list and brief review of some publications on barrier-free design and related subjects. Though such information is essential for people with disabilities, its relevance does not end there. Barrier-free design is based largely on user needs and on ergonomics, or human engineering. This approach can contribute to all projects, not just those for disabled clients.

The Minnesota Housing Finance Agency publishes a mimeographed "Home Accessibility Information Series," available from the Minnesota State Documents Center (117 University Ave., St. Paul, Minn. 55101; $6.00). It consists of nine short discussions of key areas such as movement, ramps, steps, lifts, bathrooms and grab bars. Each covers the design principles and problems involved, and summarizes typical solutions. Series #3, "Ramps," gives maximum pitches for different conditions, and explains why they apply. Wheelchair ramps, for example, should rise no more than 1 in. for every 12 in. of run. Steeper ramps are usually beyond the strength of people propelling their own wheelchairs, are dangerous for motorized wheelchairs, and can cause back problems for attendants who push wheelchairs. Information of this type is much more useful than simple specs and codes.

One of my favorite tools is "Humanscale 1/2/3" (Niels Diffrient, Alvin R. Tiller, Joan C. Bardagjy, MIT Press, 28 Carleton St., Cambridge, Mass. 02142, 1974; $12.50 each, $39.95 for the set), a portfolio of information on human engineering. It consists of three clever data cards, with dimensioned diagrams on both faces inside the card and a wheel that spins inside the card. You dial the age, school grade, height or category (average adult, etc.) of the person or group you are designing for, and the corresponding dimensions appear in little windows. "Humanscale #1" shows dimensions of the human body. For example, someone 65 in. tall would have a shoulder height of 53.2 in., an eye level of 60.9 in., a high grip of 72.6 in., and an arm-reach radius of 24 in. measured from the shoulder. This presentation gives designers a handy way to get greater precision when designing storage and work centers or when laying out window heights, door openings, hall widths and other features. "Humanscale #2" is on seating and table design, and #3 is on wheelchair users and disabled and elderly people.

Perhaps the best single book on the problems faced by disabled people and on how designers can help create solutions is *Design for Independent Living: The Environment and Physically Disabled People* (Raymond Lifchez and Barbara Winslow, University of California Press, 2120 Berkeley Way, Berkeley, Calif. 94720, 1982; $9.95). It tells the story of the Center for Independent Living in Berkeley, Calif., a workshop and growth center for physically disabled people. The area is a mecca for disabled people, and the CIL is the main reason.

While the book does discuss specific problems and their solutions, much of it is devoted to the design approach developed at the Center, which the authors call "the interactionist position." It de-emphasizes the traditional drawing-board approach to design, and advocates working with and observing disabled clients in order to design for their particular needs.

Independent Living for the Handicapped and the Elderly (Elizabeth E. May, Nova R. Waggoner, and Eleanor B. Hotte, Houghton Mifflin Co.) illustrates layouts, devices, tools and designs that make independent living more possible for people with specific disabilities. It is based partly on the work of Lillian Gilbreth, a pioneer in this field. Unfortunately this book is out of print, but it's worth checking for in libraries and used-book stores.

How to Create Interiors for the Disabled (Jane Randolph Cary, Pantheon Books, 201 E. 50 St., New York, N. Y. 10022, 1978; $5.95) is an excellent nuts-and-bolts book. It has chapters on ramps, doors, windows, storage, kitchens and similar topics. It shows how spaces can be laid out, what clearances are generally best, and mentions hardware and equipment that may be useful in particular situations. The book emphasizes simple, low-cost solutions, using readily available supplies. The author gives sources and product names, which is very useful.

Housing Interiors for the Disabled and Elderly (Bettyann B. Raschko, Van Nostrand Reinhold Co., 115 Fifth Ave., New York, N. Y. 10003; 1982. $39.95) is also a comprehensive and up-to-date book on barrier-free design. But it is more academic in approach and surveys research results and technical information more thoroughly than does Cary's book. The solutions it features tend to be more costly and highly technical, requiring specialized, hard-to-find equipment.

My favorite book of this type is *The Accessible Bathroom* (Karen Nickels, The Design Coalition, 1201 Williamson St., Madison, Wis. 53703, 1985; $5.00). The bathroom justifies a book-length treatment because existing bathrooms are often very difficult to adapt. Nickels' book is clear, well illustrated and complete. For example, she points out that most houses or apartments have hallways that are 32 in. to 36 in. wide, and for a wheelchair user to make the right-angled turn into the bathroom, the doorway needs to be at least 36 in. wide. She also recommends that the door swing out in order to conserve space inside the bathroom and because of the potential danger of a wheelchair user falling and blocking a door that swings in. The sample layouts in the book are particularly useful.

Karen Nickels treats a different subject in a similarly practical way in her book *An Accessible Entrance: Ramps*. More than just a discussion of slopes, this book also covers different configurations of ramps and platforms, handrails and slip-resistant surfaces. There's even a section on landscaping.

All kinds of supplies can be located by consulting "The System" (Ronald L. Mace, AIA, Information Development Corp., 360 St. Alban Court, Winston-Salem, N. C. 27104), prepared by an architect who uses a wheelchair and who specializes in design for disabled people. This two-volume set is a looseleaf compilation of illustrated design information, accessibility specs and standards, and product information. At $299.95, "The System" may not be for everyone, but it's well worth consulting. Architectural firms and architectural libraries are most likely to have copies.

I found much of the above information at the Adaptive Environments Center (621 Huntington Ave., Boston, Mass. 02155). AEC is the New England distributor of "The System" and sells or distributes various literature, including some of the items described here. However, their primary function is to serve as a design, consulting, advocacy and educational agency on barrier-free design, and to operate a reference library on this subject. They also hold training sessions for small groups, including builders. —*S. C.*

The Kitchen Cabinet
How to design and build one with basic tools

by Will Hasson

The fundamental building block in every successful kitchen is the below-the-counter cabinet. It supports the work surface above and makes for organized storage beneath. Though this essential built-in can take on a multitude of styles and refinements, at heart the construction requirements are all the same. A sturdy case and framework, easily operable drawers, doors that fit and proper scale are common to good cabinets, whether made of painted plywood or expensive hardwood. In this article, I will describe the basic steps involved in building an uncomplicated, yet handsome, kitchen cabinet unit for about $140 in materials.

The cabinet shown above is the standard 24-in. depth, and is designed for the typical ¾-in. thick by 25½-in. plastic-laminate countertop. Its 35¼-in. height, also standard, accommodates appliances such as dishwashers and trash compactors, and presents the countertop at a level on which most people can work comfortably. These dimensions are used widely in the trade, but you can change the height to suit yourself just by adding or subtracting an inch or so. The 54-in. length here is arbitrary, but it makes good use of a single sheet of plywood and has room enough for a small sink to be let into the countertop. Also, a cabinet of this general size is small enough to move easily from shop to site—an important consideration.

Starting out—Constructing cabinets should always begin with a drawing of exactly what you have in mind. The drawing is indispensable for working out proportions, making cutting lists and for seeing the relationships between the different parts. You can use the drawings and cutting lists on the facing page as models for preparing your own design and material requirements. If you do as much as you can on paper before you cut any wood, you'll save yourself a lot of time and frustration.

Almost all cabinets have the same parts: a case (or carcase), a face frame, doors and drawers. The cabinet shown here is designed to feature wood, and therefore has a carefully joined face frame and panel doors. The face-frame members are doweled together, and the whole frame is then applied to the front of the case. It provides jambs for the cabinet doors, defines the openings for the drawers and generally stiffens the carcase and helps it resist lateral racking. The doors and drawers have ⅜-in. rabbeted inner edges so they overlap the face frame ⅜ in. to form a lip on all sides, and so the drawer fronts and door frames project ⅜ in. beyond the plane of the face frame. This arrange-

From *Fine Homebuilding* magazine (June 1982) 9:32-38

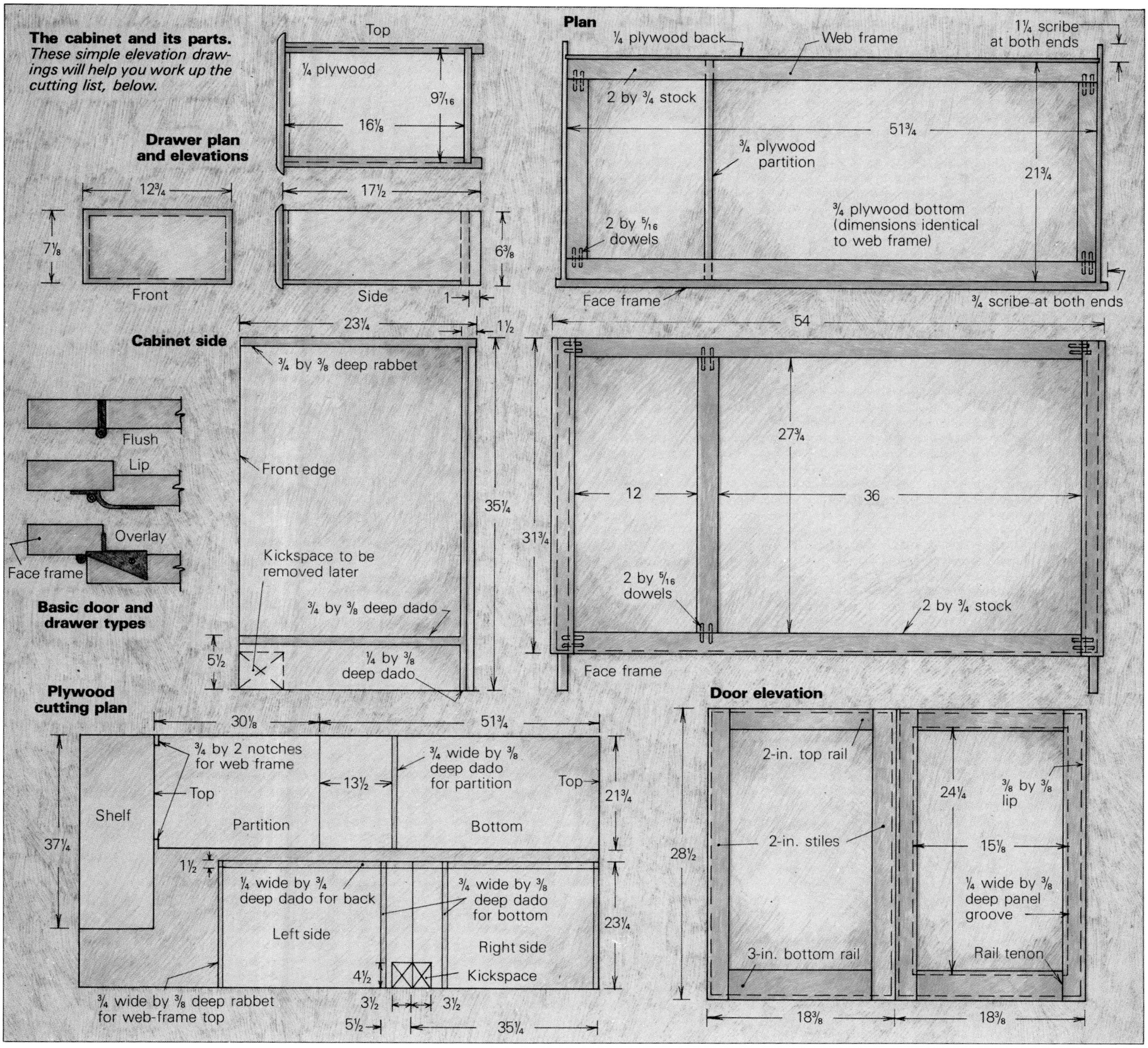

The cabinet and its parts.
These simple elevation drawings will help you work up the cutting list, below.
Drawer plan and elevations
Top
¼ plywood
9 7/16
16⅛
12¾
17½
7⅛
6⅜
Front
Side
1
Plan
¼ plywood back
Web frame
1¼ scribe at both ends
2 by ¾ stock
51¾
¾ plywood partition
21¾
¾ plywood bottom (dimensions identical to web frame)
2 by 5/16 dowels
Face frame
¾ scribe at both ends
Cabinet side
23¼
1½
¾ by ⅜ deep rabbet
Front edge
35¼
31¾
Kickspace to be removed later
¾ by ⅜ deep dado
5½
¼ by ⅜ deep dado
Flush
Lip
Overlay
Face frame
Basic door and drawer types
54
27¾
12
36
2 by 5/16 dowels
2 by ¾ stock
Face frame
Plywood cutting plan
30⅛
51¾
¾ by 2 notches for web frame
Top
Shelf
Partition
13½
¾ wide by ⅜ deep dado for partition
Top
Bottom
21¾
37¼
1½
¼ wide by ¾ deep dado for back
Left side
¾ wide by ⅜ deep dado for bottom
Right side
23¼
4½
Kickspace
¾ wide by ⅜ deep rabbet for web-frame top
3½
3½
5½
35¼
Door elevation
2-in. top rail
24¼
⅜ by ⅜ lip
2-in. stiles
15⅛
28½
¼ wide by ⅜ deep panel groove
3-in. bottom rail
Rail tenon
18⅜
18⅜

ment looks good, and the rabbets allow considerable latitude in fitting doors and drawers into the cabinet. Once the face frame is made and attached, however, you can choose between either overlay or flush detailing, as shown in the drawing above.

In our shop, we make the face frame extend ¾ in. beyond the sides of the case so the cabinet can be scribed to fit snugly against interior walls and against other adjacent cabinet units.

You can build the entire cabinet unit with just a few tools. A table saw or radial arm saw is useful for ripping frame members and drawer sides to width and for crosscutting them accurately to length. The case sides and back, however, are best cut with a skill saw, since in many cases it's almost impossible to wrestle a full sheet of ¾-in. plywood onto a saw table. You will also need an electric drill with a sharp 5/16-in. bit (preferably a brad-point bit) and a doweling jig for joining frame members.

It's possible, but not advisable, to get the job done without a table saw or radial saw. Without standing power tools, you would have to use a circular saw for all the ripping and crosscutting and a router for cutting the grooves, rabbets and dadoes. By hand-planing the frame members and drawer sides to finished width, you could certainly get accurate results, though it would take you considerably longer this way than if you were to use a standing power saw.

Making the face frame—Construction begins with the face frame. Rip ¾-in. solid stock into 2-in. wide strips and cut them to length. A crosscut jig for your table saw can be a great help in cutting accurate 90° angles. One way you can build a jig like this is described in the

Cutting list

Part	How many?	Size (in.)
Case		
Partition	1	30⅛ x 21¾ x ¾-in. ply
Bottom	1	51¾ x 21¾ x ¾-in. ply
Sides	2	35¼ x 23¼ x ¾-in. ply
Shelf	1	37¼ x 14 x ¾-in. ply
Back panel	1	51¾ x 30½ x ¼-in. ply
Web frame	2	51¾ x 2 x ¾
	2	17¾ x 2 x ¾
Face frame	2	50 x 2 x ¾
	2	31¾ x 2 x ¾
	1	27¾ x 2 x ¾
Doors		
Stiles	4	28½ x 2 x ¾
Rails	2	15⅛ x 2 x ¾
Rails	2	15⅛ x 3 x ¾
Panels	2	15⅛ x 24¼ x ¼-in. ply
Drawers		
Fronts	4	7⅛ x 12¾ x ¾
Sides	8	6⅜ x 17½ x ¾
Backs	4	6⅜ x 9 7/16 x ¾
Bottoms	4	16⅛ x 9 7/16 x ¼-in. ply
Kickplate	1	54 x 3½ x ¾
Hanger bar	1	37¼ x 3½ x ¾

The frame. With the doweling jig indexed on the pencil mark (1) Hasson bores out the end grain in a frame member. The hole is bored to the proper depth when the electrical tape on the drill bit is flush with the top of the jig, which is a self-centering dowel-guide made by Dowl-It (Box 147, Hastings, Mich. 49058).

For joining face-frame members, a single pencil line (2) marks the intersection of an upright. Lines to mark bore centers have been extended with a combination square down the edges to ensure accuracy in locating holes.

Crosscut jig

A simple table-saw attachment is especially useful for cutting frame members to length. We have four different versions for cutting various angles and sizes of work. The one drawn below is for making precisely square cuts in stock up to 2 ft. wide.

The guide rails on the bottom of the jig fit into the two miter grooves milled into the saw table on either side of the blade. We use oak or maple for the rails because these woods are hard and slippery. The runners should slide easily without any side-to-side movement.

The rails must be exactly perpendicular to fence A, which is rabbeted on its underside. In our latest version, I placed the rails in the table grooves and put a dab of glue atop their ends. Then I positioned fence A on the glue points and adjusted it perpendicular to the rails with a combination square. When the glue had set up, I applied glue to the edge of a ½-in. plywood panel and carefully slid the edges into the rabbet at the bottom of fence A, clamped it in place, and screwed the plywood to the runners, without moving the assembly from the table saw. Later I glued fence B to the top of the plywood. It keeps the ends of the plywood from flopping around and gives ballast to the front of the jig.

Passing the jig over the sawblade a few times will cut a workable slot in the plywood table. If you use the jig with a dado blade, make several shallow cuts to form the blade slot.

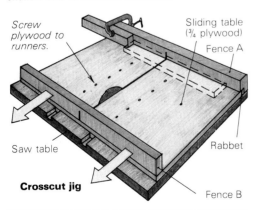

Screw plywood to runners.

Sliding table (¾ plywood)

Fence A

Saw table

Rabbet

Crosscut jig

Fence B

1

sidebar at left. Lay the frame members on a flat surface in the positions they belong in and label both sides of each joint. Holding one piece tightly in position with your fingers or a clamp, draw two lines across the joint. These lines mark the centers of the $\frac{5}{16}$-in. dowel holes, so don't put them too close to the edges of the stock—about ½ in. in is good. Next, carry the marks over the edges and ends of the strips with a combination square. A doweling jig is crucial to this operation because it ensures that the dowel hole is square to the surface and in just the right spot. Center the indexing mark of the doweling jig (mine is self-centering) on the lines and bore $\frac{5}{16}$-in. dia. holes slightly more than 1 in. deep for 2-in. dowels (photo 1, above). Drill a test hole to the right depth, and mark the drill shank with a piece of electrical tape where it's flush with the top of the jig. The tape will mark the depth for all the holes.

Before you join the frame members, think which parts should go together first. Generally, the rule is to work from the inside out. With large, complicated frames it is sometimes useful to glue up the frame in sections, letting the glue in each section dry before assembling it into a complicated whole. After drilling all the holes, baste the dowels on one end with a thin coat of yellow (aliphatic-resin) glue, and drive them home (2). To assemble each section, apply glue first to the end-grain edges, letting it soak in and reapplying as necessary. Then coat the dowels and close the joint.

Clamp the frame together with bar clamps, and use wooden pads between the clamp jaws and the face frame to avoid crushing the edges and to direct the clamping force to the joint area (3). Small pieces of paper between the clamp and the frame will prevent the glue from reacting with the metal and staining the wood black. Don't rush. Work steadily and carefully, making certain that everything is flat and square. After the glue dries, tool off the squeeze-out with a sharp chisel or paint scraper. Plane or sand the face frame with a belt sander to even out the joints; then set it aside.

3

4

When gluing up the face frame (3), check for square, and position clamp blocks to direct clamping pressure across joint lines.

The basic case (4): ³⁄₄-in. plywood sides, bottom and partition are glued and nailed in place with 6d cement-coated nails. Notches in the top of the partition will receive the web-frame top.

Apply the face frame (5) with the cabinet laid on its back. Before gluing face frame to carcase, check the scribe depth (the amount by which the frame overlaps the sides). Re-check periodically while tightening the clamps. The web-frame top has already been glued and nailed into notches in the partition and into rabbets in the case sides.

5

The case—The case or carcase determines the interior space of the cabinet. The sides, bottom and interior partition and shelf in this cabinet are all ³⁄₄-in. plywood, and the back is ¹⁄₄-in. plywood. We use lauan plywood for these parts because it's easy to work, and has an unobtrusive color and grain pattern that doesn't clash with the solid woods on the face of the cabinet. A web frame, similar to the face frame, is fitted into rabbets and holds the carcase together at the top. The bottom of the case is housed in dadoes in the sides.

Now lay out the cabinet sections on the plywood in the most economical fashion (drawing, p. 31). Cut the plywood for the sides, bottom and partition, and mark the positions of the dadoes and rabbets. Remember there are two opposing sides, one the mirror image of the other. Avoid making a pair of identical sides by accident, and having to scrap one.

Set your table saw or router to cut a groove ³⁄₄ in. wide by ³⁄₈ in. deep. Now rabbet the tops (inside) of the case sides and dado the bottoms

as shown in the drawing on p. 31. Then cut ¹⁄₄-in. wide by ³⁄₈-in. deep grooves for the plywood back.

Next, dowel-join and glue up the web-frame top just as you did the face frame. It has the same outside dimensions as the plywood bottom panel, and is held in the rabbets cut into the top of the case sides and in two notches cut into the partition top. The web frame holds the top of the case together, and serves as a cleat for attaching the countertop.

When the carcase components are cut to size, nail and glue them together from the bottom up (4). Use 6d cement-coated nails, and draw a centerline opposite the dadoes to aid in locating the nails. Lay the partially assembled case on its back and align the side and partition while nailing the web frame in place. Make sure the distance between the partition and the sides is equal at the top and bottom.

After assembling the case, attach the face frame (5). If the cabinet is to be painted or if nail holes are not objectionable, the face frame

can be glued and face-nailed to the body with 6d finishing nails. A neater way is to glue and clamp the face frame to the case, though this requires a good supply of bar clamps and C-clamps. Whichever method you use, leave an equal overlap at each side for scribing. When the frame is glued in place, saw out the kickspace notches.

Drawers—Doors and drawers fall into one of three categories, depending on how they relate to the face frame. Lip doors and drawers are the traditional choice. Overlay doors and drawers are used almost exclusively in mass-produced kitchen cabinets, mainly because they are so quick and easy to install. But they also give a kitchen a clean, solid look. Flush doors and drawers (they fit flush with the face frame) make the cabinets look like furniture, and are by far the most difficult to install, as each one must be hand-fitted.

The details for drawer construction depend upon the type of drawer (lip, overlay or flush)

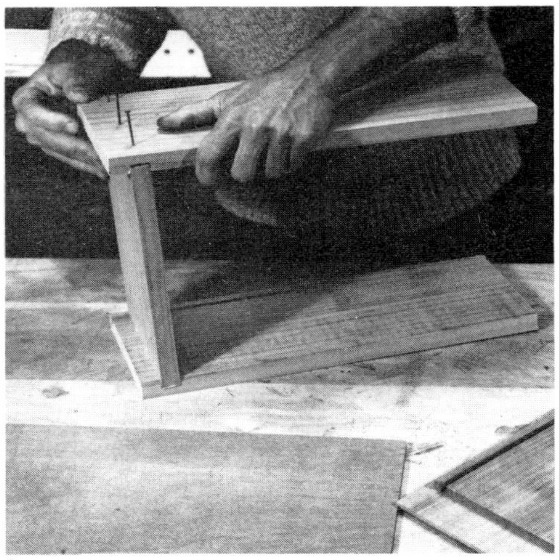

6

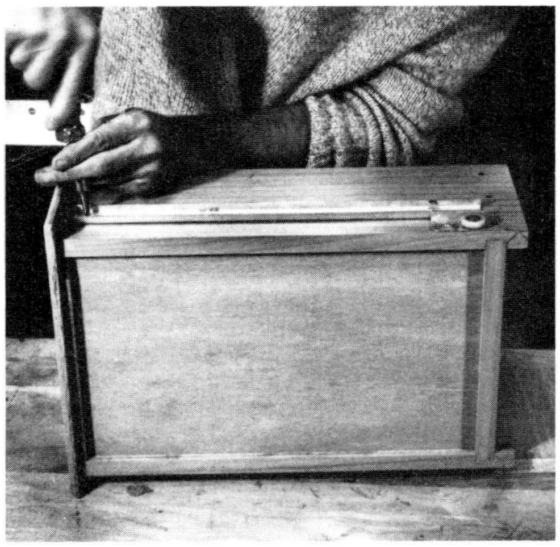

7

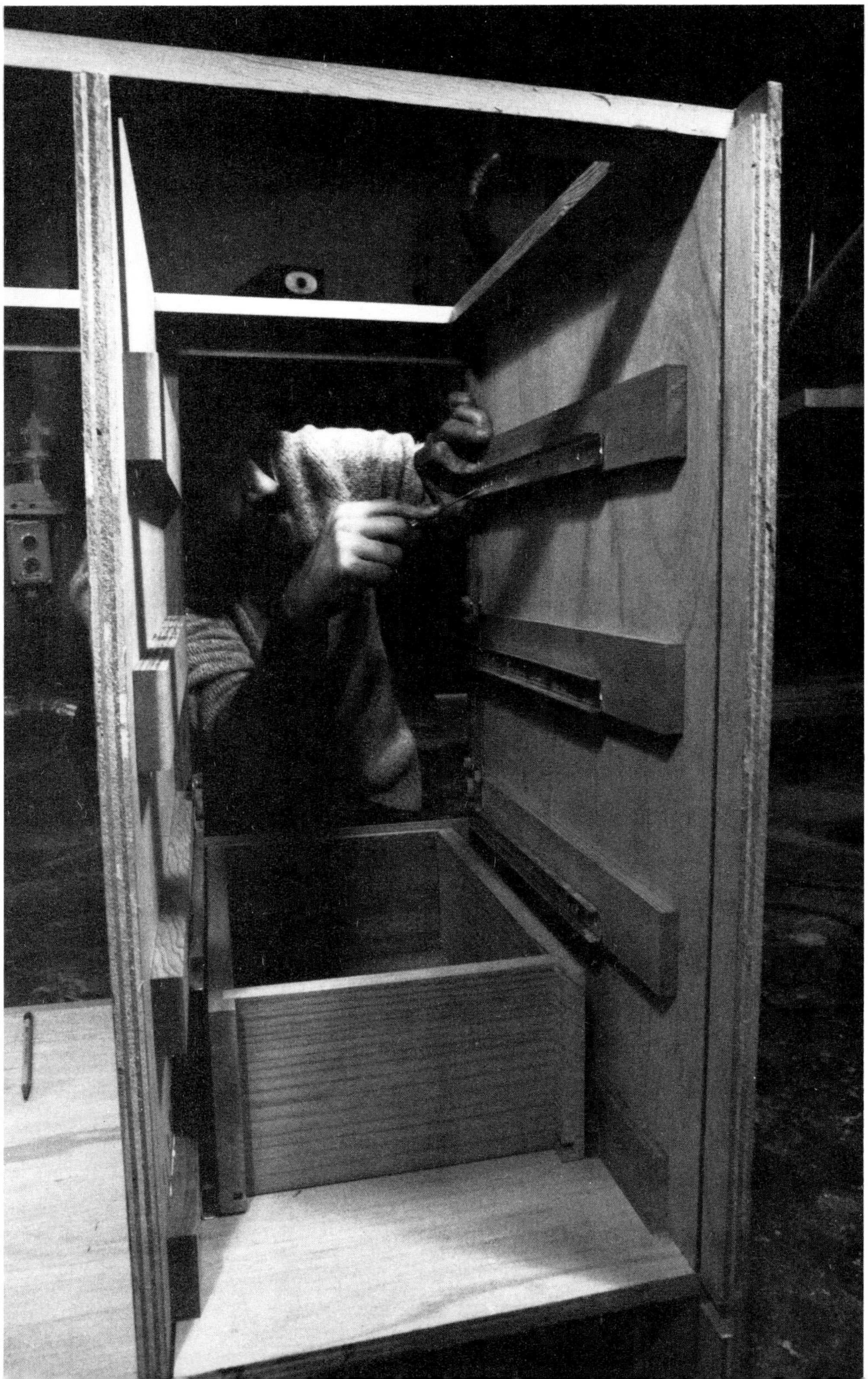

8

Section through drawers

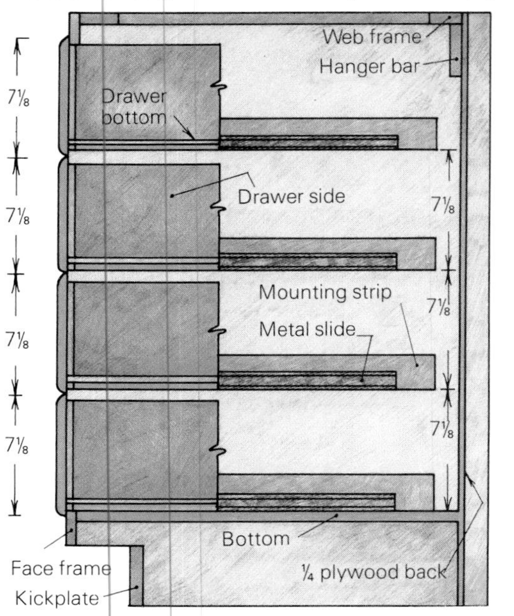

1¼ scribe
Web frame
Hanger bar
Drawer bottom
Drawer side
Mounting strip
Metal slide
7⅛
7⅛
7⅛
7⅛
7⅛
7⅛
7⅛
7⅛
Bottom
Face frame
Kickplate
¼ plywood back

Plan of drawers and slide

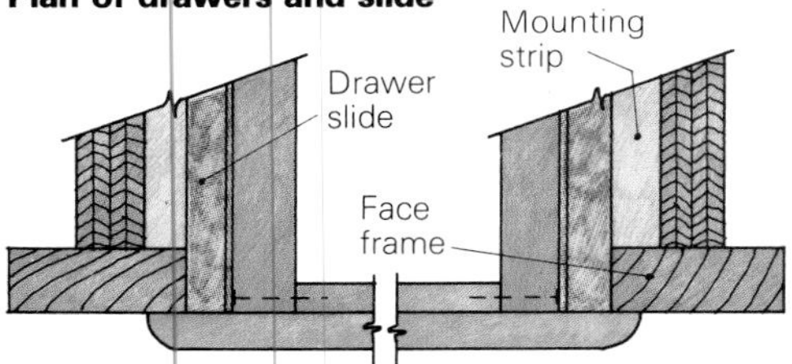

Mounting strip
Drawer slide
Face frame

Drawers. **After cutting the components (drawing, above), assemble the drawer by gluing and nailing the dadoed sides to the back (6). Slide the drawer bottom into its groove, and cap the box with the drawer front. Bore pilot holes for nailing the sides into the rabbeted front to avoid splitting the wood. The front edges of the drawer front have been shaped with a router and a ⅜-in. rounding-over bit.**

Screw the slides to the drawer sides (7). The wheel flange should be flush with the side's bottom edge, and the track parallel to the edge.

Inside the cabinet (8) drawer slides are fixed to a mounting strip that holds them flush with the face frame. The mounting strips are glued and screwed to the case sides.

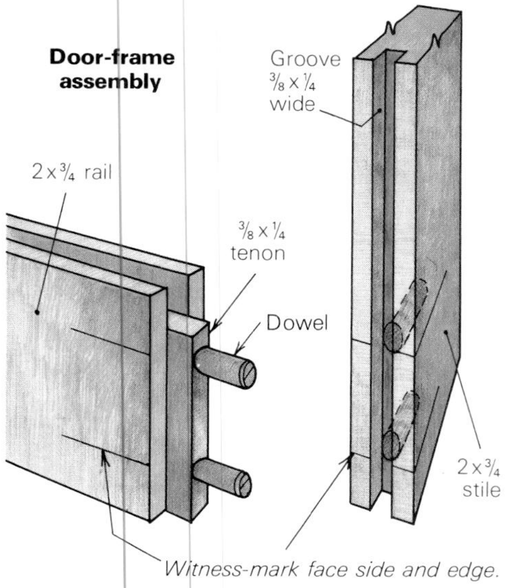

Door-frame assembly
Groove ⅜ x ¼ wide
2 x ¾ rail
⅜ x ¼ tenon
Dowel
2 x ¾ stile
Witness-mark face side and edge.

A bottom rail, with doweled tenon and panel groove. The stubby tenon adds strength and lets you plow unstopped grooves in the stiles.

and the kind of drawer-slide mechanism you use. We use metal slides with nylon rollers for mounting the drawers because they are easy to install and because drawers glide smoothly and quietly on them. The slides come in a number of sizes, based on the dimensions of the drawer and the expected weight of its contents. Each drawer requires a pair of slides, which fit into a corresponding pair of tracks mounted on the inside of the cabinet. The slides in this cabinet are Grant #336 (Grant Hardware Co., High St., West Nyack, N.Y.; and 16651 Johnson Dr., City of Industry, Calif. 91745).

Begin laying out the drawers by considering the inside dimension of the opening in the face frame into which they will fit. In this cabinet, the drawer opening is 12 in. wide and $27\frac{3}{4}$ in. high. To keep things simple, we'll construct four identical drawers (drawing, facing page, top). Add the opening height plus the width of two lips ($27\frac{3}{4}$ in. + $\frac{3}{8}$ in. + $\frac{3}{8}$ in. = $28\frac{1}{2}$ in.) and divide the total by four to determine the height of each drawer front ($7\frac{1}{8}$ in.). The length of the drawer front is the width of the opening plus the width of two lips ($12\frac{3}{4}$ in.).

Cut out the drawer fronts and calculate the width of the rabbet on the inside of each drawer front required to overlap the drawer sides, the metal slide and the face frame. The side thickness is $\frac{3}{4}$ in.; almost all metal slides require $^{17}/_{32}$ in. between the drawer side and the face frame; and the lip width is $\frac{3}{8}$ in. This adds up to $1^{21}/_{32}$ in.

Cut the rabbets in the drawer fronts, and set them aside while you make the other drawer parts. The width of the sides will be the drawers' front height less the width of the two $\frac{3}{8}$-in. lips (in our case, $7\frac{1}{8}$ in. − $\frac{3}{4}$ in. = $6\frac{3}{8}$ in.). The drawer length of $17\frac{1}{2}$ in. in this cabinet is arbitrary. Drawers can be as long as the depth of the cabinet will allow.

The drawer sides, back and front are grooved along their bottom inner edges to receive the $\frac{1}{4}$-in. plywood bottom. Plow the groove $\frac{1}{4}$ in. deep and $\frac{3}{8}$ in. from the bottom edge. The sides have a $\frac{3}{4}$-in. wide dado cut 1 in. from the rear edge to house the drawer back. Nail and glue

the drawers together, making sure they are square (6). Apply glue to the joints but not to the bottom panel, which should float freely in the groove. This is especially important if the drawer bottom is made of solid wood rather than plywood, because gluing it will cause it to crack eventually.

Half of the drawer slide is screwed to the drawer sides (7); the other half is attached to the sides of the cabinet on a spacer strip that brings it flush with the face frame. Locate the bottom edges of the spacers the same distance apart as the height of the drawer fronts. This will give you a guide for attaching the slides (8). All metal slides come with slotted holes to allow up-and-down and in-and-out adjustments. Use the slotted holes until the drawers run properly, and then drive the rest of the screws to lock the slide in place. You'll probably have to shave the top and bottom edges of the drawer fronts with a plane to regularize the spaces between them.

Panel doors—Frame-and-panel construction is common to most cabinet doors because it can be varied in so many ways. The inner edges of the frame may be molded with a router or shaper, be treated with applied molding or just be left square. The panel may be flat or raised, or glass may be used instead of wood.

Construction is basically the same regardless of the details. The first step, again, is to make a cutting list. Door stiles should be equal to the height of the door opening plus $\frac{3}{4}$ in. for the lips top and bottom. Calculate the width the same way. For a pair of doors, the opening plus $\frac{3}{4}$ in. is divided by two to get the width of each individual door. The length of the rails equals the width of the door less twice the width of the stile plus twice the depth of the panel groove for cutting a short tenon on the rail ends. In this cabinet, rail length is $15\frac{1}{8}$ in. ($18\frac{3}{8}$ − 4 + $\frac{3}{4}$). Typically stiles and top rails are 2 in. wide. Bottom rails are $1\frac{1}{2}$ times as wide to add visual weight and to increase the amount of wood involved in the joint.

After ripping the stiles and rails to width and

cutting them to length, arrange the pieces on a flat surface and mark the joints for dowels. Keep the holes far enough from the edges to prevent cutting into the dowels when rabbeting the outer edge for the lip and grooving the inner edge for the panel (drawing facing page, bottom). Mark the inner edge of each piece so rabbeting, grooving and drilling get done in the right spots. Then bore for dowels.

Make a $\frac{1}{4}$-in. wide groove in a scrap piece of wood for testing the thickness of the rail tenons. Now cut the tenons $\frac{1}{4}$ in. thick by $\frac{3}{8}$ in. wide on both ends of the rails. Do this on a table saw or with a router, or clamp the rail in a vise and cut the tenon with a good backsaw. Make sure the tenons fit snugly, but not too tightly in the test groove.

The next step is to groove the inner edges of the frame members to receive the panels and tenons. Be certain to mark the outside face of each member and hold that face against the saw fence when plowing the grooves for the panels. Cut the $\frac{1}{4}$-in. plywood panel to fit, and then assemble the frame around it. Again, don't glue the panel into the groove. Be sure the doors are square and flat; otherwise they won't lie flat against the cabinet when closed.

Once the glue has dried, cut the $\frac{3}{8}$-in. by $\frac{3}{8}$-in. rabbet all around the door's inner edges (9), and you're ready to put on the hinges. Hinges are made for all three kinds of doors, and each style requires a specific type of hinge. It is best to install the hinges for lip doors on the doors first, spacing them one hinge length down from the top and the same up from the bottom. Next, set the cabinet on its back, put the doors in place and mark the position of the hinges (10). Drive one screw into each hinge and see if the door swings freely and lies flat. If it does, drive in the rest of the screws. If the fit is skewed, remove the screws, readjust the hinges as necessary, and try again. Now install catches to keep the doors flat against the face frame. Mount the catches opposite the door pulls. We use the common roller variety. Screw the male half to the top of the door stile, engage the two halves and screw the catch plate to the mount-

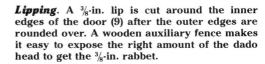

Lipping. A $\frac{3}{8}$-in. lip is cut around the inner edges of the door (9) after the outer edges are rounded over. A wooden auxiliary fence makes it easy to expose the right amount of the dado head to get the $\frac{3}{8}$-in. rabbet.

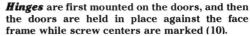

Hinges are first mounted on the doors, and then the doors are held in place against the face frame while screw centers are marked (10).

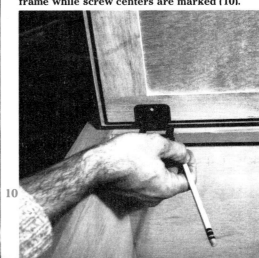

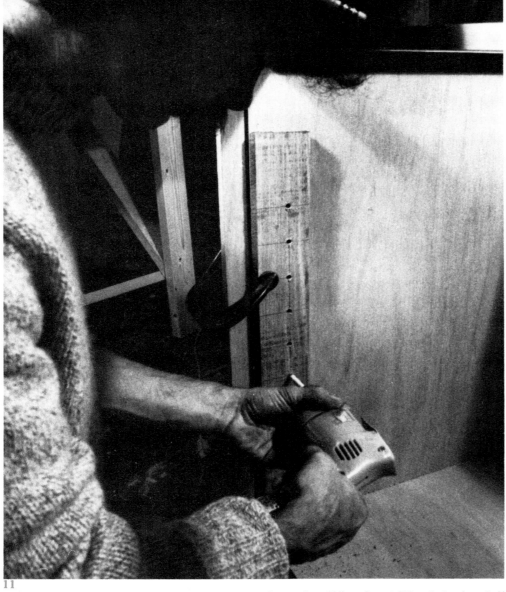

11

A template (11) makes drilling holes for shelf rests quick and accurate.

The hanger bar for attaching the cabinet to the wall is glued and nailed to the bottom of the web frame (12). The kickplate overlaps the side by the same amount that the face frame does.

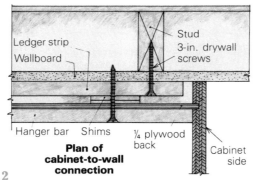

12

Plan of cabinet-to-wall connection

Ledger strip
Wallboard
Stud
3-in. drywall screws
Hanger bar   Shims
¼ plywood back
Cabinet side

Attaching adjacent cabinets

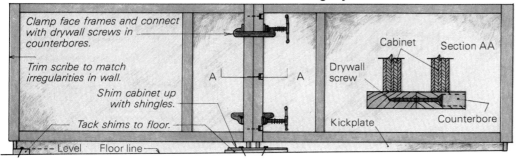

Clamp face frames and connect with drywall screws in counterbores.

Trim scribe to match irregularities in wall.

Shim cabinet up with shingles.

Tack shims to floor.

Level   Floor line

A   A

Cabinet   Section AA

Drywall screw

Kickplate   Counterbore

ing block with the door closed. Magnetic catches are also good, but best of all are self-closing hinges, which let you do away with catches all together.

While the back is still off, bore holes for the shelf rests. Make a drilling jig like the one shown in photo 11 with ¼-in. dia. holes, 2 in. on center, for press-in shelf rests. Use a piece of tape on the drill bit to regulate the depth of the hole. I drill the vertical rows of holes about a foot apart toward the back of the cabinet. The shelf should be about 14 in. wide, rather than span to the front of the cabinet. This narrower shelf lets you get at pots and other stuff stored in the rear of the cabinet.

A 1x4 hanger bar for installing the cabinet should now be nailed and glued to the bottom of the web frame and to the sides of the cabinet (12). Finally, slide the ¼-in. plywood back into its groove and nail it in place. Give everything a good sanding, and protect the wood with the finish of your choice. For wood finishes, we prefer Watco Danish Oil or lacquer, but for cabinets that are used frequently, polyurethane is the best choice.

Installation—Chances are good that the space your cabinet will occupy is neither level, square nor bordered by perfectly flat walls. These imperfections are usually slight and of no structural consequence, but they can drive the meticulous installer crazy. A few tips:

First, measure the highest and lowest points in the room and determine the differential. If the difference is an inch or less, I shim up the bottom of the cabinets, starting at the lowest point in the room. If the difference is more than 1 in., I split it by adding shims at one end and cutting the bottoms off the cabinets at the other. When the cabinets are level, pull them away from the wall and attach 1x4 ledger strips to the wall opposite the hanger bars.

Return the cabinets to their intended positions and check any counter-to-wall intersections for fit. If the wall is irregular, plane the scribing strip to match the wall contour (for more on scribes, see the next article).

When the cabinets are scribed and level, clamp the neighboring face frames together (if you've got more than one cabinet) and attach them with three counterbored drywall screws. Don't worry about plugging the counterbores—they won't show, and you can easily remove the cabinets if you decide to take them with you. Once the face frames are joined, screw the hanger bars to the wall ledgers, filling any gaps between the two with shims. It doesn't take a lot of screws for a solid connection; two per cabinet should do it.

Cut the kickplate to fill the gap at the back of the toe-space, and attach it in place with 6d finishing nails. We recommend finishing the juncture between the flooring and the kickplate with dark-colored vinyl coving. The coving makes this busy but hard-to-reach kitchen cranny easier to clean, and protects the kickplate from scuff marks. □

Will Hasson is a partner in Fourth St. Woodworking, Berkeley, Calif.

Counter Intelligence

Some tips on working with plastic-laminate countertops

by Jesus Granado

For the past 25 years, plastic-laminate surfaces have been the most popular countertop finish in the kitchen and bathroom. They come in a wide variety of colors, patterns and textures, and the material is affordable, durable and easy to clean.

Plastic laminates are manufactured by several large companies (see box, p. 39) and sold under a variety of names, the best known of which is Formica, but they are all basically the same. Five to seven layers of kraft paper, with a final colored or patterned top layer, are saturated with melamine plastic and subjected to heat and pressure in excess of 1,000 psi in a large press. The result is a hard, thin panel, about $\frac{1}{16}$ in. thick. A final skin of melamine is applied to the top, and the product is ready for use.

The standard countertop is 25½ in. wide, with a 3½-in. high backsplash. Typically, the substrate is made of ¾-in. high-density particleboard, although plywood is sometimes used. On commercially constructed tops, the plastic laminate is bonded to the core under heat and pressure. This allows one piece of plastic to wrap the entire counter from backsplash to nosing and eliminates dirt-catching junctures of horizontal and vertical surfaces. The tops are

designed to cover the common 24-in. wide cabinet, leaving a 1-in. overhang. The remaining ½ in. is a scribe allowance at the top of the backsplash for fitting the counter to irregularities in the wall.

Custom cabinet shops and large building-supply centers frequently carry post-formed countertops from 6 ft. to 12 ft. in length, or can have them made to order. These stock countertops come in a limited range of colors, and cost $5 to $7 per running foot. Your supplier should also have matching sidesplash and open-end trim kits for finishing an installation. For more money, you can get an extraordinary selection of colors and patterns from the specialty shops, even textured and metallic finishes.

Installing a post-formed countertop—Putting in your own counter isn't very difficult, and it's a good way to save between $100 and $200. The easiest top to install is the straight section, with one open end and no miter (more about miters later). Begin by measuring the distance from the end of the cabinet to the wall, and have the counter cut to this length.

If your dealer can't cut the top to length, use a circular saw and cut from the bottom. This

will keep the upward-cutting circular-saw blade from chipping the brittle laminate as it passes through it. If you use a handsaw to make your cuts, use a crosscut with at least 10 teeth per inch, and cut from the top. For added protection against chipping, no matter which saw you use, run a strip of masking tape over the cut line, and saw through it. The laminate should be fully supported to within a few inches of the cut line. Make sure the blades are sharp on any tools used for cutting plastic laminates.

At the wall end of the counter, attach the sidesplash to the countertop with four 2-in. drywall screws in pilot bores and a bead of silicone caulk between the counter edge and the sidesplash (drawing, below). The ¾-in. thickness of the sidesplash will extend the open end of the counter to the necessary overhang for the open-end cap. If you aren't using a sidesplash, remember to add ¾ in. to the counter length for the open-end overhang.

When the unfinished sidesplash is screwed in place, position the counter on the cabinet and check for fit against the back wall. Chances are, the backsplash will touch the wall in places, with ugly gaps in between. This is where the scribe allowance comes in handy. With the

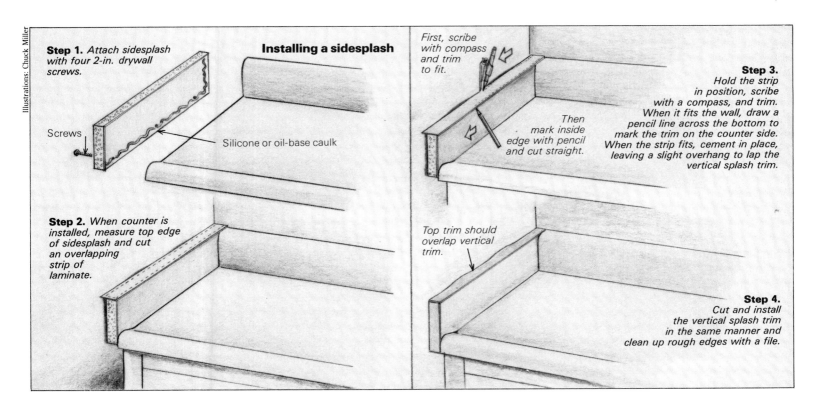

Illustrations: Chuck Miller

Step 1. Attach sidesplash with four 2-in. drywall screws.

Screws

Silicone or oil-base caulk

Installing a sidesplash

Step 2. When counter is installed, measure top edge of sidesplash and cut an overlapping strip of laminate.

First, scribe with compass and trim to fit.

Then mark inside edge with pencil and cut straight.

Step 3. Hold the strip in position, scribe with a compass, and trim. When it fits the wall, draw a pencil line across the bottom to mark the trim on the counter side. When the strip fits, cement in place, leaving a slight overhang to lap the vertical splash trim.

Top trim should overlap vertical trim.

Step 4. Cut and install the vertical splash trim in the same manner and clean up rough edges with a file.

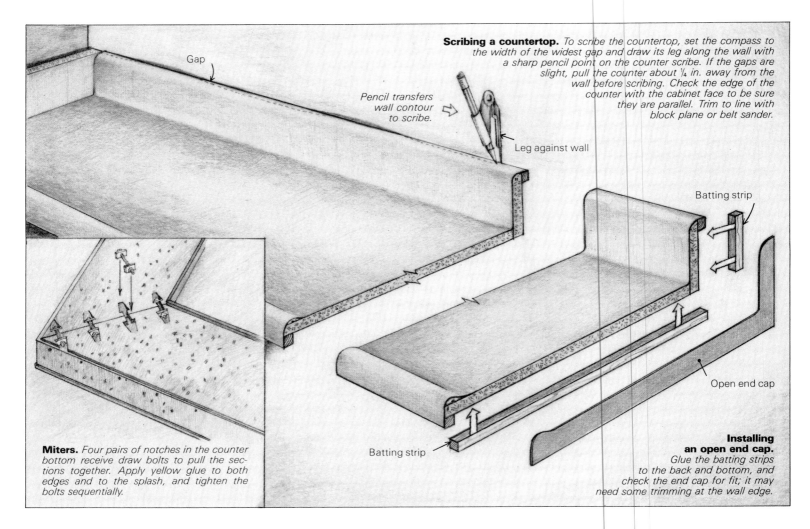

Scribing a countertop. *To scribe the countertop, set the compass to the width of the widest gap and draw its leg along the wall with a sharp pencil point on the counter scribe. If the gaps are slight, pull the counter about ¼ in. away from the wall before scribing. Check the edge of the counter with the cabinet face to be sure they are parallel. Trim to line with block plane or belt sander.*

Gap

Pencil transfers wall contour to scribe.

Leg against wall

Batting strip

Open end cap

Batting strip

Miters. *Four pairs of notches in the counter bottom receive draw bolts to pull the sections together. Apply yellow glue to both edges and to the splash, and tighten the bolts sequentially.*

Installing an open end cap. *Glue the batting strips to the back and bottom, and check the end cap for fit; it may need some trimming at the wall edge.*

counter against the wall and parallel with the face of the cabinet, run a compass, set to the width of the widest gap, along the top of the backsplash (large drawing, above). As the compass is drawn along, the wall's contour is transferred to the scribe allowance. Trim to the pencil line with a block plane or a belt sander until the counter fits tightly against the wall.

Counters often need to be cut out for sinks, which are usually centered below windows or above cabinet doors and set back 2 in. from the counter's front edge. Mark the shape of the opening in the right place on the underside of the counter. Cut straight lines with a circular-saw pocket-cut, and connect them with saber-saw cuts at radiused corners.

Reposition the counter on its cabinet and make sure it's flat. Sometimes a top will be slightly twisted and one corner will not touch the cabinet, and then you'll have to use screws. Usually the cabinet's web frame for attaching the counter is ¾ in. thick. If so, use 1¼-in. screws to avoid penetrating through the ¾-in. thickness of the counter. You don't want screw tips poking through your nice new top. Place the screws 10 in. on center, and at all corners. If the top rests flat, use panel adhesive to secure it to the cabinet—it's quicker than screws. Spread a bead of adhesive on all the cabinet surfaces that will touch the bottom of the counter and put the counter back on for the last time. In 24 hours, the adhesive will have cured enough for you to use the counter.

When the top is secured, finish the sidesplash

trim and the end cap. The splash kit will include a strip of laminate for covering the raw edges. Cut a strip long enough to cover the top, hold it in place and scribe it with the compass. Trim it along the pencil line with a pair of tin snips. When it's tight to the wall, run a pencil along the underside, against the inside edge of the splash, for trimming the outer edge. Finished, this piece should conform to the contour of the wall and to the straight edge of the sidesplash, covering any gap between the two. To glue it in place, coat both surfaces with contact cement and press it into position. Bevel the rough edges with a file.

A strip of laminate cut to the cross-sectional shape of the countertop is supplied by the dealer to finish the open end. Glue the batting strips to the bottom of the counter and the back of the splash (drawing, above right), and cement the end cap in place. Some end caps are precoated with heat-activated glue; use an electric iron to install them.

The length of a wall-to-wall counter, plus the thickness of its two end splashes, should be ½ in. shorter than the space it will occupy. The ½ in. will give you some room to maneuver the top into position. Center the top on the base cabinet, with equal gaps at both side walls, and trim as shown, letting the scribed laminate cover the gaps.

Miters—An L-shaped or U-shaped counter arrangement is more complicated than a straight one. A 90° corner in a countertop is the same

as in a picture frame, but the miter cut is nearly 3 ft. long and has to be dead on. It's impossible to make this cut without special equipment, so buy sections of counter with the 45° miter already sawn. Some suppliers have a random selection in stock; others will have to order counters cut to your specifications. You can also take your counter to a custom shop that will make cuts on a miter saw for a fee.

To provide a bearing surface for draw bolts at the miter joints, cut tapered notches with a router in the counter bottom. The draw bolts, along with yellow glue in the joint, will hold the sections together (drawing, above left). It's best to scribe a mitered top to the walls before the sections are joined. When both counter pieces fit their respective walls, and the miter joint is tight, you can glue the sections together.

Gluing can be done in place, or the sections can be moved to a bench and glued upside down. I prefer gluing in place. It's a little more cumbersome, but the assembled top doesn't have to be moved around. Whichever method you choose, apply glue to both edges and align the surfaces of the two counter sections at the miter before the glue dries. Lightly tap a block of wood up and down the seam until the surfaces are perfectly flush.

Rolling your own—Even without a high-pressure press, you can make a durable countertop, and by ordering your laminates through a custom shop, you can get the color and texture you want. A counter you make yourself won't have the rounded nosing and curved backsplash like the post-formed ones, but you do have the option of varying the width of the counter and the height of the backsplash.

The substrate should be high-density particleboard. Don't use ordinary floor underlayment; it's just too soft. Glue and nail batting (boards that thicken the edges) and scribe strips to the underside of the show edges (drawing, right). Next cut the plastic-laminate to cover the counter surface so that it overhangs the visible edges about ⅛ in., and fits flush with edges that butt into walls. With the top surface applied, cut the laminate strips to cover the edges. Do this on a table saw, and use a veneer-cutting blade (carbide-tipped blades cut smooth and chip-free). Contact-cement the strips into place, butting them hard against the underside of the overhanging top. Finally, trim the overhang off with a bevel or flush-cutting plastic-laminate bit in your router. The bit you use must have a ball-bearing pilot. A bit with a solid pilot can burn and otherwise mar the plastic surface it bears against.

Another method is to glue on the edge strips first, trim them flush with the top and bottom edges with a 90° laminate-trimming bit, apply the field (countertop) laminate second and finally trim the overhang with a bevel-cutting laminate bit.

When you're bonding the laminate to the particleboard substrate, take care to apply the contact cement evenly to both surfaces. Covering large areas with a brush leaves tiny ridges in the cement and hinders bonding. Instead use a cheap, short-napped paint roller to get complete, uniform coverage. Once the cement is dry to the touch, press the two surfaces together to activate bonding. Be certain that the laminate is properly aligned before you lower it onto the substrate, something best done by two people. Once contact is made, that's it; there's no ungluing. Use a linoleum roller to flatten the countertop and to bring the two surfaces into intimate contact. A rolling pin or veneer roller will do for pressing the edges. To avoid air bubbles, start in the middle and work toward the edges.

Maintenance—I tell my customers to treat their countertops the way they treat their furniture. Don't use abrasive cleansers on plastic laminate; the top layer of melamine will erode and eventually it will stain and peel. Use a liquid cleanser like 409 or Fantastic and a sponge to clean the top, and then treat it to a coat of liquid furniture wax every four to six months. The wax will protect the plastic and make it easier to clean. Don't use the top as a cutting surface, and don't put a pot straight from the stove on the counter. The temperature of boiling water is the hottest the surface can get without blistering. There are also several chemicals that will harm plastic laminates; hydrogen peroxide is the most common. Drain cleaners shouldn't come in contact with your countertops either. □

Jesus Granado makes and installs countertops in Richmond, Calif.

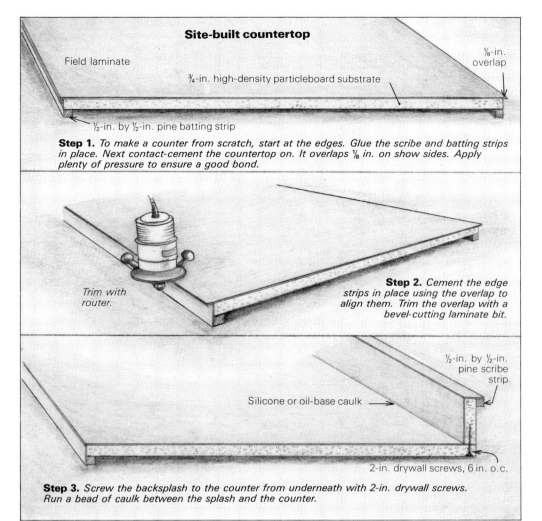

Site-built countertop

Field laminate

¾-in. high-density particleboard substrate

⅛-in. overlap

½-in. by ½-in. pine batting strip

Step 1. *To make a counter from scratch, start at the edges. Glue the scribe and batting strips in place. Next contact-cement the countertop on. It overlaps ⅛ in. on show sides. Apply plenty of pressure to ensure a good bond.*

Trim with router.

Step 2. *Cement the edge strips in place using the overlap to align them. Trim the overlap with a bevel-cutting laminate bit.*

½-in. by ½-in. pine scribe strip

Silicone or oil-base caulk

2-in. drywall screws, 6 in. o.c.

Step 3. *Screw the backsplash to the counter from underneath with 2-in. drywall screws. Run a bead of caulk between the splash and the counter.*

Buying plastic laminates

Plastic laminates were first used as an electrical insulating material in the early 1900s. They were a lighter and less expensive alternative to mineral and glass insulators. The addition of colors and designs printed on the top layer of paper, underneath the transparent resin surface, produced the first decorative laminates. Radio manufacturers, who were using laminates as insulators, began making imitation wood-grain cabinets.

The National Electrical Manufacturers Association (2101 L St. N.W., Washington, D.C. 20037) sets the standards for this industry. These include tests for thickness, dimensional change, formability and resistance to wear, scuff, impact, heat, staining, light and blistering. NEMA publishes Standards Publication #LD 3-1980, *High Pressure Decorative Laminates* ($12.55 plus 20% for postage and handling). This overpriced 60-page pamphlet has an excellent section on fabricating and installing plastic laminates. However, this same information is free of charge in the advertising literature of all the major manufacturers.

Nearly all high-pressure decorative plastic laminates in the U.S. are made by seven companies—Consoweld Corp. (700 DuraBeauty Lane, Wisconsin Rapids, Wis. 54494); Formica Corp. (10155 Reading Rd., Cincinnati, Ohio 45241); Lamin-Art (6430 E. Slauson, Los Angeles, Calif. 90040); Nevamar Corp. (8339 Telegraph Rd., Odenton, Md. 21113); Pioneer Plastics (Pionite Rd., Auburn, Maine 04210); Westinghouse Electrical Corp. (Hampton, S.C. 29924); and Wilsonart (600 General Bruce Dr., Temple, Tex. 76501).

Decorative plastic laminates are produced in several grades. Standard grade can be used for most applications. Some manufacturers make plastic laminates for use on countertops that are thicker and more durable than the material used for walls or other vertical-surface applications. Post-forming grade is specially made to bend under pressure, and the maximum bending radius and other data are available from the maker. Fire-rated plastic laminates can also be purchased. Sheet sizes for all these grades vary from one manufacturer to another, although 24 in., 30 in., 36 in., 48 in. and 60 in. are standard widths, and 6 ft., 8 ft., 10 ft. and 12 ft. are standard lengths.

Other variables are color, pattern, texture, and finish, and these determine price. Sold by the square foot, laminates with deeply textured surfaces, detailed patterns, and exotic (called "decorator") colors cost more. Solid white is the least expensive, in the $1.10 to $1.50 range. Shopping around will definitely pay off. —*Paul Spring*

The Flush-Fit Cabinet

Custom building with techniques well suited to the small shop

by Paul Levine

In some ways, technology seems to have left the small cabinetmaker behind. It can be rough for a little guy to compete with a cabinet fabricator equipped with sliding-table panel saws, two-part polyester sprays, high-temperature curing rooms and tilting spindle shapers with automatic feeds. With little space and scant funds to buy machinery, can a one-man show still make it?

I believe so. With a garage or basement to work in, a Sears Roebuck nearby, a little talent and a lot of hard work, the small cabinetmaking shop can steal away a very nice slice of the pie.

Custom cabinetwork requires so many different skills and turns up so many surprises that the modularity big businesses thrive on is not of much use. Larger woodworking concerns are of necessity more rigid and thus less responsive to the needs of the client. Making a cabinet 6 in. deeper becomes a six-month ordeal for the big guy, and changing the radius of a countertop's

curve becomes an impossibility. The small cabinet shop, on the other hand, can rise to the occasion, and give the customer truly custom work.

Good hardware—Keeping up to date on hardware options is important if you want to attract custom jobs. I use Accuride (12311 South Shoemaker Ave., Santa Fe Springs, Calif. 90670) full-extension ball-bearing slides on all my cabinet drawers. These slides work silently and smoothly, and they permit the drawer to open its full length (photo facing page, top right). Every time your clients go into someone else's kitchen and open a drawer, they will be reminded of how conveniently and effortlessly their own custom-made cabinets work. Lasting impressions like this mean referrals, and referrals are bread, butter and gravy for the small cabinetmaker.

Hinges are another key hardware item. The European style flush-fit cabinets that I specialize

in are to a great extent designed around high-quality concealed cup hinges. These hinges let you build cabinets that have no face frames. The hinges mount against the side of the cabinet's carcase and are let into the back of the door. The door is built to the full outside dimension of the cabinet front. The Grass hinges that I use (Grass America, Box 1019, Kernersville, N. C. 27284) can be adjusted in all three dimensions after they're installed, and will open to nearly 180° (photo facing page, bottom right). Fully opening cabinet doors are nice because they never act as barriers to people walking by or working in the kitchen.

Pulls for door and drawer fronts are the final hardware category. The custom cabinetmaker needs to be able to supplement the standard selection of pulls with a few innovative or unusual handles. At the moment my favorites are small, cylindrical pulls made of soft rubber. Available

From *Fine Homebuilding* magazine (December 1985) 30:58-62

from Forms & Surfaces, Box 5215, Santa Barbara, Calif., these pulls are pleasant to touch and very easy to clean. Also, they double as bumpers for doors.

Plywood and the carcase—I don't build the kickspace into my base cabinets. Instead, I prefabricate a base-rail system in my shop, using 4½-in. wide lengths of ¾-in. plywood and 1x1 pine cleats. These rails run under all base cabinets; one along the back, close to the wall, and one in the front, set back 2½ in. from the cabinet face to create the kickspace. I cut sections of railing to length and set them down against layout lines on the floor. Then I find the highest point along the rail's top edge and shim the entire rail system level. The rail is fastened to the floor by screwing through the 1x1 cleats (drawing, next page).

Once all the rails are level, the base cabinets can be set down on top of them and screwed to the rail and to each other. This method of building and installing base cabinets is used widely in Europe, and it really speeds the work. Shimming a rail level is much easier than shimming an entire base cabinet. And because the rail system is separate from the cabinet, it can have its own special treatment in terms of finish. I've even designed a special kickspace rail that hinges up in one section to provide extra storage space underneath the cabinet.

With the kickspace and face frame eliminated from the carcase itself, my cabinets are just basic boxes. Each has a top, two sides, a bottom

and a back. The front—what you see after a wall of cabinets has been installed—consists of either drawer fronts or doors.

I use ¾-in. thick hardwood plywood for everything but the back of the box, which is ¼-in. hardwood-faced ply. Many lumber dealers now sell hardwood-faced plywood with fir veneer cores. I don't like to use this stuff. Fir veneer is naturally wavy and unstable, and this can mean sand-throughs in the hardwood face veneers on a sheet. There can also be a large number of voids to contend with. Generally, the quality range of fir veneer-core plywood from one order to the next is very wide, and this can add a lot of anxiety and frustration to a job. To eliminate this, I always use lumber-core plywood with poplar or lauan cores. These are relatively soft, stable hardwoods with even grain.

Medium-density hardboard is my second choice if cost prohibits the use of good plywood. Available in thicknesses up to 1⅛ in., MDH is very stable as long as it doesn't get wet, and it's an excellent base for veneering. Particleboard runs a poor third. If extra weight and reduced strength won't be a problem, then it is the most economical material to use. I don't like to handle particleboard sheets because they're so heavy. I also don't like the formaldehyde-laced material that comes back in my face from the saw.

As soon as the plywood gets to the shop, I rip the sheets to finished width. For base cabinets, this is usually 23½ in.; for wall cabinets, 12 in. By processing the material immediately, I don't

The flush-fit cabinet owes its elegance to cabinetmaking skill and good hardware. Concealed hinges, above, eliminate the need for a face frame. This one mounts in a 1⅜-in. dia. hole bored in the inside face of the cabinet door. A shoe screwed to the side of the carcase holds the detachable hinge mechanism, which allows the door to open nearly 180°. Full-extension, ball-bearing drawer slides, top, are also part of the custom kitchen. Facing page and above left, doors and drawer fronts are covered with plastic laminate; their edges are trimmed with solid wood. The wood trim creates a nice contrast and also cushions edges from blows and abrasions that might chip a laminate edge.

have to contend with storage or handling problems. Full-size sheets can really steal space in a small shop, and every time you have to move a sheet you risk damaging an edge.

Good edges are essential, whether I'm gluing on a hardwood lip to cover the laminations or running a router bit along an edge to flush-trim laminated plastic or wood veneer. The factory edge is never smooth or straight enough. By cutting the plywood to finished width immediately, you get pieces that are easy to handle and edges that you can confidently work off of.

To make accurate cuts in 4x8 plywood sheets, I built extensions for my Unisaw. The right-side extension was built using Rockwell's Unifence accessories and enables me to set up the rip fence 48 in. from the blade. The other extension is on the outfeed side and is just long enough to provide 4 ft. of surface area beyond the blade (photo facing page, top left). Both extensions are simple plywood tables with adjustable legs and plastic-laminate tops. Before building these, I tried using adjustable rollers, but they encouraged the plywood to "walk" away from the cut. With my table extensions and rip-fence setup, I have no trouble making finished edge cuts in large sheets without assistance.

With all the carcase stock cut to width, I next cut it to length. Sides for a cabinet will be the same length, as will top and bottom. I join the top and bottom of the cabinet to its sides with the combination rabbet/dado joint shown in the photo facing page, bottom left and in the drawing below. These joints are glued and stapled with a pneumatic gun. I used to clamp the carcase together until the glue dried. This took far

too long, so I switched to driving screws with a screw gun. Power-stapling is better yet. It's faster, and staples have the advantage of being drift-free, which you can't say about nails or screws in plywood. The staple enters the wood so fast that the parts don't have a chance to move.

I use yellow Titebond aliphatic-resin glue for all wood-to-wood joints. It's a little more moisture resistant than white PVA (polyvinyl acetate) glue, a little stronger at higher temperatures and easier to sand. It won't gum up belts or paper, as white glue sometimes does. Whenever possible, I buy glue in 1-gal. or 5-gal. quantities to save money. Titebond's manufacturer, Franklin Chemical Industries (2020 Bruck St., Columbus, Ohio 43207), has some helpful brochures on gluing techniques and on the various types of aliphatic-resin glues.

Fastening the ¼-in. plywood back onto the cabinet—the next step—enables me to square up the carcase. I used to rabbet the back into the sides, top and bottom, but this didn't increase the strength of the carcase appreciably, and it took a lot longer than stapling down a glued joint.

To attach the back, I first set the carcase down on the floor, back edges up, and get the sides, top and bottom as close to square as possible. Then I run a scant glue bead around the back edge and spread it evenly with a brush or finger. I place the back on, put two staples along one edge, and square the corner. This should square the entire carcase. Stapling the rest of the back down takes about 30 seconds.

To complete the carcase, I cover its exposed plywood face edges with ³⁄₁₆-in. thick flat hard-

wood lipping (or edging). I use cherry, maple, birch or oak molding strips, depending on how the carcase will be finished. The strips can simply be glued in place, using masking tape to compress the joint while the glue sets. For less expensive jobs, I butt-join the molding strips at corners, but a mitered corner looks better. The best way to miter the molding is with a picture framer's trimmer (photo facing page, right). This razor-sharp, lever-actuated tool is expensive and can be a bit dangerous to operate, but it's a worthwhile investment if you do a large volume of edging.

The faces—Door and drawer fronts, the faces of the cabinet, are the most important parts of the job. You can use pre-veneered plywood, or do your own wood veneering over a plywood substrate. A third alternative is to glue plastic laminate to both sides of the door or drawer front. This is where the client's preferences and the cabinetmaker's creativity should interact. There's a wide range of options you can offer, and dressing up the doors and drawer fronts allows you to trademark your work, setting it apart from what's available through catalogs or from other woodworkers.

If you're gluing down wood veneer or plastic laminate, the inside face of the door or drawer should get the same treatment as the outside face. Otherwise, the substrate may warp as a result of uneven shrinkage or moisture absorption.

There are many plastic laminates on the market now that didn't exist several years ago. Though the range of colors is amazing, I often end up using black or white. I don't like plastic that's made to look like other materials, especially wood. Wilsonart Laminates (Wilsonart, 600 General Bruce Drive, Temple, Tex. 76501) has a designer line of laminates that's especially suited for non-horizontal use. These laminates have a grid pattern incised in the plastic that creates a textured, non-glossy surface. It's an ideal material for door and drawer fronts in a modern kitchen, but I think it looks best when framed by a solid wood edge (photos pp. 40 and 41). The wood edging looks and feels a lot nicer than a plastic-to-plastic corner, and won't show bumps or dings as dramatically.

Working with plastic laminate can be a real chore if you're not careful about gluing, cutting and trimming. Special plastic-cutting circular-saw blades are available, but I use a Freud 80-tooth, Teflon-coated combination blade in my Unisaw because it will produce glass-smooth cuts in wood as well as plastic. This enables me to cut plastic and wood that have already been laminated together.

When I'm building doors that will have plastic on both faces, I prefer to do all my laminating first and then cut the door to finished size on my table saw. I start with an oversize sheet of plywood (enough for two or three cabinet doors) and glue a single sheet of laminate to both sides. When laminated, the plastic should be about ½ in. or so shy of two adjacent plywood edges that are perfectly square. These are the first edges to register against the saw's rip fence to produce your first finished edges. If you have these, making the remaining cuts is easy. Once

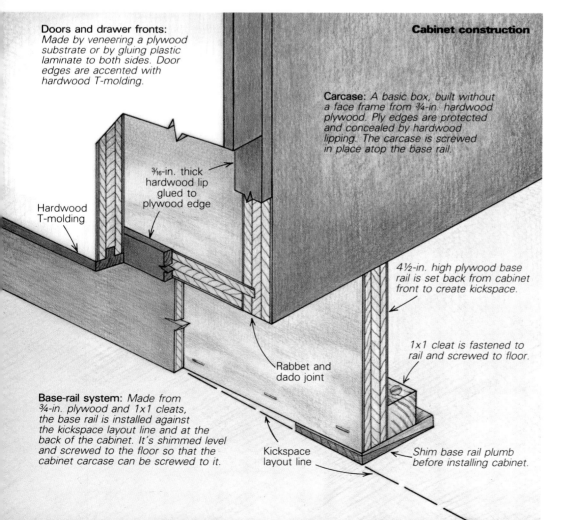

Doors and drawer fronts: *Made by veneering a plywood substrate or by gluing plastic laminate to both sides. Door edges are accented with hardwood T-molding.*

Cabinet construction

Carcase: *A basic box, built without a face frame from ¾-in. hardwood plywood. Ply edges are protected and concealed by hardwood lipping. The carcase is screwed in place atop the base rail.*

³⁄₁₆-in. thick hardwood lip glued to plywood edge

Hardwood T-molding

4½-in. high plywood base rail is set back from cabinet front to create kickspace.

1x1 cleat is fastened to rail and screwed to floor.

Rabbet and dado joint

Base-rail system: *Made from ¾-in. plywood and 1x1 cleats, the base rail is installed against the kickspace layout line and at the back of the cabinet. It's shimmed level and screwed to the floor so that the cabinet carcase can be screwed to it.*

Kickspace layout line

Shim base rail plumb before installing cabinet.

Drawing: Elizabeth Eaton

Extension tables on two sides of the table saw, left, allow the author to cut large sheets of plywood or laminate accurately and safely. Plastic laminate tabletops make a low-friction surface.

Carcase construction. Cabinet sides are dadoed to receive the rabbeted top and bottom, above. All joints are glued and gun-stapled. Levine switched to pneumatic stapling because nails and screws were too time-consuming. The carcase is squared when the ¼-in. plywood back is attached. The back has to be cut perfectly square, and after one corner is stapled down, right, the rest of the carcase is held square while the remaining sides are stapled.

To miter the solid wood lipping that covers the edges of the doors and drawers, Levine uses a razor-sharp picture framer's trimmer, above. An accurate chopsaw with a finish-cutting blade will also work. Details of flush-fit cabinet construction are shown in the drawing, facing page.

you've prepared laminated doors this way, you'll never go back to using a router and trim bit.

I've tried the latex contact cements, but the bad-smelling, solvent-based cements work better. If you do a lot of laminate work, buy your glue in 5-gal. buckets. Single-gallon prices are far higher. The fastest way to apply contact cement is by spraying, but this is done only by large-scale countertop fabricators. A reasonable alternative is to roll on the adhesive with a thin-napped paint roller. I always apply two coats to each surface. A single coat isn't reliable.

Once the contact cement has dried on both surfaces, I stand the plywood substrate up against the wall with its square edges up and glue side facing out. Holding the plastic with both hands, I then press it in place. The next step is to lay the lamination flat and roll the plastic tight against the substrate. If you don't have a roller, hammer against a block of wood covered

with felt to flatten the laminate out. This same procedure is repeated to laminate the other side of the substrate.

By cutting doors and drawer fronts ½ in. shorter and narrower than their finished dimensions, I leave room for a ³⁄₁₆-in. thick T-molding along all four edges and a minute space between adjacent doors. I cut the slot in the door's edges with a dado blade in my table saw; the T-molding is run in my shaper, and its corner joints are mitered on the Lion trimmer. As with the flat molding, I glue the T-molding to the door edges, and clamp it fast until the glue sets. Then the molding has to be flushed up to the door surface with a router and flush-cutting bit. Finally, I ease the corners of the molding with a very sharp, low-angle block plane.

I've just described the techniques I use to make wood-edged, plastic-laminate covered doors and drawer fronts. The same techniques

could be used to veneer a plywood door with wood, and this is an attractive option. The solid wood edging is still a good idea on wood-veneered doors.

Mounting concealed hinges—When the doors are complete, they are drilled out to receive their hinges. Like most concealed hinges, the Grass #1200s that I use have a metal cup that has to be sunk and fastened in a precisely drilled hole in the back of the door. Suppliers that sell hinges also sell the 1³⁄₈-in. dia. (35mm) Forstner bits required to bore this hole.

It's best to bore the back of the doors on a drill press. I locate the holes ³⁄₁₆ in. from the edge of the door and 3 in. from the top and bottom. On the carcase side, the hinge has a surface-mounted shoe that simply screws in place. The shoe has a track that accepts the door-mounted part of the mechanism. Screws in

Finger joints for drawers. Levine builds drawers with finger joints, using the table-saw jig shown here. It consists of a guide pin equal to the slot dimensions and offset from the dado blade by exactly one slot width. The dado is set up to cut the exact width of the pin. The guide pin fits into a slot cut in an auxiliary fence screwed to the saw's miter gauge. (A test joint on scrap material is cut first in case the guide pin has to be adjusted slightly left or right.) The first cut, top left, is a slot cut with one edge of the stock butted against the pin. Subsequent cuts, left, are aligned by placing the previous slot over the guide pin. The result, above, is a tight, strong fit that can be quickly repeated in drawers of different sizes.

the track enable you to align the door exactly and also to demount it easily. The hinge design is complex, but it's not difficult to install. And the adjustment capability can compensate for slight installation inaccuracies.

Finger-joint drawers—For a long time I shied away from using finger joints in my cabinet drawers in favor of template-cut dovetails. But router-cut dovetails turned out to be fairly fussy themselves. The time I spent blowing out my jig and aligning and clamping the stock started to dull my enthusiasm for dovetails. The system I now use for cutting finger joints has made drawer building much easier. I'm able to use my table saw, which is a lot less tiring than using a router. Here's how I do it.

First I joint and surface the stock (I prefer to use oak, cherry, or ash) and rip it to width. I like to use ½-in. thick wood for small to medium drawers, and ⅝-in. thick stock for larger ones. When cutting the drawer sides to length, I add ⅛ in. for trimming.

After squaring the table-saw blade to the table and the miter gauge to the blade, I screw an auxiliary fence to the miter gauge. I usually use ¾-in. thick plywood 4 in. high and 30 in. long, extending the gauge an inch or two across the path of the sawblade. I put a dado set into the saw, set to cut ¼ in. wide and 9/16 in. high if the stock is ½ in. thick. The extra 1/16 in. is for trimming after the drawer is together.

Now I run the auxiliary fence through the blade to create an indexing slot. I remove the fence from the miter gauge, make a mark to the left or right of the slot that's equal to one slot width, and screw the auxiliary fence back on the miter gauge. The fence is aligned so that the blade will cut out this new slot width exactly.

I make a hardwood guide pin to fit into the first slot and glue it in place (photo top left). It should be about 2 in. long. Now the jig can be tested on some scrap stock. I always cut a test corner before using the jig on drawer stock. With the stock butted against the guide pin, I run it through the saw. Then I reposition the stock so that the slot I just cut fits over the guide pin. I cut the second slot, reposition, and cut the next, until I complete this half of the joint.

In a finger-joint corner, one side of the joint

will begin with a pin, while the other side begins with a matching slot. To start a side with a slot instead of a pin, first butt a piece of scrap against the guide pin and cut a slot. Now rotate the scrap 180° and set this slot over the guide pin. Butt the drawer against the scrap and you're ready to cut your first slot. After this, remove the scrap and continue to cut slots and fingers until the side is done.

If the width of your drawer stock is an even multiple of the width of each finger, your finished pieces will start with a pin and end with a slot, or vice versa.

If your test-fit joint is too loose, readjust the auxiliary fence so that the guide pin is a little farther away from the sawblade. If the joint is too tight, move the guide pin slightly closer to the sawblade.

When the body of the drawer is complete, you can attach its face. I build my drawer faces the same way that I build cabinet faces, laminating plastic or wood veneer to both faces of the front and edging with hardwood T-molding. □

―――――――
Paul Levine lives in Sherman, Conn.

European Cabinet Hardware

A look at cup hinges and drawer slides

by Paul Levine

My customers usually want cabinets overnight, or better yet, yesterday. Of course, they make this demand after a prolonged period during which they can't decide on style or hardware, or even whether they want cabinets at all. Then when they are finally ready to order, they're surprised that I can't produce the cabinets instantly.

One fellow who had a hard time making up his mind ended up needing cabinets so badly that he couldn't wait for an order of high-quality drawer slides to come in. "Build them with anything," he said, so I substituted another slide for the ones I usually use. He got his cabinets, but once he saw the difference in the slides he wanted them removed, and paid me to install the ones I had originally ordered. There is no substitute for high-quality hardware, particularly in cabinets that you're building for yourself.

European-style hardware is part of a modular, production-oriented cabinetry construction system (the 32mm system) developed in Europe for efficient construction and installation. Basically, the casework consists of a plywood box with no face frames; hinges and drawer slides are attached directly to the inside surface of the box. High-quality hinges and slides are integral to the system, and a glimpse of this hardware will provide an understanding of why the 32mm system is becoming popular with American cabinetmakers and amateur woodworkers.

The concealed cup hinge—The concealed cup hinge is the key element in European-style cabinetry (photo right and next page). Entirely hidden behind the door, these hinges let the design maintain clean lines, without hinge knuckles poking out. The hinges themselves are not much to look at, but their forte is function.

Concealed cup hinges are adjustable in all three dimensions, and the adjustments are quick and easy to make. When I'm working on a project, I always imagine the worst. What if the cases aren't perfect—will the doors line up? What if the walls aren't plumb—will that rack the cases out of square? If adjusting the hinges is so easy that I can show the home owner how to do it in a few minutes, alignment will be ensured even under difficult conditions. Another advan-

The concealed cup hinge makes possible the clean lines of European-style cabinetry. The hinge is hidden behind the cabinet door, and is mounted to the inside surface of the casework.

From *Fine Homebuilding* magazine (February 1988) 44:69-71

tage of cup hinges is that they distribute the weight of the door quite well. The bearing surface is the entire rim of the cup—over 4 sq. in. Standard hinges put all that weight on just two or three screws.

Although it is difficult to obtain exact weight ratings on these hinges, the manufacturers do offer rules of thumb for figuring out how many hinges to use in given situations. The standard cabinet door requires two hinges; on doors that are larger than 39 in. high by 15 in. wide, a third hinge, centered between the top and bottom hinges, becomes necessary.

In my cabinets, the workhorse (black and white photo below) is the Grass #1200 full overlay hinge, with 176° swing (Grass America, Inc., P.O. Box 1019, 1377 South Park Drive, Kernersville, N. C. 27284). The #1200 is more expensive than hinges with lesser opening capacity, but the money is well spent. Hinges that will open only to 90° or 110° can be dangerous in the kitchen. If a cabinet door is jutting out into the path of someone carrying a tray of food, the

door will not give way, and the resulting collision may rip the door from its mounting (it won't be good for the tray carrier, either). A door that is mounted on 176° hinges will open almost flat back to the cabinet. If it happens to obstruct someone's path, the collision will simply bump the door out of the way.

The thing that allows cup hinges, particularly the 176°-opening hinges, to swing the cabinet door clear of the sides of the case is a series of pivots, shown in the photos below. Standard leaf hinges have a single pivot, and thus a limited range of movement.

Specialty cup hinges—In addition to standard cup hinges, there are several kinds of special-purpose cup hinges. For example, lots of my customers want their cabinets to include pull-out trays, or drawers concealed behind a cabinet door. While most hinges leave the door jutting into the path of the tray or drawer, a hinge like the Grass #1203 moves the door out of this path when opened 90° to the face. This

also means that the tray can be made with little or no allowance for the door.

There are specialty hinges for just about any cabinet combination you can think of. Mepla (Mepla, Inc., P.O. Box 1469, 909 W. Market Center Dr., High Point, N. C. 27261-1469) has a catalog full of them. Blum (Julius Blum, Inc., Hwy. 16-Lowesville, Stanley, N. C. 28164) makes what they call a blind corner cabinet hinge (Blum #99M950) that allows mounting to a parallel surface. It will open 95°, which is fine where the adjacent wall's cabinets will obstruct any greater opening. Blum also makes a hinge that can be mounted to a surface that's 135° to the face of the cabinet.

Special hinges are available for unusually thick doors. Any door that's over ⅞ in. thick, particularly full overlay doors, will bind against the cabinet unless the hinge pivots slightly away from the case. There are hinges for glass doors and also for mounting two doors to a common partition (these are called half-overlay hinges).

Though hinges that open only 90° or 110° can

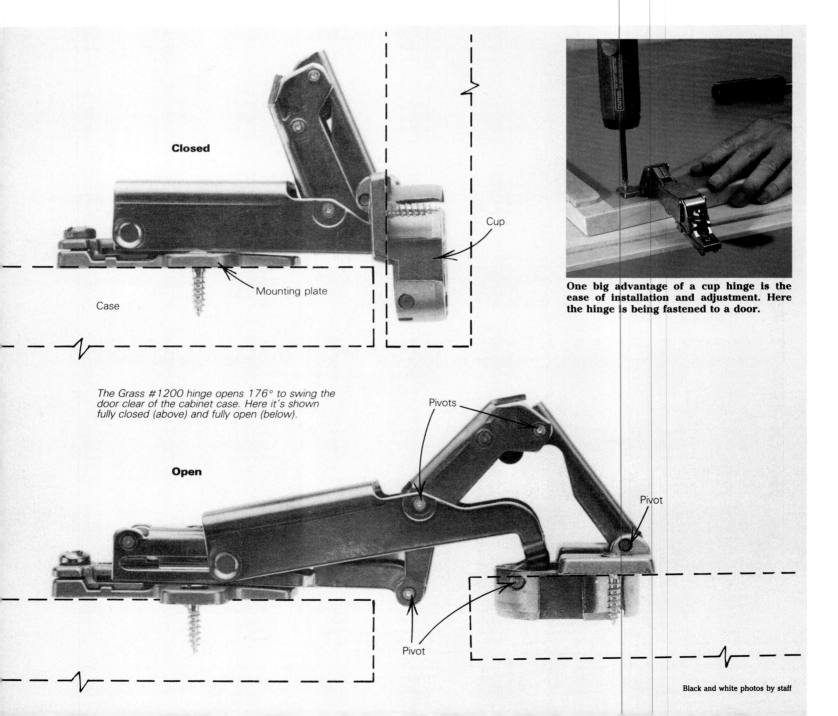

Closed

Case

Mounting plate

Cup

One big advantage of a cup hinge is the ease of installation and adjustment. Here the hinge is being fastened to a door.

The Grass #1200 hinge opens 176° to swing the door clear of the cabinet case. Here it's shown fully closed (above) and fully open (below).

Pivots

Open

Pivot

Pivot

Black and white photos by staff

be problems elsewhere, they're useful when cabinets run into a corner and a partial swing is all that's needed. Partial-swing hinges cost less so you can save some money by using them where they're appropriate. Full-opening hinges may be difficult to adjust under circumstances where they cannot be opened more than 90°.

The great success of cup hinges has led to a curious phenomenon. Cup hinges are now being made for face-frame mounting. This allows the hinge to be completely concealed, yet the cabinets retain the look of traditional face-frame cabinets. As far as I'm concerned, though, the innovation is a poor one. Face-frame cabinets obstruct full access to the interior of the cases, and adding a cup hinge makes the problem worse. The only advantage I can see in putting cup hinges on face-frame cabinets is that the cup hinge installs and adjusts so easily.

Mounting cup hinges—All cup hinges mount in a similar fashion, though each has its idiosyncrasies. First, a 35mm hole is bored in the door;

this becomes the mortise for the hinge cup. The cup is then pressed into the mortise and fastened with two small screws (photo facing page, right). The hinge is held in place securely because of the precise fit between cup and hole and will even stay in place for the moment without screws, which makes it easier to fasten.

To mount the door, a metal mounting plate is screwed to the inside of the case. A mating piece on the hinge slides over it, and a screw in the hinge is tightened to lock everything in place. If it sounds simple, you understand it entirely—it *is* simple, much more so than mounting a flap hinge. Once you see how solidly cup hinges mount into their holes and how easy they are to install, I'll bet you won't go back to whatever hinge you're using now.

Adjusting the hinge is equally quick. Once the door is in place and the hinge has been locked into the mounting plate, close the door. Line it up by eye against adjacent horizontal surfaces. If it is too low or high, loosen a screw on the hinge and move the door up or down, and then

tighten the screw. This adjustment screw is located on either the hinge arm or the baseplate, depending on the specific hinge you use.

After the hinge height is adjusted, examine the spacing between doors. If the door is too close or too far away, open the door and back off or drive in the sideways adjusting screw to compensate. With some hinges a second screw must be loosened first, and then this adjustment can be made. After the adjustment is made, the second screw must be tightened again. If the door juts out or binds on closing, loosen the setting screw and pull the hinge out along its track a bit, then retighten the setting screw. It will take a little practice to know exactly which way to adjust and how much, but after adjusting several doors you should get the hang of it. □

Paul Levine is a cabinetmaker in Sherman, Conn. This article is adapted from his book on building European-style cabinetry, to be published by The Taunton Press in the spring of 1988. Photos by the author, except where noted.

A note about drawer slides

With drawer slides, as with hinges, quality is what you're looking for. In slides, this means the rails (the parts that slide past each other) will move on nylon wheels or on ball bearings—ball bearings are better. There should be no sharp edges on any metal parts. The most useful slides are full-extension slides. This means that the drawer can be opened entirely clear of the cabinet, offering ready access to the back of the drawer. The next best slide is a ¾-extension type. You can also get slides that will permit greater than full extension, and slides for peninsula cabinets that will permit a drawer to be opened from either side. The finest-quality slides have built-in bumpers to cushion the impact of collisions with the cabinet.

You can tell a good-quality slide from one of inferior quality just by picking them up—the better slides weigh significantly more. Once the slide is in place, you'll recognize quality by the fact that when you pull out a drawer, you won't hear a blessed thing. Cheap slides rattle like skeletons on a tin roof. With a good slide, the drawer will not droop when it opens. It will come straight out and stay even.

The finest slide I've ever found is made by the Accuride Co. (12311 S. Shoemaker Ave., Santa Fe Springs, Calif. 90670). These slides are fully ball bearing and the quietest on the market. Accuride full-extension slides have a load-bearing capacity of up to 150 lb. The slide itself is attached to the case wall, and a mounting rail that is non-handed (no left or right side) is mounted to the drawer. This means you can mount the slide, then the rail, and then simply drop the drawer in place.

Ease of disassembly is a big advantage. Some slides mount in an odd way that requires clearance above the drawer to enable you to tip the drawer into place. If the drawer is mounted near the top of the

case, as it is in kitchen applications, extra clearance must be provided or the drawer can't be installed.

Often you won't find this out until after you've mounted the slide on the drawer and the case and then go to install the drawer. With the Accuride full-extension, you can pull the slide all the way out of the case and engage the drawer onto the slide. Since the mounting is taking place outside the case, case allowances are of no importance.

The Accuride slide provides a detent to hold a drawer in its closed position, and bumpers to eliminate the thud when the drawer is closed. The slides are far more expensive than others, but I think they're worth it. Once my customers have tried them, they never want to go back to cheap.

Accuride makes a variety of other slide products, including an under-counter mounting slide for computer keyboards, and a TV slide that can be used in conjunction with a swivel (a nice feature for a wall unit with an enclosed TV). Accuride also makes a slide that has a hinge on one end. This permits you to make a case with a door that

swings out and then slides back into the case and disappears. Another Accuride special-application slide is the lateral-drawer file slide with a load rating of up to 250 lb.

Grant Hardware Co. (63-A High St., West Nyack, N. Y. 10994) makes a #555 and #527 full extension slide that is ball bearing and of excellent quality. I've used both slides and like them a lot. In fact, when I can't get the Accurides, I use the Grants and have no hesitation about doing so.

Every drawer slide mounts in its own peculiar way, and some are easier than others. One great time-saver is the proper orientation of the case. If you lay the case on its side and mount the part that attaches to the case, gravity will be working with you instead of against you. Just put the part where it goes and attach it with screws. I used to install the case part of the slide with the case in its normal position, i.e., sitting on the floor vertically. Now I lay the case down on its side on the bench. Not only is gravity now my friend instead of foe, but my back also thanks me every night. —*P. L.*

Drawer slides are two-piece affairs. The slide itself mounts to the inside surface of the case, while the rail mounts to the drawer. Installing the drawer simply means dropping it into place.

Bathroom Built-Ins

Precise alignment and production techniques are the key to building overlay doors and drawers

by Rob Hunt and Robert Robertson

Overlay drawers and concealed hinges give the cabinet in this master bathroom its sleek lines. Production techniques made the work go surprisingly fast, with no sacrifice in precision.

On a recent remodeling job, we designed and built all the cabinets for a master bathroom, creating clean lines and unrelieved surfaces by covering cabinet stiles and rails with overlay drawers and using concealed hinges on all cabinet doors. Our clients had found themselves with several spare bedrooms after their sons grew up and moved out, and they decided to convert one of these rooms into a spacious, comfortable bathroom—something they had always wished for but couldn't afford while their sons were still at home. They wanted individual dressing areas with built-in vanities, upper cabinets and floor-to-counter drawer units, all in teak. And they wanted teak trim everywhere in the new bathroom—door jambs, casings, around the mirrors and cabinets and around the tops of the walls.

Our job as architectural woodworkers would have been fairly straightforward, had it not been for the fact that a couple of inexperienced carpenters had made an awful mess of the framing and drywall, leaving everything out of square and out of plumb. The cabinetmaker who had originally contracted to do the trim and built-ins tried for two weeks to make things fit. His third week on the job, he threw up his hands and went off on a bender, never to return.

The careless framing and sloppy drywall work made the job a daily struggle for us too, and we ended up spending three months on it. Several tight spaces had to be filled with cabinets or built-in chests of drawers. In two instances, we had to assemble the cabinets in place because adjacent walls were so askew that a pre-assembled cabinet couldn't have been moved in and scribed to fit.

Since there wasn't a straight wall in the place, it was hard for us to make the trim details consistent around the room. A lot of planning was necessary to compensate for all the previous mistakes so the trim would work out right. We started by establishing a level line all around the room. This line would eventually become a 5-in. wide teak band 8½ ft. above the floor. Most of the door and corner trim would die into this horizontal band. We installed the vertical pieces first and then applied the band, shimming it out here and there because the walls were uneven.

The owners had decided on tile floors. Wherever tile would come in contact with trim, we made sure that the trim was plumb so that the tile setter could maintain even and

From *Fine Homebuilding* magazine (February 1983) 13:60-63

parallel rows of tile. This job had 2-in. square tile that came in big square sheets backed with plastic mesh, and we knew it would be hard to fudge very much on the grout joints to compensate for out-of-level trim.

Where we couldn't put up trim before installing tile, we used temporary grounds so the tile man would have a real edge to work to. Later we pulled these down and applied teak trim. To prevent stains, all of the teak was sealed before the tile was installed.

Trim work—Teak is nice to work, but it sure can dull sawblades and jointer knives. I wasn't prepared for all the resharpening we had to do. We began by belt-sanding all the teak to remove the mill marks. Later we touched up and slightly eased the edges with some sandpaper on a rubber sanding block.

We installed the door jambs first, taking care to plumb both directions and to make the door opening the same size from top to bottom. (We were using all custom-order doors so we didn't worry about exactly what size the openings were, just that they were consistent from top to bottom.) Next we installed the

teak casings. To close the joint between jamb and case, we glued and nailed them in place. All trim that wouldn't have to be removed later, such as mirror trim, was glued to adjacent pieces of trim.

To get good adhesion when gluing teak, you have to wipe the mating surfaces down with acetone before applying the usual yellow (aliphatic-resin) wood glue; this removes some of the oily resin from the surface fibers to allow better glue penetration. Cleaning, gluing and wiping up the mess is a slow process, but makes for better joinery.

The vanities had to be built in place because their casework had already been started when we arrived. We made the face frames in the shop and then installed them on the cases. The chest-of-drawer cabinets (photo facing page) we built in our shop and then installed. The cabinets over the chests of drawers were built without face frames, which we nailed on after installation.

Careful planning—When we build cabinets, we always do shop drawings, elevations of the cabinets without doors and drawers, showing

the face-frame members. On these drawings, we indicate how the pieces go together, with notations that show on which side the doors are hinged and how much they overlap the face frames. Above or below the elevations, plan views show how the front meets the case, with notations showing how much the front overhangs the partitions and ends. The elevations and plans are usually drawn at 1:12 scale (1 in. = 1 ft.), which is easy to convert in the shop and small enough to present the information on a manageable piece of paper. Special details are drawn at a larger scale—sometimes even full size. We use the elevations to dimension the face frames, and the plans to get dimensions for the cases.

Before drawing up your design, you've got to consider the style of your cabinets, the type of hinges and drawer guides you plan to use, and the width of reveals (spaces) you want between doors and drawers. Then you can determine the size of face-frame members. We try to make the face-frame stiles (where there will be drawers) wider than the plywood case sides by an exact plywood thickness (⅜ in., ½ in., ⅝ in., ¾ in.) so that we

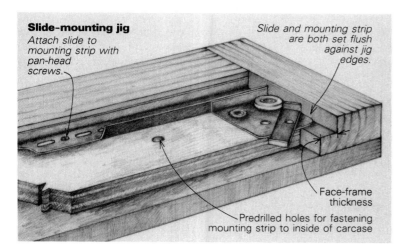

Slide-mounting jig
Attach slide to mounting strip with pan-head screws.

Slide and mounting strip are both set flush against jig edges.

Face-frame thickness

Predrilled holes for fastening mounting strip to inside of carcase

Time-saving techniques. Drawer slides were mounted on plywood strips using the jig shown in the drawing. Then the strips were screwed to the carcase sides. Above, a pneumatic stapler cut down face-frame assembly time and eliminated the need to clamp the joints while glue dried. At right, the boxwood face frame has been installed on a plywood carcase and trimmed with solid teak. Since the face frame has been sized to match the strip thickness, the slides align perfectly with their openings.

Illustration: Frances Ashforth

Achieving the overlay fit. Above, veneer strips shim drawer fronts as they are pressed against staple points in the boxes, creating registration marks for permanently fastening front to box with screws, as shown at left.

can mount the drawer slide on a plywood strip on the workbench. In production cabinetwork, it is much easier to get everything aligned if you can mount the piece of plywood with its attached slide directly to the inside of the cabinet (glue and nails), rather than trying to screw the slide to the cabinet itself as was shown on p. 34.

When our drawings were done, we made cutting tickets for the face frames. These are detailed lists describing each stile and rail, with dimensions and the location and sizes of mortises and tenons. We mortise-and-tenon face-frame members, so we add ½ in. to the drawing dimensions for the tenons. Then we cut the mortises and tenons and assemble the face frames by gluing all joints, pulling them tight with clamps and stapling through the back of the frame (through the mortise cheek into the tenon) with a pneumatic stapler.

Gluing all joints and using a pneumatic stapler and nailer is at least twice as fast as nailing or driving screws by hand, and we haven't noticed a difference in quality. Another plus is that the power nailer countersinks and drives in one step, and the surface is free of hammerhead dings—all you have is a tiny hole.

Because plywood sheets as they come from the manufacturer are not always square, we first rip the sheets to width and then check the ends for square before crosscutting. We cut all of the plywood up at the same time, label each piece, and put the pieces in piles: one pile for each cabinet. Then we lay out and make all of the special cuts and dadoes. We use a jig for the router to cut dadoes and rabbets across the grain. Grooves and rabbets with the grain are done on a router table.

When the pieces are all made, we assemble

the cases without glue and check their overall measurements before we finally glue and staple the parts together. The back is put on, glued and stapled. Cut square and fit snugly in the rabbeted back of the cabinet, the back piece squares up the box securely when it's glued and nailed. This makes it easier to position and install the face frame, which we glue and then clamp in place while joining frame to carcase with gun-driven nails.

Once assembled, everything is sanded. We belt-sand the face frames to make all of the joints flush, then finish-sand and ease all edges by hand.

Next we made the drawers and doors. Instead of making drawers with an integral front (as shown on p. 34), we made the drawer boxes first, and applied the hardwood fronts later. This allowed us to align and position the drawer fronts after installing the cabinet and drawer boxes, ensuring that the reveals between the drawer fronts were correctly aligned and uniform in width.

For drawers that have ½-in. clearance between the inside edge of the face frame and the drawer side, we usually use KV 1300 slides (Knape and Vogt Manufacturing, Grand Rapids, Mich. 49506). The overall drawer width is 1 in. less than the opening.

We made the drawer boxes from No. 2 or No. 3 1x12 white pine, which we first ripped and crosscut to rough size. Then I jointed one face and we thicknessed the stock to ⅝ in. Finally we jointed one edge, ripped the stock to finished width, and then crosscut the pieces to exact length.

The dadoes that house the drawer back and the rabbets that hold the front of the box were quickly cut on a router table, using a ⅝-in. bit. Depth of cut is important as it affects the overall width of the drawer.

To complete the cutting for drawers, we ran the grooves for the drawer bottoms with the dado blade on the table saw, and then cut out the bottoms themselves.

To assemble the drawers, we first put glue in the dadoes and rabbets; then we put the bottom into one side, attached the front and back and added the remaining side. Since we cut joints for a snug fit, we usually have to use a rubber hammer to get things together. A couple of staples through the joint makes clamping unnecessary.

Before the glue sets up, though, we check squareness with a framing square. This is a critical check when you are installing drawers with side-mount slides. We use a block plane, if necessary, to make the fronts and backs flush with the sides on the top edge. Then we round over the top edges of the boxes with a ¼-in. round-over bit, being careful not to round over the outside edge of the box front, so that when the drawer front is attached, the edge between the drawer front and the drawer box is close and tight.

Next we install the slides on the drawers. With KV 1300s, you mount the slide flush with the front and parallel to the bottom edge of the drawer. We drive one screw through the vertical slots at each end of the slide and into the side of the drawer. These slots allow some leeway for adjustment once you mount the mating slides on the inside of the cabinet.

If everything is right, the drawer will be flush with the face frame on both sides. If not, we scribe the front of the drawer box on the top and bottom edge so it will be flush with the cabinet face, and then taper it to the line on the jointer, avoiding the staples. You could also trim this taper with a hand plane.

When assembling drawers, it's a good idea to drive nails or staples from the sides into the front, rather than from the front into the sides. This way you won't nick your plane iron or jointer knives when you're trimming the front. When each drawer box fits right, we drive the rest of the screws into the slides.

Fitting overlay doors and drawer fronts— Nothing can ruin the looks of a pricey cabinet job more thoroughly than misaligned drawer fronts and doors. The overlay fit design we had decided on for the bathroom cabinets is achieved by allowing only a very narrow spacing between all drawer fronts and cabinet doors, so proper alignment was especially important. We usually do all the installing and fitting with the cabinet upright, but before the top of the cabinet is put on. This way we still have easy access to the inside of the case.

For the bathroom cabinets, we used ³⁄₁₆-in. thick plywood shims to get uniform vertical reveals between cabinet doors and drawer fronts, and ¹⁄₁₆-in. veneer shims to produce the horizontal reveals, as shown in the photo at the top of the facing page.

The first step in achieving the overlay fit is to stand the cabinet upright and slide the bottom drawer box into its hardware in the bottom opening. Then the solid drawer front is aligned on the face frame against its shims. By pushing the box up against the front and shooting two staples from the inside through the box and into the front, we joined front to box with the right alignment. Then we removed the drawer carefully (since only two staples held front to box) and fastened both parts together by driving flathead screws through the box and into the front (photo facing page, bottom). With the bottom drawer complete, we replaced it in the cabinet, then placed a shim on its top edge to space the next front. And so on up the front of the cabinet. It's important to have the cabinet sitting upright rather than on its back when installing the fronts, so that the drawers have their final gravity fit.

Some of the cabinets had to be built in place, and their tops were already attached before we installed the drawers. So when we got to the topmost drawer, it was impossible to staple the box to the front from the inside. Instead, we shot some staples through the front of the top drawer box before sliding it into the cabinet, then nipped them off just above the surface. Pressing the teak drawer front against the installed box caused the staples to make index marks in the front, which we used to align front and box when screwing them together.

Concealed hinges—To avoid having hinges interrupt the visual flow of line and plane, we used Grass concealed hinges (Grass America Inc., 1377 S. Park Dr., Kernsville, N.C. 27284) for all cabinet doors. The popularity of concealed hinges has grown in recent years. Several brands are available, but we've used only the Grass hinge. It has many advantages. The door can overlay the stile any amount on the hinge side as long as it is 1 in. or more. After installation, the doors can be taken off simply by loosening one screw on each hinge and separating the two parts, much as you would separate a butt hinge. It's easy to install, once you've done a few. The hinge has good spring-loaded action, and at $6 a pair, costs less than most concealed cabinet hinges.

There are a few things you have to watch out for when using these hinges, though. They're not well suited to plywood doors because they require a 1³⁄₈-in. dia. hole to be drilled ⅝ in. deep in the back of the door. Though this is fine in solid stock, in plywood you could easily bore into a void. The 1-in. or more overlay on the hinge side can also be a limitation, as it sometimes makes for awfully wide stiles. You've also got to have at least a ³⁄₁₆-in. reveal between doors on the hinge side. Another problem is that there are no locating bumps on the back of the fixed leaf, so it is hard to know where to screw the hinge to the face of the cabinet. One solution we've tried is to cut the heads off a couple of screws and temporarily hold them in their holes with duct tape. They should stick out of the back of the hinge just a little so that when the door is held in the proper place against the face frame, you can give it a tap with your hand and leave indentations where you will bore pilot holes in the face. Since we use these hinges in large numbers, we're going to weld some screw heads in a pair of hinges to make a permanent set of alignment hinges.

The hinges we used for these cabinets require a 1³⁄₈-in. dia. hole drilled ⅝ in. deep, with its center ⁹⁄₁₆ in. away from the door edge. This means that your bit will exceed the width of the door by ¼ in. We use a brad-point bit that we modified by filing its point off. You could also use a Forstner bit. Either way, you have to chuck your bit in a drill press to bore this hole, and I wouldn't recommend drilling them out by hand, or even with a portable electric drill. Butting a scrap piece of ¾-in. thick stock tightly against the door edge where you'll be drilling prevents tearout. It's also important to use an accurate depth stop, since you'll need to drill to within ⅛ in. of the front face of the door (assuming your cabinet doors are ¾ in. thick). For the same reason, we had to file off the center point of the bit. □

Rob Hunt and Robert Robertson own Water St. Cabinets and Furniture, in Bastrop, Tex.

Top, concealed hinges are the key to the overlay cabinet doors, and they must be mounted in precisely drilled holes. At right, tile and teak combine to give the finished master bath its simple, yet elegant, appeal.

Corian Kitchen Countertops

Combining a new material with old-fashioned ideas

by Michael O'Hare

If you think a course of shingles should overlap the course below it, you may have wondered how we put up with the conventional installation of a modern kitchen sink. The "drop-in" sink certainly ignores the requirements of normal use, which involves setting wet objects on the counter to drain, and wiping the counter down to clean it. Even with a plastic drainboard that hooks over the edge of the sink, no one has figured out how to clean a countertop hygienically. The problem, of course, is that wiping toward the sink drives dirty water under the rim into the slightest defect in the caulking. In time, this water seeps down to the particleboard counter base, swells it, heaves the sink, and wrecks the seal.

There are ways to put your faith in gravity rather than in chemistry. One solution is to make sink and counter out of a single piece of stainless steel. Commercial kitchens are built this way. The counter can be pitched to form a drainboard, or flat if you don't mind sponging. Some manufacturers do sell single and double-drainboard stainless-steel sinks, moving the rim-seal problem a couple of feet away from the sink edge, but these items are usually custom-made and quite expensive.

Another approach is to set a porcelain-enameled cast-iron sink—with or without integral drainboards—flush with a ceramic-tile countertop. No one I know of still manufactures a square-edge enamel sink, but they are available occasionally as salvage. The alternative is to use a "modern" porcelain sink, designed to be dropped onto a laminate counter, and either cut it down with an abrasive saw or contrive a way to set it flush with the tile. In either case, a sink full of hot water will expand much more than the tile around it, so the grout line between tile and sink will fail unless it is silicone.

Corian—In my own kitchen, I solved the problem in a different way, using Corian, a sort of space-age, marble-like sheet material manufactured by Du Pont. For more on this product, see p. 55. Using the techniques I'll describe, you can cut out a Corian counter and hang a conventional drop-in sink under it. This approach deals with the troublesome lip problem in a way that's effective and nice-looking.

Du Pont is reluctant to reveal the exact composition of Corian, but I infer from its texture and the odor it releases when sawn that it's made by combining acrylic and marble dust. Corian panels are available in ¼-in. (recommended for vertical applications only), ½-in., and ¾-in. thicknesses, up to 12 ft. long and either 25 in. or 30 in. wide. It comes in white, almond, and a sort of swirly white and off-white pattern vaguely reminiscent of marble but rather more like clouds.

Corian is expensive—it retails for about $15 per sq. ft. in ¾-in. thickness. But it has two important virtues. First, its beauty is not skin-deep, nor is its finish. It takes on a low-lustre patina with normal scrubbing, and its edges—factory or job-cut—are self-finished. Second, it works nicely, though slowly, with ordinary carbide-tipped tools—sawblades and router bits—and it can be drilled, filed and sanded.

Corian is fairly brittle and is not too strong in tension, although a ½-in. thick sheet 12 ft. long can be lifted by its ends. Sharp interior corners should be avoided because they increase stresses. Du Pont recommends that corners be given a ³⁄₁₆-in. minimum radius. Corian also needs fairly flexible fastenings. Indeed, the basic installation detail is to flop it onto a few dabs of silicone caulk—no screws, no clips.

If Corian has any noticeable drawback, it's the fact that Du Pont has marketed it as a direct substitute for laminate countertops. It's a much different material from any laminate, and it can be used in a number of different ways.

Kitchen design—The sink detail I used in my kitchen trades on Corian's workability and self-finished edge. I routed drainage grooves into the ¾-in. thick countertops, and set the sink under the counter. The counter drains into the sink as it should, and an overhang keeps splashes from running up the sides of the sink. You can put the plumbing on the wall where it belongs: no wiping around the faucet or water drooling under it into the cabinets below.

Corian is available in sink-counter combinations. This is an attractive option if you want a small single sink or a double sink with one small and one large basin. It still needs the drain grooves to be routed in, because the counter supplied by Du Pont is flat. I didn't use combinations for my installations, partly because they are very expensive, but principally because they aren't available with a single large basin (16 in. by 28 in.). The large basin—about the size of a conventional double sink—allows you to have a double sink when you want it simply by dropping in a plastic washbasin or two. It also allows you to wash a big pot.

In my kitchen, where two people cook, I installed two sinks to relieve the most important bottleneck. One is a washing-up sink (photo, right) next to the dishwasher with pot storage overhead. Almost everything on the rack above gets hung up wet, but it just drips onto the Corian countertop and then into the sink.

The second sink (photo facing page) is used for cooking-related tasks. It's located between the range and a restaurant cutting board (available from restaurant-supply houses in ¾-in. thickness and to-order sizes), which is installed flush between adjacent sections of Corian counter with a silicone seal. Food that spreads off the board as you work can just be swept back into place. In front of the cutting board are two

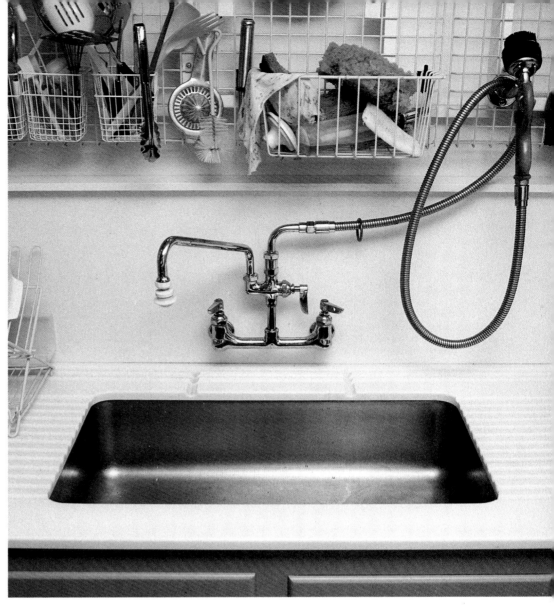

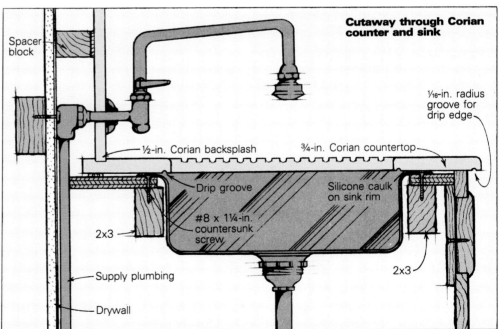

Cutaway through Corian counter and sink

Spacer block

½-in. Corian backsplash

¾-in. Corian countertop

¹⁄₁₆-in. radius groove for drip edge

Drip groove

Silicone caulk on sink rim

#8 x 1¼-in. countersunk screw

2x3

2x3

Supply plumbing

Drywall

The author installed two sinks in his kitchen, both of them beneath countertops of custom-cut Corian. The drawing above shows how the stainless-steel sinks are mounted on a 2x3 frame just below the ¾-in. thick countertop. A commercial wall-mounted faucet and rinsing nozzle complement the washing sink (photo top). Washed and rinsed pots and utensils go directly to storage in upper racks. The dishrack sits right on the drainboard that the author made by routing grooves into the Corian countertop before installing it. The cooking sink (photo facing page) is between the range and the cutting board, which is set flush with the counter. The drawer just beneath the cutting board holds removable steam-table inserts—one for cut-up food and one for scraps.

Routing the drainboard. O'Hare uses a ¾-in. carbide core-box bit and a jig that consists of tapered supports, an edge guide, and an end stop. The jig is clamped laterally to make a series of parallel, pitched grooves that will drain into the sink.

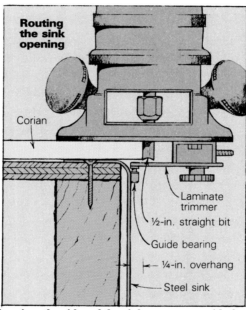

Routing the sink opening

Corian

Laminate trimmer

½-in. straight bit

Guide bearing

¼-in. overhang

Steel sink

Cutting the finished opening. As shown in the drawing, the sides of the sink serve as a guide for routing the countertop to finished size. The guide bearing in the router's laminate-trimmer base must be reversed so that it can bear against the flat portion of the sink to create a smooth edge. A second pass with a ball-bearing round-over bit and a third on the bottom with a small core-box bit, both guided by the counter edge, will finish the job.

drawers that hold removable stainless-steel steam-table dishes. One drawer, open in the photo, receives scraps for the compost pile. The other receives cut-up food to be dumped in the stew or salad. When the cutting board wears out, I will just slice the silicone, lift the old one out, and goop in a new one.

Installing the sink—The installation detail I used calls for a stock stainless-steel, drop-in style sink to be installed under, rather than through, a cutout (drawing, previous page). With the carcases in place, I began by installing a 2x3 frame to hold the top of the stainless sink about ⅛ in. below the bottom of the countertop. It would be easier to attach the sink to the counter itself from below, and Du Pont offers a screw anchor for Corian (I have also successfully tapped holes in it for other projects). But I was nervous about applying large concentrated loads

to the Corian, and a sink full of water can weigh 150 lb. So I decided to screw the sink rim to the framing beneath it, and let the Corian simply rest on the rim and framing supports. To drill the sink rim and countersink it for a few flathead screws, I had to use a slow drill speed and heavy pressure.

Drop the sink in, measure the location of its inside faces, and transfer these measurements to the countertop. If you're smart, the counter is on sawhorses outdoors; you are going to convert a good deal of it into white dust (non-toxic, according to the manufacturer), and it's nice not to have to chase it down inside the house.

Router work—The grooves for the drainboard are routed in with a simple tapering jig that's used with the edge guide shown in the top photo. I unclamped it and stepped it along the countertop to make parallel grooves pitched

toward the sink. I wanted the grooves to be ⅜ in. deep at the sink. Knowing this and the length of the grooves, I came up with a pitch of 1:96.

The router must be set to cut slightly at the very beginning of the pass. If you try to start at zero, the grooves will start irregularly owing to dust under the jig, tremors of the operator, or gremlins. I used an end stop to be sure that I started all my cuts along the same line, and I cut the grooves with a ¾-in. core-box bit. A 1-in. bit might be better because it will give you wider, more easily sponged grooves. Use a powerful router (I used a Stanley 90150), not a hobby machine; Corian is hard and dense.

If you're like me, you'll find that routing a $350 piece of material concentrates the mind wonderfully. Washing dishes is bad enough without looking your mistakes in the eye every night. On the first sink, I cut a 20-in. long drainboard. The grooves were too deep at the sink end, and had to be wiped individually. To fix this, I went over the countertop with the same jig and a straight-face bit, lowering the lands between the grooves for the last 10 in. or so. The second installation has a shorter drainboard, so the lands didn't need this treatment.

You might also want to add (subtract) a soap dish while you're routing.

The next step is to jigsaw the rough sink cutout slightly smaller than the finished opening. The finished edge in the Corian around the sink will be cut with a router, using the sides of the sink as the guide. I used an 18-tooth-per-inch metal-cutting blade in a jigsaw with an orbital stroke, and it moved right along. As an experiment, I reduced orbit to zero (vertical motion only), and it slowed down remarkably.

Once the hole was cut, I brought the counter back inside, set it on the cabinet dry and clamped it in place to rout the final opening. You want the finished Corian edge to overhang the sink by about ¼ in. for a drip groove and to conceal the sealant. Using the sink to guide the router requires some jury-rigging; the drawing at left shows the method I came up with. I used a Sears laminate trimmer with the guide bearing mounted upside down. The bearing must be far enough below the bit to ride on the flat side of the sink, not on its rounded top corner. I set the bearing ¼ in. ahead of the bit's cutting arc to get the overhang, and used a ½-in. carbide-tipped straight bit with a ½-in. shank. You have to do this routing in the kitchen, so it helps to have an assistant follow the router around the sink with a shop vacuum.

Now take the counter back outside and finish it. If you plan to use a Corian backsplash, rout a ⅛-in. deep rabbet for it along the back edge of the counter. I used ½-in. Corian for my backsplashes, so I made two passes with a ½-in. bit to give myself a fraction of an inch of play. Round over the top corner of the sink opening and the front edge of the counter (use a Robert Adam double-reverse ogee elegantissimo bit if your taste in decoration is more exuberant than mine). Rout a drip groove around the underside of the same edges with a ⅛-in. veining bit, and then ease the bottom corners with a flat file (routed corners of Corian are sharp enough to cut you). This completes the countertop.

Photos this page: Debra Sanderson

Installing the counter—You install the countertop on a few dabs of silicone caulk on the top edges of the supporting cabinets (photo top right) and on a continuous fat bead of silicone all around the top of the sink. (This sink-counter seal should be clear silicone; it's not visible from most angles but you might as well not have an irregular white band under the counter.) Clean all the surfaces you're going to caulk with alcohol, and remember to mask where you don't want silicone; dried silicone smears are hard to remove. The kitchen will smell like an explosion in a vinegar factory for an hour or so because the silicone releases acetic acid as it sets.

Du Pont sells adhesive kits for edge-joining Corian. The adhesive (photo middle left) glues two pieces together and hardens into a bead that won't show after you sand it flush (except with the cloud-patterned type of Corian). If you need to join two pieces, be sure that the edges of the Corian are absolutely clean (sanded and alcohol-rubbed); otherwise, dirt will be trapped and show as a black line. A dowel wrapped in aluminum foil (photo middle right) makes a nice fillet if this joint occurs at an inside corner.

With the counter set, you can drop the backsplash into its rabbet in a thin bead of silicone. I found I could tool a neat small fillet in the silicone with a ¼-in. dowel as long as I ran strips of masking tape along each side of the bead so the inevitable smears could be peeled off. The top of the backsplash can be held in place in several ways; I used silicone for the wash sink but had to use screws in sloppy holes, drawn up lightly with washers, for the cooking sink. The cooking-sink window also got a Corian stool cap so the potted plants can drip freely when watered.

Plumbing—The wall faucet is installed through the backsplash into female ½-in. threaded fittings. Eccentrics in the faucet itself allow some misalignment in these rough-ins, but you'll be lucky (or very foresighted) if the joints make up just as the faucet flanges come snug (a little more silicone here) against the backsplash. Don't overtighten the faucet flanges because this will stress the Corian.

A serious gap in the plumbing catalogs is a wall-mount faucet with a sprayer in residential grade. If you want a sprayer and you agree with me that plumbing doesn't belong on the deck, you will have to buy a piece of expensive restaurant hardware. When you do, you get a wonderful sprayer and—if you want it—a 9-ft. hose that will reach all the way to your range for filling stock pots.

The counters have worked out as well as I had hoped. They're easy to clean and they look nice. My pride in this project, however, was rather dampened upon its completion. Admiring my work with a beer, I realized that I had merely recreated, in plastic and stainless, the same basic design that builders used 100 years ago, hanging a zinc sink beneath a marble counter. □

Michael O'Hare was trained as an architect and engineer, but for reasons he still does not fully understand, teaches public management and policy analysis at Harvard's John F. Kennedy School of Government.

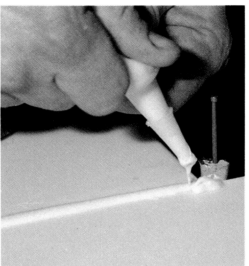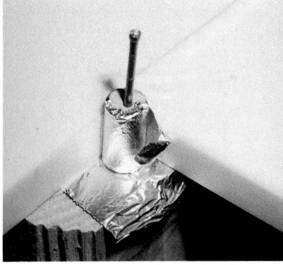

Installing the countertop. **As long as all its edges are supported, Corian can be held in place by its weight and a few dabs of silicone spread on the framing beneath it, top. Where lengths of Corian butt, above left, a special adhesive supplied by Du Pont is used. The adhesive will harden into a bead that can be sanded flush to blend imperceptibly with the rest of the countertop. Above right, a dowel wrapped in aluminum foil can be used to create a fillet of adhesive material at an inside corner. Rounding the corner this way reduces stress concentrations.**

Information on Corian

Editor's note: Du Pont publishes a helpful booklet, several brochures, and a series of technical bulletins on Corian. The "Professional Installer's Guide for Corian Countertops" (45¢) is a 29-pp. manual that includes instructions on preparing cabinets for Corian, cutting and joining the panels, installing the backsplash and applying decorative edge treatments.

The "Reference and Specification Guide" (50¢) is a 20-pp. brochure that describes available Corian products—three thicknesses of sheet goods (¼ in., ½ in. and ¾ in.) in various panel dimensions for countertops and tub surrounds, precast single-bowl and double-bowl lavatories and precast kitchen sinks and bar sinks. Also listed are Corian accessories—caulk, sealant, installation hardware, cleaning pads and conductive tape (required for cooktop applications.)

There's also the "Corian Idea File of Unique Edge Treatments" (50¢), which shows you how to make six kinds of decorative edges using wood, metal and plastic. Unless you're really stuck for details, you won't need this one.

Finally there are the following free technical bulletins—"Using Joint Adhesive to Repair Countertop Joints," "Corian Building Products Fabrication Methods," "Weatherability of Corian," "Corian Flammability Ratings," "Performance Properties of Corian Sheet," "Chemical Resistance of Corian Building Products" and "Corian Care and Maintenance."

To order any of the literature mentioned above, write E. I. Du Pont de Nemours & Co., Inc., Corian Building Products, Room x40859, Wilmington, Del. 19898. To locate distributors in your area, call 1-800-441-7515, or check the Yellow Pages under Kitchens or Bathrooms.

Corian is a registered Du Pont trademark.

Random-Fitted Panels

Creative cabinetwork transforms a cramped kitchen into a pleasant workspace

by Fletcher Cox

Ideas for using a random-fitted board design for paneling and cabinets had been in my head for a while before I got to try them out in a kitchen remodeling job in Jackson, Miss. The house was a 1908 Italianate in which the original kitchen had been in a separate building. Much later, the pantry in the main house was converted into an indoor kitchen. It was long and narrow (21 ft. by 8 ft.), its cabinets were rickety, and the green-painted walls made the room dark and depressing.

To make the room lighter, we decided to

Woodworker Fletcher Cox lives in Tougaloo, Miss. Photos by the author.

paint the walls white and use white Formica on the new countertop. A wood ceiling would warm the room up some, but straight, tongue-and-groove boards would have been inappropriate in this long space. Random-fitted boards seemed a good idea. I decided to use ash; it's easy to work, and pale enough to preserve the light, airy feeling we were striving for. The boards I bought from a local supplier were ¾ in. thick, surfaced on two sides, and 4 in. to 10 in. wide.

I began the ceiling by nailing up a layer of ¾-in. plywood overhead for a nailing surface. Then I started putting up the random boards, working out from one corner and trying to

keep a good proportion of long, wide and angular pieces. To decide on shape, what I did was to pull a board out of my truck, hold it up to the ceiling, and mark several critical angles. Then I'd pull the board down, connect the marks with a chalkline or a long straightedge, and cut it. I used a saber saw to cut the boards to size and a plane for trimming to fit and beveling the edges. All the ceiling pieces were butt-joined, and rather than trying to hide the nails, I showed them off, using 6d, cement-coated nails in predrilled holes. Ash can split easily, so the pilot holes were necessary. The cement coating rubbed off on the hammer, so I had to clean its head frequently

Upper cabinet design

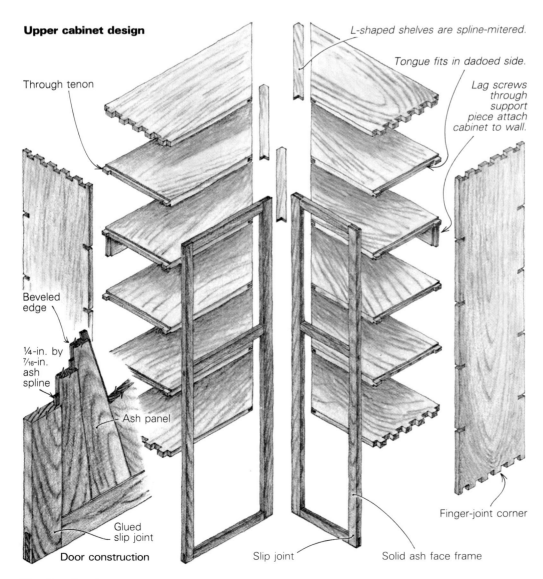

Through tenon

Beveled edge

¼-in. by ⁷⁄₁₆-in. ash spline

Ash panel

Glued slip joint

Door construction

L-shaped shelves are spline-mitered.

Tongue fits in dadoed side.

Lag screws through support piece attach cabinet to wall.

Finger-joint corner

Slip joint

Solid ash face frame

Construction details for wall-mounted corner cabinets and spline-fit, random-panel doors are shown in the drawing at left. Custom built-ins include a pan-shaped drawer, top, to hold pans and skillets. Behind the snouted door is storage space for cookie sheets. The large, pull-out cutting board, above, was made from strips of ash, walnut and cherry.

Illustration: Christopher Clapp

in solvent to keep from leaving brown stains on the boards.

As the ceiling progressed, we discussed what to do with the rest of the space, and decided to build in a long counter on the east wall, which was broken with two windows looking out toward the backyard (photo, right). Even with a stove and dishwasher tucked in under the counter, there would still be plenty of room for me to put in all the things I would want in my own kitchen: a pull-out cutting board, a skillet drawer shaped like the pans that are stored there, and a snouted cabinet with a rack for cookie sheets (photo facing page).

Along with these elaborations, I wanted to continue using random boards in the cabinetwork. I designed the cabinet doors to hold random-fitted pieces held together by splines. The only glue in the doors is at the corners, where I used slip joints (see the drawing on the facing page). Fitting the ash pieces together wasn't too difficult because I'd had plenty of practice on the ceiling. I cut each door's interior pieces and fit them together, then temporarily inserted a thin paper shim between each piece before trimming the perimeter pieces to fit the opening. The shim space serves the important purpose of allowing the wood to expand. Without it, the pieces could easily burst their frames apart during warm, humid weather.

To cut the spline slots in each piece, I used a piloted slot-cutter chucked in a router mounted upside-down on a small table. I've used this kind of homemade shaper before and it sure saves time. The splines were 7⁄16-in. by ¼-in. ash, so I cut the slots ¼ in. wide and ¼ in. deep. Beveling the edges was the last step in preparing the fitted random boards. The door frame also had to be slotted to receive splines. Gluing up the four corners of each frame locked the interior paneling in place. The face frame for the base cabinets was built from solid ash, and I used ash plywood for the carcase and shelves.

The corner cabinets above the counters required more intricate work because they were built from solid wood. I made both cupboards in my workshop and then hauled them to the house to be installed. The L-shaped shelves are joined together with splined miters, and let into the cabinet sides with dadoes and through mortises (drawing, facing page). I glued an ash face frame to the assembled shelves and sides, and then installed piece-panel doors like the ones I'd built for the base cabinets. The upper cabinets weren't built with backs, so to fasten them to the wall I glued cleats to two shelves and simply lag-screwed them into studs in the wall.

The pull-out cutting board took shape in my workshop as the project went along. It's laminated from strips of ash, cherry and walnut, and measures 24 in. wide by 36 in. long. I soaked it in boiled linseed oil before installing it in the kitchen. The finish for the cabinets was a wash coat of equal parts of gloss polyurethane and mineral spirits, followed by three coats of satin polyurethane. □

Random-panel cabinetwork enlivens this long, narrow kitchen. The white plastic-laminate countertops and pale ash boards make the most of a limited amount of natural light.

From *Fine Homebuilding* magazine (October 1983) 17:68-69

Installing a Sheet-Vinyl Floor

Whether flat-lay or coved, use a felt-paper pattern for best results

by Terry Shrode

People still call it linoleum, even though it isn't, and the chances are good that the floors in your bathroom and kitchen are covered with it. It's properly called resilient flooring, and it also turns up in the family room, workshop and utility porch—any place where a durable, low-maintenance and affordable floor is a requirement.

Resilient flooring is available in a wide price range, from as little as $3 a square yard to over $30 a yard, and it comes in colors and designs that will suit just about anybody's taste. Along with the outlay for supplies, you can figure an equal amount for the installation labor. This article is about how to install resilient flooring in two different ways. One is the relatively easy flat-lay method. The other is the more complicated coved style that used to be common with linoleum floors.

Flat-lay is the term for a floor that meets the wall at a 90° angle. This junction is covered by a baseboard or a toe molding. A coved floor requires a little more material than a flat-lay floor, and it wraps right up the wall, where it is finished with a J-section trim piece called cap metal (drawing, facing page). The floor-to-wall intersection is backed with radiused blocking called cove stick. At inside and outside corners, the flooring is mitered—it's the floor mechanic's version of the carpenter's crown-molding problem. A coved floor is more difficult to install than a flat-lay floor, but I think it looks classier, and it's easier to keep clean at the perimeter.

There are two basic types of resilient floors available today (sidebar, facing page): sheet goods, which come in 6-ft., 9-ft., 12-ft. and 15-ft. widths; and tiles, which are usually 1-ft. square. Most sheet goods and tiles are made of either vinyl compositions or pure vinyl. I'm going to concentrate on sheet vinyl because it's the most popular, and it comes in the greatest variety of colors, grades and designs.

Vinyl-tile floors follow the same basic installation procedures as sheet-vinyl floors, and the boxes of tile usually include easy-to-follow instructions. But I think vinyl-tile floors have one serious drawback: they have lots of seams for water or dirt to invade. This can be a serious problem, especially in wet locations with wood subfloors. Don't get me wrong—I've seen properly maintained inexpensive

Terry A. Shrode is a flooring contractor in Richmond, Calif.

vinyl-tile floors over wood substrates that have lasted for many years, but this is the exception and not the usual case.

Estimating materials—The rule of thumb is to lay out the floor with the fewest seams, and with the least amount of waste. There are only two possible directions to run the vinyl, and one is usually better than the other.

In the kitchen plan below, I've shown the layout lines for an installation using 6-ft. wide goods (the most common width available) running the two possible directions. The east-west direction leaves me with both more waste and more seams than the other option, so the north-south orientation is clearly the best choice here. Two pieces, or drops, are needed for this floor. The west-side drop is 14 ft. 6 in. plus an extra 3 in. that should be added to any length to allow for trimming. This floor will be coved, which requires about 4 in. of material per wall, thereby adding another 8 in., for a total of 15 ft. 5 in. If the plan calls for doorways to be covered, this will add to your total—be sure to include them.

The east-side drop is 2 ft. shorter, because of the cabinets, for a sum of 13 ft. 5 in. The tiny gap in the southeast corner will be filled with a piece of scrap from the cabinet cutouts.

The total amount of material you need to order depends on the "pattern match" for the particular piece of flooring in question. If the

Determining the drops

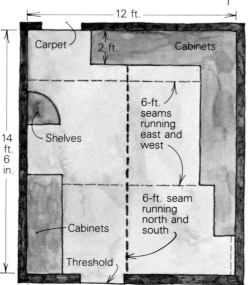

piece has no definite design, no extra material is needed. If, on the other hand, there is a recurring design, the distance between repetitions has to be added to each drop after the first one. The design in the material chosen for this kitchen repeats itself every 18 in., so the east-side drop totals 14 ft. 11 in. If there were a third drop, it too would need another 18 in. added to it, and so on. The grand total for this kitchen is 15 ft. 5 in. plus 14 ft. 11 in. With 6-ft. goods, this comes out to 20¼ sq. yd.

Subfloor—It often takes more time to prepare the base under the sheet goods than it takes to install the new flooring, and this is one of the most important steps in the entire process. Every ridge, bump or gouge will telegraph through the new floor, inviting premature wearout. Termite and water damage are the other big problems, and you should take care of any major structural upgrades before you begin work on the new floor. Check to see that the existing floor is securely fastened to its joists. Eliminate squeaky spots or loose floorboards with a few ringshank nails.

A lot of the floors that I install are over existing vinyl or linoleum surfaces. They are adequate subfloors if they are free of wax or grease. I cut back any small imperfections, such as loose seams, gouges or bumps, to solid underlayment, and fill the resulting gaps with a patching compound like Fixall (Dowman Products, Inc., Box 2857, Long Beach, Calif. 90801).

A floor with more extensive damage should be covered with ⅜-in. or thicker plywood or particleboard. This includes old T&G floors that have cupped or twisted. Install the plywood finished side up; if you use particleboard, get the best underlayment grade you can find. Where I work on the West Coast, we don't have the wide humidity swings that are common in other parts of the country. Consequently, I leave about a ³⁄₁₆-in. gap at the walls, but I don't leave much of an expansion gap between the sheets. I just loosely butt them together in a staggered pattern and secure them to the subfloor with ⅞-in. staples. I use staples because they are fast, and because they don't leave dimples in the underlayment the way nails might. If you choose nails, make sure they are ringshanks. Don't use sheetrock nails—they will work their way out over time. In either case, nails or staples should reach ½ in. into the subfloor, and they should be

From *Fine Homebuilding* magazine (August 1984) 22:44-49

Two 3-ft. wide pieces of builder's felt are butted together and taped to make a pattern for the first drop in the kitchen shown in the drawing on the facing page. Here the finished pattern has been taped onto the flooring, and Shrode is trimming the material to fit. The corner cut-out at the bottom of the photo indicates that this will be a coved floor.

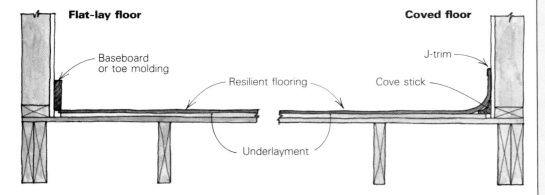

Flat-lay floor

Baseboard or toe molding

Resilient flooring

Underlayment

Coved floor

J-trim

Cove stick

Illustrations: Frances Ashforth

Resilient flooring

A hundred years ago, an Englishman named Walton coined the word linoleum to describe a pliable floor covering made of wood pulp, cork, turpentine, pigments and oxidized linseed oil. This mixture was applied to a burlap or canvas backing, and it was ready to install. Linoleum is still an excellent floor covering, but it requires lots of maintenance and is now made only by the Krommenie Co. in Holland and distributed by the L. D. Brinkman Co. (14425 Clark Ave., Industry, Calif. 91745). People also use it for countertops and drafting boards.

Today's resilient flooring also includes cork and rubber-base products. But by far the most common are vinyl floor coverings. Vinyls are petroleum-base plastics that are made into floor coverings in two basic ways.

The first is the inlaid method, which produces hard-surface goods. Millions of tiny vinyl bits, with color built right into them, are spread out and compressed at high temperature into a thin layer, which is then bonded to a backing material for strength. Inlaid floors are very durable because the color runs deep into the material. They also have a very hard surface and they are quite stiff, which makes them difficult to install.

Rotogravure is the second method. Rotogravure floors make up the bulk of the sheet-goods business, and the cushion layer built into them makes them comfortable to walk on and resistant to dings. To produce them, rolls of blank flooring are run through printing presses. A plate on the press carries the photographic image of the design, which is embossed into the flooring. A thin layer of vinyl above the cushioned core then receives colored dyes from the press to complete the design. A clear layer on top takes the wear.

Once they are installed, cushioned floors have to be sealed at their seams with a special solvent made for each type. It comes in applicator bottles from your supplier, and it welds the two pieces of flooring together to keep out dirt and moisture.

Both inlaid and rotogravure vinyl floorings are available in what manufacturers call wax or no-wax finishes. No-wax means the floor looks waxed, but you don't have to wax it. Wax means you have to wax it. In the past, I avoided cushioned floors with no-wax finishes. They had a thin layer of PVC over the flooring and didn't wear very well. But recently, the manufacturers have come out with new coatings that seem much more durable.

Another change is in the backing material. For years, asbestos backing was the standard. It resisted heat, moisture damage and mildew, but as we now know, is an awesome health hazard. The industry still hasn't settled on its replacement. Some floorings now have vinyl backings, which are an added expense. Others have a fiberglass backing, which can leave you scratching at the end of the day when you install it. But both of these are improvements over asbestos.

In the vinyl-flooring business, new products are being introduced all the time, some of which require new installation procedures. Some call for different adhesives, others shouldn't be back-rolled during installation. It's important to ask your supplier about the specific procedures to follow for your floor.

In general, you get what you pay for in resilient flooring, but after a point your money is spent on style rather than durability. Around here, $20 per yard will buy you a floor that should last for 20 years. Check with your local flooring contractor for the brands and styles that are available. And try this test for durability when you're shopping for a vinyl floor: Scratch the surface of the floor sample with your fingernail. If you can gouge a hole, or come close to it, stay away from it. —*T. S.*

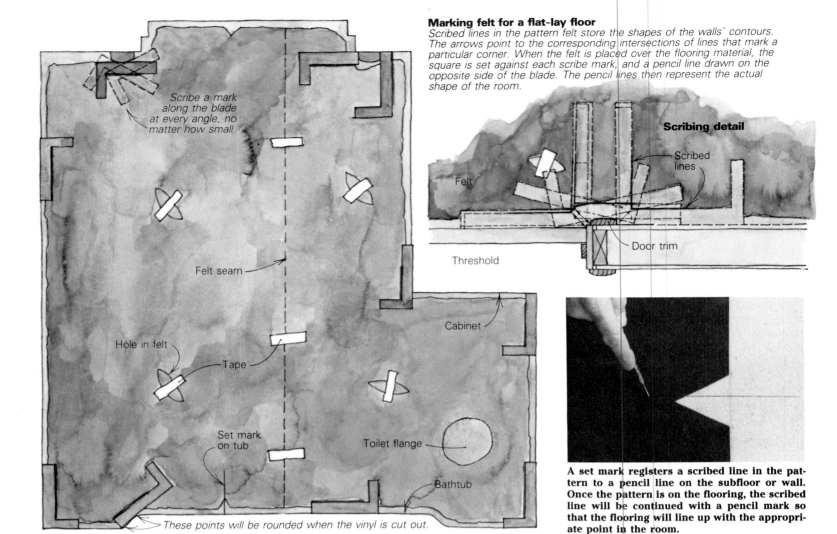

Marking felt for a flat-lay floor
Scribed lines in the pattern felt store the shapes of the walls' contours. The arrows point to the corresponding intersections of lines that mark a particular corner. When the felt is placed over the flooring material, the square is set against each scribe mark, and a pencil line drawn on the opposite side of the blade. The pencil lines then represent the actual shape of the room.

Scribing detail

Scribed lines

Felt

Door trim

Threshold

Scribe a mark along the blade at every angle, no matter how small.

Felt seam

Hole in felt

Tape

Set mark on tub

Cabinet

Toilet flange

Bathtub

These points will be rounded when the vinyl is cut out.

A set mark registers a scribed line in the pattern to a pencil line on the subfloor or wall. Once the pattern is on the flooring, the scribed line will be continued with a pencil mark so that the flooring will line up with the appropriate point in the room.

spaced ½ in. from the seams 3 in. o. c. around the edges and 8 in. o. c. in the field.

Adding a new floor over two or three layers of old flooring is fine. Before you do this, though, check for height problems. Building up the floor this way will sometimes trap the dishwasher or prevent the refrigerator from fitting back into its nook. You may have to remove the old floors. If the old surface is a cushioned-type resilient floor, don't install hard surface goods over it—foot traffic may crack the new material. If the old floor is smooth, you can lay the new one right over it, without new underlayment. Be sure to give it a thorough cleaning with TSP (tri-sodium phosphate) so that the adhesive will stick. Don't sand the old flooring—it might have asbestos in it. If it's a coved floor, cut out the portion that wraps up the wall and remove the old J-trim, but leave the old cove stick. It will work fine for the new floor.

Making a flat-lay pattern—There is nothing mysterious about laying a vinyl floor, even with coving. The key to success is the pattern. The pattern is made of felt paper (15-lb. builder's felt is fine) pieced together with duct tape or masking tape to approximate the shape of the floor. In a room where it takes only one piece of material to cover the floor, I make a pattern (drawing, above left). It begins with a piece of felt butted against the longest wall,

followed by consecutive pieces until the floor is covered.

If the floor is to have more than one drop, I strike a chalkline to mark the first seam. The placement of this line is critical, because the rest of the floor will be affected by its position. When I'm using 6-ft. goods in an area with more than one drop, I use two 3-ft. wide lengths of felt butted together to simulate each drop. One edge of the pattern corresponds with the seam in the vinyl. In either case, I cut eye holes out of the pattern so I can tape it to the work, and I avoid creasing the felt.

Once the pattern paper is secured to the floor, I make set marks, registration points that I mark with a scribed line on the pattern and a pencil line on the underlayment, tub edge or wall (photo above). I notch the pattern with a V at these points to make them easy to find. I like to use at least two set marks for each drop—usually one along the length and one along the width. These marks will later be transferred to the vinyl flooring.

The pattern is cut about an inch shy of the walls all around. This allows me to transfer the shape of the room onto the pattern. I do this with a square with a 12-in. long blade that is 1½ in. wide. The blade spans the gap between the pattern and the wall, and I make a scratch on the room side of the blade (drawing, above right). Then I work my way around the room, marking every angle, no matter how

small, with a scratch on the pattern paper. I make the marks at least 4 in. long. If I have to use the square's short leg, which is 1 in. wide, I make a note on the pattern to remind myself that something out of the ordinary was done. Later, when I use the pattern to mark the correct perimeter on the actual goods, I just reverse this whole process.

I mark curves by moving the square around them at short intervals. These marks will later be connected and rounded off when the material is cut. These scribe marks can look like unintelligible scratches at first, especially around door casings and pipes. Study the drawings to see how the scribe marks capture the room's contours.

Trimming the seams—If the floor will have a seam, the material has to be trimmed. Factory edges must never be used for seams. They will be crooked, gouged or dirty, and all vinyl sheet goods are slightly oversize to allow for trimming.

Sheet goods are installed with reversed seams, unless the manufacturer says otherwise. This means that a roll of sheet goods has a left edge and a right edge. Installed, a right edge butts against a right edge, and a left edge butts against a left edge. Therefore the drops will alternate in direction. I cut the pieces individually, then butt them together at the seam because I've found this to be the quickest and most accurate way for me. Others cut both layers at once.

Roll the flooring out, face up, on a clean, smooth surface. Garage floors are nice if they aren't oily. Don't lay the material in direct sunlight, which will cause it to shrink. Now back-roll the flooring, and roll it out flat again. This also shrinks the material, but since you have to back-roll it during installation, you want the shrinkage to take place before the material is cut.

Where to cut the seam depends on the design of the floor. If it has one with straight lines, they will have a certain width—usually ⅛ in. to ½ in.—to simulate grout lines. Trim to one side or the other; if you leave the line on the first drop, cut it off the next drop. Some floors have extra-wide grout lines at the edges. They have to be trimmed down to match the grout lines in the rest of the design. If the material has no design, take off about ½ in.

Position a long straightedge at the appropriate spot along the border of the material. Kneel on one end, and steady the other end with your hand (photo above left). Use a utility knife with a fresh blade to score the surface. The hand will naturally make a bevel, so turn the knife inward slightly to make sure the blade follows the straightedge. Make a smooth cut approximately 2 or 3 ft. long—whatever length is most comfortable for you. Stop, but don't remove the knife. Slide your hand and knee down the straightedge and repeat the cut. When you get to the end of the straightedge, don't remove the knife. Just slide the straightedge down the border, line it up, and keep cutting.

Use the linoleum knife to finish the seam (photo above right). Place the curved part of the blade in the groove made by the utility knife. Pull gently, letting the knife follow the score mark.

Using the pattern—Align the pattern felt along the edge of the seam, and adjust it so that the design in the vinyl breaks the same way at each end. If the pattern felt covers the entire floor, adjust it to be as square to the design in the flooring as possible, with equal design breaks around the edges. This is usually a matter of compromises, since four walls are rarely square. Using the eye holes in the felt, tape the pattern to the material.

Now transfer the marks on the felt to the flooring. Place the square next to each mark, and make a pencil line on the opposite side of the square onto the material. When you're finished, you have a picture of the floor. Using the utility knife, cut on the waste side of the pencil line. This will make the material a little fat and ensure a tight fit. Round off the corners slightly, and be careful not to cut into the main sheet. For long, straight runs, use the straightedge. Take your time.

Installation—Sweep the floor clean, back-roll the vinyl again to make it easy to carry, and lay it in place to check the fit. Trim any areas that need it, and make sure the set marks are telling the truth. Remove the floor-

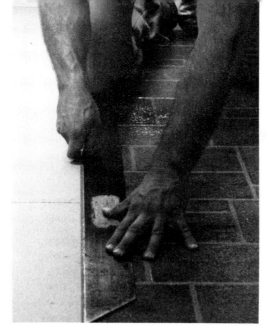

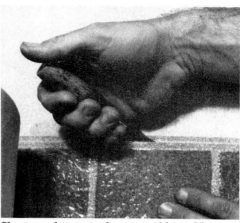

Sheet goods are made extra wide and have to be trimmed at the seams. The author prefers to cut one sheet at a time, using a long straightedge and a utility knife to score the vinyl, left. The cut is finished with a linoleum knife, above.

Shrode uses notches cut in the pattern felt to register the second drop to the first. The notches are placed three design repetitions apart, and let him accurately position the pattern on the material.

ing, and use a ³⁄₃₂-in. notched trowel to spread latex adhesive over the area of the first drop. Stop the adhesive 3 in. shy of the seam line. This area will be spread with adhesive when the second drop goes down. Make sure there are no puddles in the adhesive, and set the flooring into it while it's still wet. One person can do this, but it's a lot easier with two. Position the areas with the set marks first, spread the floor out and use a moist rag to pick up excess adhesive. Immediately use a floor roller, which you can rent, to squeeze the material down into the adhesive. Work from the center toward the edges. After rolling, a few bubbles may persist. They should disappear by morning, because the latex draws the flooring downward as it dries.

The second drop—Matching the design is the challenge of the second drop. For this kitchen floor, I made notches in the pattern felt that corresponded to the grout lines in the flooring design. I lined up these notches with the appropriate grout lines in the second drop. Whether the flooring has a design or not, I make a set mark along each seam to help align the drop (photo above).

This floor is a hard-bodied, inlaid type from Armstrong called Designer Solarian, and it needs an epoxy adhesive under its seams to prevent water penetration. Before the second drop went down, I mixed up a batch of epoxy (Armstrong S-200), lifted up the unglued edge of the first drop, and spread the epoxy under it about 3 in. with a small-notch trowel. I con-

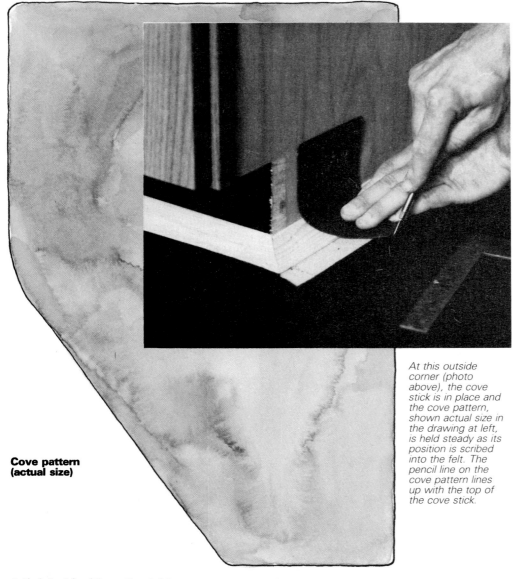

**Cove pattern
(actual size)**

At this outside corner (photo above), the cove stick is in place and the cove pattern, shown actual size in the drawing at left, is held steady as its position is scribed into the felt. The pencil line on the cove pattern lines up with the top of the cove stick.

A finished inside and outside corner on a coved floor. Material is removed to fashion the inside corner, while a patch is added to create the outside corner—you can see a faint seam on the right-hand side. Cap metal, held in place by brads, finishes the top edge.

tinued the epoxy another 3 in. out from the seam, and then I troweled latex adhesive over the rest of the drop area. With the second drop in place, I butted the seams together with pressure from my foot, and taped together spots that wanted to separate until the adhesive set up (about an hour).

Coved flooring—A coved floor is essentially the same as a flat-lay floor with a few extra steps. For one, cove stick has to be installed. This looks like a tiny crown molding with a concave face, and it backs the coved flooring. It's mitered at the corners and nailed in place. The pattern felt is laid out the same as in the flat-lay sequence, but the seam line for the drop will be 4 in. closer to the wall, because of the extra material required for the coving.

I trim the felt pattern as closely as possible to the base of the cove stick. Then another pattern comes into play. This one is made from a piece of scrap vinyl, and it duplicates a short section of coving with an inside corner cut on one end (drawing, left). This cove pattern fits over the cove stick just like the finish material. First I decide how high the coving will be—usually 2 in. or 3 in. above the stick. Then I make a pencil mark on the cove pattern to correspond with the top of the stick (photo above left). Starting at the door casing, I align the pencil mark with the stick. Then I note the position of the cove pattern on the felt with scribe marks about every 3 ft. around its base. When the felt is placed over the vinyl to mark the cutlines, I reposition the base of the cove pattern on the marks in the felt. With a pencil, I mark the cutline on the vinyl at the top of the cove pattern.

Inside corner cuts are marked by holding the pattern firmly on the cove stick and fitting the curved side into the corner. Mark the corner of the pattern into the felt. The pencil mark on the pattern won't necessarily line up with the stick. Once the material is cut, the inside corners will look like a square cut-out with a tapered notch in one corner. Installed, the cove flaps fold up and the notch forms a crease in the corner (photo below left).

Outside corners—This is the trickiest part of the job, because it requires cutting a patch of material to fill a gap in the coving. This means matching colors and designs, and making accurate cuts, some with beveled edges. The fill piece usually goes on the less conspicuous side of the corner.

Mark each outside corner on the felt pattern by making a notch in the felt that bisects the angle, then runs parallel with the wall about 1 in. from it (drawing, facing page, top left). This notch indicates which side the fill piece goes on. When all the room's features have been noted on the pattern, place it on the material. Allow room around the edges for the coving, and keep the pattern breaks in mind.

Once the pattern is positioned, tape it down and transfer the scribe marks to the material, using the square around the door trim and the coving pattern along the walls. Connect the cove height marks with the straightedge, and

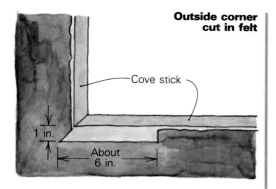

Outside corner cut in felt

Cove stick

1 in.

About 6 in.

Cutting outside corner in flooring

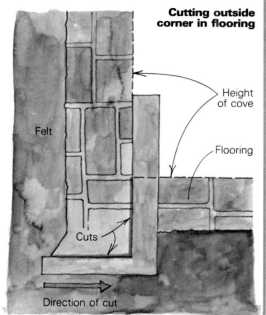

Height of cove

Felt

Flooring

Cuts

Direction of cut

Flat-lay floor around door casing

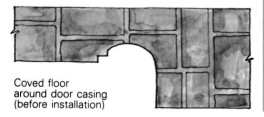

Coved floor around door casing (before installation)

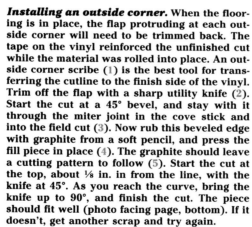

Installing an outside corner. When the flooring is in place, the flap protruding at each outside corner will need to be trimmed back. The tape on the vinyl reinforced the unfinished cut while the material was rolled into place. An outside corner scribe (1) is the best tool for transferring the cutline to the finish side of the vinyl. Trim off the flap with a sharp utility knife (2). Start the cut at a 45° bevel, and stay with it through the miter joint in the cove stick and into the field cut (3). Now rub this beveled edge with graphite from a soft pencil, and press the fill piece in place (4). The graphite should leave a cutting pattern to follow (5). Start the cut at the top, about ⅛ in. in from the line, with the knife at 45°. As you reach the curve, bring the knife up to 90°, and finish the cut. The piece should fit well (photo facing page, bottom). If it doesn't, get another scrap and try again.

cut the material as you would a seam. Stop the cut at an outside corner where the two cove height marks intersect. Begin the outside corner by placing the square along the notch in the felt (drawing, second from top). Cut along the square with the utility knife—these are small seams and must be square and straight. Once this cut is finished, find a piece of scrap that matches the pattern of the 90° corner. This is a fill piece that will be used to complete the corner. Label it, and set it aside. Now reinforce the material around the point of the cut with some tape to keep the vinyl from tearing during installation. The photos above show the installation sequence.

At doorways, you have to deal with a transition from flat-lay to cove. Here the flooring is

cut around the contours of the trim on the door side, then rises in a curve to cove height on the wall side (drawing, above left).

Coved installation—This sequence is the same as the flat-lay process, with an extra step: corner seams have to be spread with epoxy before the field receives its latex adhesive. Spread the epoxy around the door casings, along the tub or shower, in front of the dishwasher, on both sides of an outside corner—wherever water may have a chance to seep in. When both adhesives are spread out, carefully unroll the flooring and tuck it into its corners. If it's cold, hard surface goods may be stiff and reluctant to bend at the cove. Warm it up by passing a hair dryer back and

forth over it, and tack it down with some brads at the top of the coving.

When all the corners are complete, I take out the temporary brads, and install the cap metal with brads 6 in. o. c.

Maintenance—Different types of floors need different types of care, so ask your flooring supplier for warranty information and cleaning instructions. What I have found to work best in my own home is to damp-mop the floor regularly with warm water. Occasionally I add a little mild dish detergent to the mop water, followed by a thorough rinse. I sweep or vacuum the floor frequently, but never use anything abrasive on it. Any vegetable cooking oil will remove scuff marks. □

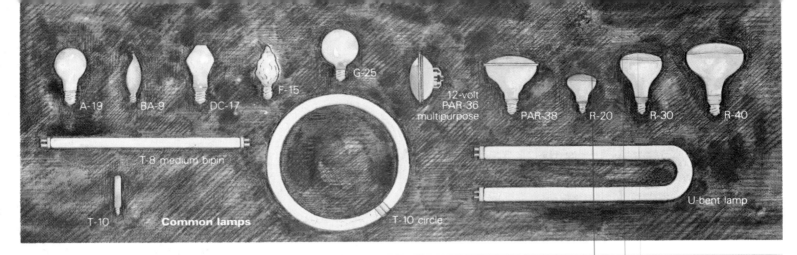

A-19 BA-9 DC-17 F-15 G-25 12-volt PAR-36 multipurpose PAR-38 R-20 R-30 R-40

T-8 medium bipin

T-10 **Common lamps** T-10 circle U-bent lamp

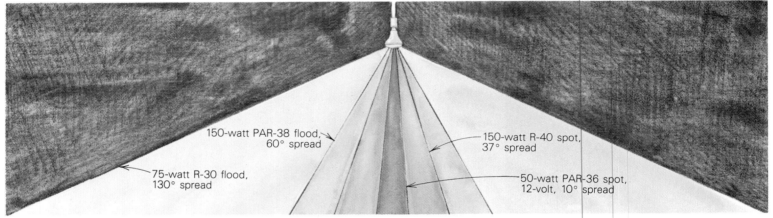

150-watt PAR-38 flood, 60° spread

150-watt R-40 spot, 37° spread

75-watt R-30 flood, 130° spread

50-watt PAR-36 spot, 12-volt, 10° spread

Toward the Right Light
On lamps, fixtures and illuminating principles

by Bart Smyth

Lighting is an important design element all by itself, and not just for aesthetic reasons. Proper lighting can make the difference between feeling comfortable or uneasy in a room, between feeling alert or fatigued at work, and between safety and jeopardy at a shop bench. And new energy-efficient lighting products that can save money also work better than old equipment.

Frequently, the lighting plan for a new home or remodel isn't much more than a map of where the junction boxes and switches are supposed to go. Maybe a notation, such as "recessed downlight at entry," will appear on the plan, but this is the exception rather than the rule. Lighting often takes last place on the design priority list. I know, because before I specialized in the business of lighting design, I worked as an architect, and lighting was largely ignored in architecture school.

To do a good job of residential lighting design, you need to know some basic terminology and principles, and you need to be familiar with the various kinds of hardware available to you. Let's begin with a look at what creates the light, and the devices that hold these light sources in place.

Lamps—What most people refer to as light bulbs are technically called lamps. There are many types on the market, but for simplicity's sake, I'm going to stick to the common ones that are best suited to residential use.

We're all familiar with the incandescent lamp. It has a tungsten filament that heats up when an electric current is passed through it. Along with the heat, the filament gives off light. Incandescent lamps that are rated above 25 watts are filled with argon, an inert gas (below 25 watts there is no gas in the vacuum). If oxygen were allowed into the chamber, the filament would burn very brightly, but not for very long—you've probably seen this happen when a lamp cracks slightly. The light flares suddenly as the filament burns up, and then goes out with a pop.

Incandescent lamps use a lot of energy compared with other light sources, but they also produce a pleasant and easily controlled light. For every watt (watts = amps × volts) of energy, they produce 15 to 20 lumens. For our purposes, suffice it to say that a lumen is a standard unit used throughout the industry to measure the light output of a lamp.

The most common incandescent lamp is the one with the drawn-out, rounded shape found in just about every tabletop fixture around the house. This type is known as an A lamp, and the commonly used variety, 40W to 100W, is known as an A-19 lamp. The 19 refers to its dimension across at its widest point in ⅛-in. increments. For example, an A-19 lamp measures ¹⁹⁄₈ in. (2⅜ in.) across. In addition to the A-type configuration, lamps come in many other shapes, some of which are shown in the drawing at the top of this page. Some lamps are almost spherical; others are more tubular. Each has a range of wattages.

The reflector lamp is the other commonly used incandescent light source found in the home. Reflector lamps (drawing, above) are shaped to reflect light in a particular direction

From *Fine Homebuilding* magazine (June 1983) 15:54-57

Incandescent and fluorescent lamps come in a wide variety of shapes, wattages and colors (facing page, top). Bases also vary from lamp to lamp, so be sure the fixture you intend to use is compatible with the light source.

The beam spreads of many lamps fall between the extremes shown on the facing page, and a few go beyond them. The 12-volt spot has the tightest pattern on this chart, while the 110-volt flood has the widest. The drawing at right shows some common track fixtures.

12-volt fixture with built-in transformer and narrow-beam spotlight

Projector

Wallwasher with floodlight

Track fixtures

and concentration, with either one of two beam spreads: spot or flood. The spot is a relatively tight cone of light, concentrated into a narrow beam. The flood is a broader, more diffuse beam. Common reflector lamps come in 75W and 150W, and are designated as R or PAR lamps. The R lamps are designed for use indoors, while the PAR lamps have a sturdy bulb of Pyrex glass and are designed for outdoor applications. You've probably seen them blasting a patio or garden area at night.

Stamped on the face or base of every incandescent lamp is the name of its manufacturer, the wattage and the amount of voltage the lamp is designed to take. Some lamps are rated for 120 volts; others, for 130 volts. If you install a 130-volt lamp in a fixture that gets 110 volts, you won't get quite as much light as advertised (about 20% less), but the lamp will last up to three times longer. The 130-volt lamp costs a little more, but if it's installed in a hard-to-reach spot, it's worth the extra cash.

Fluorescent lamps—Known technically as hot cathodes, fluorescent lamps are the other typical residential light source. They generate light by producing ultraviolet radiation within a glass cylinder. As this radiation bounces around, it interacts with the layer of phosphor crystals that coat the inside of the lamp, producing visible light. For each watt of energy invested, a fluorescent lamp pays back 60 to 80 lumens—three to four times more than an incandescent lamp.

Many of my clients aren't keen about using fluorescent lamps, except in the kitchen or workshop. They usually complain that they don't like the color of the light, that it's too flat and diffused, or that they are sensitive to the 60-times-per-second on/off cycle of these lamps. But the efficiency of fluorescents can't be ignored, so I try to combine them with incandescent sources whenever I can. Also, phosphor coatings that closely duplicate the range of light produced by incandescent lamps are available.

Low-voltage lamps—A new trend in lighting design is to bring low-voltage lamps into the house. These are incandescent lamps; the majority are rated to work at 12 volts. Most of the ones I use belong to what is known as the PAR-36 series—Pyrex glass with a reflector, ³⁶⁄₈ in. (4½ in.) across. They are similar to the lamps used in cars with twin headlights, and in small-aircraft landing lights.

Many people associate low-voltage lighting with weak light, but in fact just the opposite is

true. After all, those 12-volt headlights coming down the road are mighty bright. PAR-36 lamps between 25W and 50W put out a lot of light, and a wide variety of well-defined beam spreads is available throughout the series.

Low-voltage lamps moved indoors in a big way when designers started using them as accent lights in display windows. The filament in a low-voltage lamp is much smaller than its 110-volt counterpart—it's almost a point source. Two advantages result. A point source is easier to manipulate with the lamp's reflector than the larger filament found in a 110-volt lamp. This means that the light from a low-voltage lamp can be gathered into the kind of tight cone that makes a good spotlight. More important, a low-voltage lamp is more efficient than a 110-volt lamp, making it a money-saver in the long run. The problem is getting to the payback point. A low-voltage installation currently costs about 50% more than conventional lighting. The fixtures aren't as common, and the system requires a transformer to step the household current down to 12 volts. Some fixtures have transformers built into them, others are plugged into a system that has a large transformer that's capable of supplying juice to more than one lamp. I think it's just a matter of time before competition drives the price down, and low-voltage lamps and fixtures become commonplace. They are simply more efficient than most other 110-volt lamps. Like their 110-volt equivalents, the life expectancy of low-voltage lamps is vastly increased when they are used with dimmers.

I like to mix the two basic types of incandescent light to meet particular needs while minimizing energy use. For example, in my living room I have a 6-volt lighting system that I use mostly to accent paintings. It's on a track, and I use 12-volt PAR-36 lamps in the fixture, which increases lamp life from its de-

signed 2,000 hours to an astonishing 2,000,000 hours. From this track I do all my highlighting with just under 50 watts of power. I supplement this with a standard, shaded tabletop fixture with a 75-watt A-19 lamp on a dimmer; I use it at half to three-quarters intensity. In all, I use a little under 100 watts of power to illuminate my entire 225-sq. ft. living room. For some, this may be a little dim, but it's an experiment, and it keeps changing.

Fixtures—The thing that holds a lamp is called a fixture, and I break fixtures down into five categories: track, surface-mounted, recessed, portable and decorative.

Track fixtures are designed to do various lighting tasks, such as accenting, wall-washing and general down-lighting. They come in a wide variety of shapes and sizes, and they can accept reflector or non-reflector lamps (drawing, above). A locking device at their base hooks into the electrified channel anywhere along the track.

Framing projectors are a very specialized type of track fixture. They are adjustable beam-shaping fixtures that are designed to focus a precisely shaped patch of light on some target area. They are used most often to illuminate paintings or prints, and they can create the illusion that the artwork is floating in space. Different projectors cast circular light forms or square light forms. As you might expect, these projectors are expensive—well over $100—and they are relatively inefficient, so I recommend them only when I think they are really appropriate.

Surface-mounted fixtures, as the name suggests, are mounted directly on a wall or ceiling. They're available in many different styles. They can throw a diffuse light, or a directed one. After track-mounted fixtures, surface mounts are the easiest to install, but because

Downlight

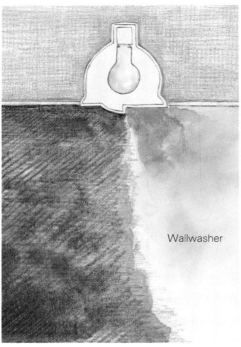

Wallwasher

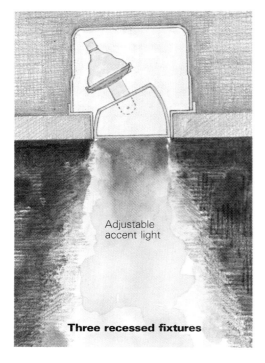

Adjustable
accent light

Three recessed fixtures

their location is fixed, they have their limitations and work to best advantage as part of an overall lighting plan.

Recessed fixtures are mounted flush to a surface. Some are installed in walls or even floors, but the vast majority are mounted in the ceiling. There, they usually cast their light straight down, but some can play their beams at an angle. Others have an adjustable lamp socket that enables them to throw light in different directions. Flush-mounted framing projectors are also available. They aren't quite as flexible as their track counterparts, but they can be used to dramatic effect.

There are both interior and exterior recessed fixtures, and there are lots of different trim packages to go with different house styles. Three kinds are shown at left.

Portable fixtures. If a fixture has a cord and a plug, it's considered portable. If it's anchored down with fasteners or adhesives, it can lose its Underwriters' Laboratory rating. The most common kind are the shaded fixtures used in living rooms and dens, on tables or floors. Another type is the uplight; it's usually a deep cylindrical or rectangular fixture, and it's most often found behind a piece of furniture or under a leafy plant. It casts its light upward, articulating shapes that might otherwise be lost in shadow.

Decorative fixtures. Some fixtures are designed primarily to be seen, rather than to provide illumination. These are the decorative fixtures, and they are usually portable or surface-mounted. Sometimes their purpose is to complement the style of the building—for example, carriage lights on either side of a Tudor-revival entry. Authentically used, they would be dim, to mimic the original oil lamp or candle. A hidden light source, such as a deeply recessed fixture in the soffit over the door, might provide the needed illumination.

Light-level control—In the 1950s, rheostats were all the rage in mood lighting. You could simply install one in your switch box, and dial it to bring the lights up or down. Rheostats do this well, but they do it by resisting a portion of the electricity on its way to the lamp. This diverted juice is turned into heat, and unless you need a warm spot on the wall, they are a waste of energy.

These days, light levels are usually controlled with dimmers, solid-state devices that actually alter the electric current and send only the desired amount to the lamp. Both rheostats and dimmers extend lamp life, and dimmers also save energy.

There are several kinds of dimmers, and they are all rated at different load capacities. I've had my best luck with the Lutron brand (Coopersburg, Pa. 18036). A good dimmer shouldn't interfere with radio or TV, as some of the less expensive ones do. There are small dimmers that go between a lamp and its socket, and there are also dimmers on their own cords, known as tabletop dimmers, that can control portable fixtures. And of course, there are the standard, wall-box mounted units with a rotary dial or slide control.

Applying the light—Lamp types, fixtures and dimming devices are the lighting designer's raw materials. My basic rule of thumb is that you should see what you're lighting, not the source of the illumination. This principle is often violated at the front door. How many times have you seen that carriage-style fixture on the front porch partially blinding guests with intense, unshaded light? Yes, it tells everybody where the front door is, but does it invite anyone to approach? A better solution would be the one I mentioned above: using the carriage-style fixtures as architectural elements to complement the house, with the actual illumination coming from a hidden fixture. Combining the various types of lamps and fixtures this way is the challenging part of lighting design. The right combination depends on the specific kind of job the light is asked to perform.

Task lighting—Task lighting is designed to illuminate a work area. The kitchen is the most frequently used workplace in the home, and it suffers more from inadequate lighting than any other room in the house. Many of the kitchens I see have one or two fixtures mounted on the ceiling near the middle of the room. They can be blazing away, filling the room with light, but sometimes it's hard to see what you're trying to chop on the counter because your hands are in shadow. Your body is blocking the light. The goal of task lighting is to get the light where it's needed.

One common solution for this kind of problem is to mount a tubular lamp in a strip fixture on the bottom of the cabinets above the counter. Usually the fixture is mounted against the wall. Wrong. Against the wall, the lamp will probably be visible from a distance, and when you're sitting at a nearby table it becomes a glaring nuisance. I prefer to place the fixture at the edge of the cabinet farthest from the wall (photo and drawing, facing page, left). If the fixture is presentable, I leave it visible. Otherwise I trim it with a strip of wood. The fixture I use, Lektra (Lighting, Inc., 2465-B 4th St., Berkeley, Calif. 94710), will accept either fluorescent or incandescent lamps. If you choose a fluorescent, though, make sure it produces a warm white light. The standard cool white is on the blue/green side of the spectrum, and it makes food look awful.

If there aren't any cabinets above the counter to hold tube fixtures, I specify recessed lights mounted close enough together to cross-light the work area or counter. This way shadows are kept to a minimum. To eliminate the side glare caused by the recessed lamps, I like to use the deeper fixtures, such as the #H44 series by Halo, or the 7705 fixture by Lightolier, when there's enough room in the ceiling to accommodate them. When teamed up with a polished black aluminum trim, called Alzak in the trade, it's hard to tell from the side that the fixture is a light source (photo facing page, right).

Another kind of task-lighting fixture, the two-armed, clamp-on adjustable variety, can be easily positioned over your desk, work-

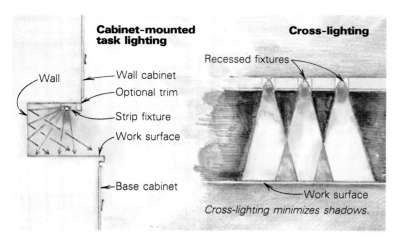

Cabinet-mounted task lighting

Wall
Wall cabinet
Optional trim
Strip fixture
Work surface
Base cabinet

Cross-lighting

Recessed fixtures
Work surface

Cross-lighting minimizes shadows.

Incandescent strip fixtures mounted under the wall cabinets illuminate the work surfaces in the remodeled kitchen in the photo above. In both this kitchen and the one at the right, the sink counter is cross-lit by recessed fixtures. The highly polished trim reflects the strong light downward onto the work surface and eliminates side glare.

bench or carburetor. With these fixtures, you can adjust the distance and the angle so they will shine on the work surface along your line of sight. Otherwise, reflected glare will strain your eyes. But concentrated task lighting without background lighting is a bad idea.

Background light is referred to as ambient light. It can be the diffused result of a mixture of light sources, or it can be the work of a purposeful arrangement of fixtures, perhaps controlled by dimmers. Whatever the source, ambient light is necessary to reduce the contrast levels created by task lighting. Too much contrast is bad for your eyes. This balance also means a great deal psychologically. It can mean the difference between wanting to enter a room and stay there, or taking a peek in and beating a hasty retreat.

Accent lighting—This type of light is used to focus attention on some object, such as a painting or a piece of sculpture. Track fixtures are especially well suited to this job. Sometimes I use a combination of low-voltage and line-voltage fixtures on the same track, for maximum flexibility. A well-placed recessed fixture with the right lamp and trim package can also be a very effective accent light.

Indirect lighting—Ambient light levels are frequently adjusted with indirect lights bounced off reflective surfaces (an excellent

job for fluorescents). Remember that both the color and texture of the reflective surface have a dramatic influence on the overall effect of this type of illumination.

You can also use indirect light for purely decorative purposes. Ceilings are frequently the target of such schemes, but they are almost always lit so intensely that the room's focus becomes skewed. People feel small and uncomfortable when the ceiling is too brightly lit. Ceilings that merit highlighting should be illuminated with low-level uplighting. The effect should be subtle, and the scale produced by the light sources in the living area should be unaffected.

Once you become aware of the qualities that make for a well-lighted place, you'll be much more sensitive to illumination wherever you go. Look at the different fixture types around you, and decide if they're used properly. Why does the lighting succeed in one room and fail in another?

You can try out the ideas and suggestions discussed in this article by playing with an assortment of 110-volt lamps, most of which you probably own already. For instance, start with some A lamps, a 75-watt R-30 spot and flood, and a 75-watt PAR-38 spot and flood. Get some long pieces of lamp cord, and put sockets on one end and plugs on the other. You might even add a portable dimmer to one of the lamps for some level control. Then you

can begin to experiment. Set up your lamps, then move them around. Look at the different kinds of light these lamps create, the different beam spreads and what they do to a room when they're aimed in a variety of directions and combinations. This is really the best way to familiarize yourself with the basics of lighting. Experiment, and you will become more conscious of the way that lighting has been handled around you.   □

Bart Smyth is an architectural lighting consultant in San Francisco.

Sources of supply

Track and recessed fixtures:
Capri Lighting, 7020 E. Slauson Ave., Los Angeles, Calif. 90040.
Halo, 400 Busse Rd., Elk Grove Village, Ill. 60007.
Juno Lighting, Inc., 2489 S. Wolf Rd., Des Plaines, Ill. 60018.
Lightolier, 346 Claremont Ave., Jersey City, N.J. 07305.

Lamp manufacturers:
General Electric, 1705 Noble Rd., Box 2494, Cleveland, Ohio 44112.
Sylvania, GTE Products Corp., Lighting Center, Danvers, Mass. 01923.
Westinghouse, Lamp Division, Bloomfield, N.J. 07003.

Making Wooden Light Fixtures

With nice ones so hard to find, creating your own makes sense

by John Birchard

Trying to find the right manufactured light fixture can be a discouraging experience. They soon begin to look all the same, and the prices can be astounding. When my wife and I were building our own home, we installed several reasonably priced cylindrical fixtures only to discover later that they were so poorly made that we couldn't remove spent bulbs without twisting the wires inside the fixture—a ridiculously dangerous situation. Because we could find nothing else that fit our decor, I eventually replaced them with fixtures I made myself. The techniques involved in building fixtures are fairly basic, and the latitude for creativity is great.

Safety—The first consideration in constructing a light fixture should be safety. You may want to consult with your local building inspector to clarify any particular questions you have, but the following guidelines taken from the Uniform Building Code are a good place to start.

1. Combustible materials should never be exposed to heat in excess of 90°C (194°F). Incandescent light bulbs produce lots of waste heat. In

Birchard started making his own light fixtures (right) when he found commercial ones expensive and flimsy. Now he makes them professionally for clients who like the effects of custom wood fixtures. The valance (top), built by Robert Lasso, has translucent panels, though it could have a solid wooden bracket instead. This kind of fixture works just as well along a blank wall as over a window. The drawing at top left on p. 70 shows how such a wall bracket can be built.

wall-mounted fixtures this heat can usually be dissipated by leaving most or all of the top of the fixture open. Ceiling fixtures can be suspended or spaced down an inch or so from the ceiling. Where this approach isn't practical, recessed fixtures can be ventilated into the attic. Never insulate within 6 in. of such fixtures, or over their tops. Since fluorescent tubes produce very little waste heat compared to incandescent bulbs, consider them for large fixtures where ventilation is a problem.

2. Wiring should never be exposed to heat in excess of its rated capacity. If the first rule is followed carefully, this won't be a problem, but in ceiling boxes where the wiring runs through the box, check the insulation rating on the wire you use, and make sure it's adequate.

3. There should be no exposed wires or connections. I generally design my fixtures so that wiring is concealed within their structural parts, but there are exceptions to the rule. Exposed connections are acceptable more than 8 ft. above the floor, and exposed wiring may be necessary for hanging fixtures. Pulley cord, vacuum-cleaner cord, and some lamp cords are rated for this kind of use. Wiring that supports a fixture must be firmly clamped to prevent tension on the connections. Use stranded conductors (wires made up of many small strands twisted together) for movable or flexible fixtures. Romex is too stiff and brittle for these applications. You should also be careful not to run wires across sharp edges or areas where they can be abraded by movement or vibration.

4. Fixtures should be firmly attached to fram-

From *Fine Homebuilding* magazine (June 1985) 27:60-63

ing members (usually joists or studs). Fixtures up to 50 lb. can be supported by outlet boxes as long as the boxes are firmly attached to framing members. This is especially important if the switch is located on the fixture, which means that people will be coming into contact with it.

Design considerations—Besides safety, fixtures have to look good and provide the right kind of light for their location and function. The design possibilities are endless, but they break down into two basic categories. I think of *built-ins* as including ceiling-mounted, wall-mounted and most suspended lamps. *Portables* are plug-ins—usually table or floor lamps. Both types can be designed to provide different qualities of light. Sometimes a bright beam is needed in a fairly confined area (direct lighting). In another situation a softer, more general source of light is called for (indirect lighting). I'll be talking mostly about built-ins in this article.

Ceiling boxes—Perhaps the simplest approach to room-lighting is to create ceiling boxes by nailing wooden channels or troughs along the bottom of ceiling joists and blocking, as shown in the drawing, top right. You can use one or more low-wattage sockets in these boxes, and cut rigid translucent plastic that will fit into rabbeted trim pieces tacked to the undersides of the joists. The inside of the box, top and sides, should be painted white or lined with gypboard or aluminum foil for reflectivity.

Depending on its size, a ceiling box could require a number of 25-watt or 40-watt bulbs spaced a foot apart. Using more bulbs in one box means that each bulb should be of lower wattage. This will prevent heat build-up problems. In long narrow boxes, consider using the cooler fluorescent tubes.

A simple ceiling box can be set flush with the ceiling or suspended in a carefully crafted wooden frame for a look that is reminiscent of Greene and Greene, as shown in the photo at right. This same type of light box can also be built in conjunction with a skylight (drawing, middle right). The skylight cuts down on your use of electricity during the day, and also allows for better dissipation of waste heat from the bulbs at night. Because of the tendency of moisture to condense on skylights in cold weather, use exterior spots or floods in a skylight light box because of their weather resistance. They also allow you to direct the light downward. Bulbs this powerful should be at least 18 in. from the diffusion panel. The farther away you can put them, the more even their light will be.

Wall brackets and valances—Another approach to indirect lighting is to reflect light off the ceiling from a wall bracket or valance strip (photo facing page, top). The term valance once

Ceiling boxes can be built flush by setting them between the joists (drawing, top right). They can also be suspended from the ceiling in a frame (photo right). A suspended box can carry out the design scheme of the rest of the room, and it can be built with translucent panels in its sides as well as its bottom surface.

Photo this page and facing page, bottom: John Birchard

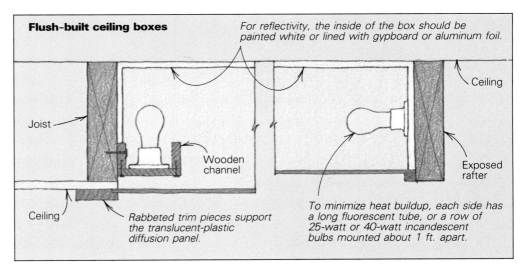

Flush-built ceiling boxes

For reflectivity, the inside of the box should be painted white or lined with gypboard or aluminum foil.

Joist

Ceiling

Wooden channel

Rabbeted trim pieces support the translucent-plastic diffusion panel.

Ceiling

Exposed rafter

To minimize heat buildup, each side has a long fluorescent tube, or a row of 25-watt or 40-watt incandescent bulbs mounted about 1 ft. apart.

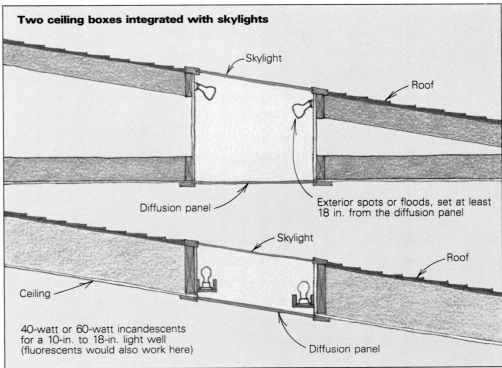

Two ceiling boxes integrated with skylights

Skylight

Roof

Diffusion panel

Exterior spots or floods, set at least 18 in. from the diffusion panel

Skylight

Roof

Ceiling

40-watt or 60-watt incandescents for a 10-in. to 18-in. light well (fluorescents would also work here)

Diffusion panel

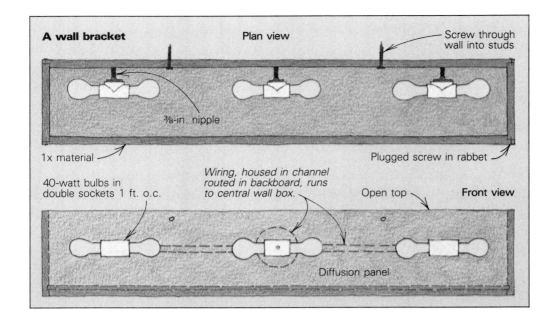

A wall bracket

Plan view

Screw through wall into studs

⅜-in. nipple

1x material

Plugged screw in rabbet

40-watt bulbs in double sockets 1 ft. o.c.

Wiring, housed in channel routed in backboard, runs to central wall box.

Open top

Front view

Diffusion panel

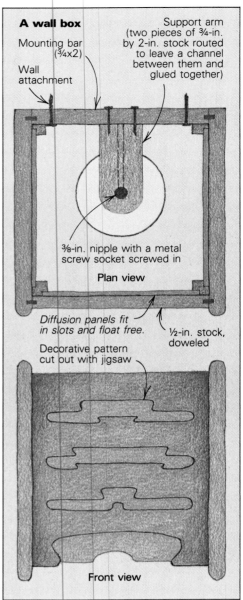

A wall box

Mounting bar (¾x2)

Support arm (two pieces of ¾-in. by 2-in. stock routed to leave a channel between them and glued together)

Wall attachment

⅜-in. nipple with a metal screw socket screwed in

Plan view

Diffusion panels fit in slots and float free.

½-in. stock, doweled

Decorative pattern cut out with jigsaw

Front view

Lasso built the wall bracket above using the techniques detailed in the drawing at top. Housing the plastic panels in slots solves potential shrinkage problems.

referred to a decorative strip along the top of a window to hide drapery tracks, but it is now also used to refer to a wide strip of wood or other material used to hide lighting along the top of a window. A wall bracket is simply a valance without a window below it. Wall brackets can be especially useful in large, open rooms where conventional ceiling lighting may fail to illuminate areas close to the walls.

You can build a valance or wall bracket that's closed on the bottom to direct light to reflect off the ceiling, or you can leave the bottom open and let the light shine down as well. Install this type of lighting at least 2 ft. from the ceiling or you may get a lot of glare.

The backboard, an inner strip of wood screwed to the studs, holds the bracket to the wall and also supports the light sockets. In the

drawing, top left, a series of double cluster sockets are anchored to the inner strip by ⅜-in. nipples (small threaded pipe nipples, through which wiring can be run, and which can hold a socket in place), and the wiring is run in a channel on the wall side of the backboard. Leave at least 1 in. of clearance between the bulbs and the front strip, and leave the top of the bracket open for ventilation. The front strip of a wall bracket should generally be at least 6 in. wide to hide the bulbs, and the ends should be capped. If you want light to shine out the bottom, consider a diffusion panel to help prevent glare.

Wall-mounted boxes—These squarish spotlights can produce either direct or indirect light, depending on your design and the materials you use. In some areas you may want your boxes to

transmit light from all sides, and in others you may want a box that is opaque on the sides and open only on the top and bottom.

Wall-mounted boxes, like the one in the photo at left, provide a chance for real creativity. The Greene brothers designed some exquisite light boxes employing both leaded glass and intricate wood joinery. This style is still a source of inspiration for many home builders today, and is well documented in books like Randell L. Makinson's *Greene and Greene* (Peregrine Smith, Inc., Salt Lake City). Vol. II has many fine photographs of light fixtures and other details from Greene and Greene homes.

One of my favorite approaches to making wall boxes is to cut designs out of flat pieces of ½-in. thick wood with a scrollsaw. I glue these pieces of wood together to form a three-sided box, and then attach translucent plastic to the inside with stops. I tried gluing the plastic in, but it came loose because of wood shrinkage caused by the heat from the bulbs. For incandescent fixtures, it's important to construct them so that they won't pull themselves apart when the wood shrinks. For this reason, I try to attach the shade to the support arm at only one place. Leave

Photos, except where noted: Robert Lasso

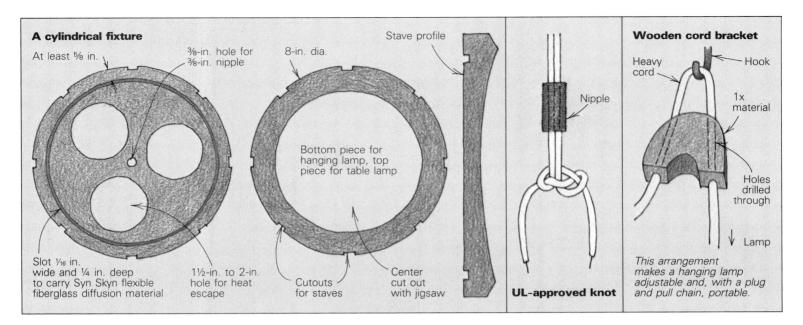

A cylindrical fixture

At least ⅝ in.

⅜-in. hole for ⅜-in. nipple

Slot ¹⁄₁₆ in. wide and ¼ in. deep to carry Syn Skyn flexible fiberglass diffusion material

1½-in. to 2-in. hole for heat escape

8-in. dia.

Bottom piece for hanging lamp, top piece for table lamp

Cutouts for staves

Center cut out with jigsaw

Stave profile

Nipple

UL-approved knot

Wooden cord bracket

Heavy cord

Hook

1x material

Holes drilled through

Lamp

This arrangement makes a hanging lamp adjustable and, with a plug and pull chain, portable.

---

space for the plastic to move around, too, so the wood can move without stressing the joint.

My friend, Robert Lasso, who has built many wall boxes over the years, has had few shrinkage problems. He dowels or laps all joints (drawing, facing page, right), and cuts thin slots in his frames with a fine-toothed table-saw blade or a slotting cutter on a router table to hold the plastic diffusion panels. With the plastic floating free in the slot, a little shrinkage is no problem.

Hanging lamps—Lasso also makes cylindrical hanging lamps (photo right). He begins by cutting out two discs of wood about 8 in. in diameter. Then he drills a ¼-in. hole through the center of the discs so he can bolt them to an adjustable jig that holds a small router at the desired distance from the center. He uses a ¹⁄₁₆-in. straight bit to rout ¼-in. deep slots around the circumference of both discs, at least ⅝ in. from their outside edges.

Lasso usually cuts most of the center out of the disc that won't hold the socket, leaving a ring through which light can shine (drawing, above). He drills a ⅜-in. hole in the center of the other disc, through which he passes a ⅜-in. nipple to run the wire through. He also drills three 1½-in. to 2-in. holes in this disc, to let heat out. There are a number of ways to connect the top and bottom discs. The drawing shows staves, but you could just as easily use dowels.

A metal shell socket is screwed to the inside of the nipple, and the wire is then passed through the nipple and into the socket. Two-strand lamp wire can be tied in the UL-approved knot (drawing, top center) inside the socket to relieve the strain on the connections. Crimp-on strain relievers can also be used for heavier wire like vacuum-cleaner cord. If the fixture is to be hung on the wall, the socket is at the top. For a table-top cylindrical lamp, it is on the bottom.

For his cylinders and other curved shapes, Lasso uses as a diffusion panel a flexible material called Syn Skyn, made by Tap Plastics (3011 Alvarado, San Leandro, Calif. 94577). This flame-resistant fiberglass comes in three grades of coarseness. The finest grade looks almost like

For diffusion panels on cylindrical fixtures like the one above, Lasso uses a thin fiberglass material called Syn Skin. The cylinders work as table lamps or, with a simple cord bracket (drawing top right), as hanging lamps.

Japanese rice paper, and bends easily to a radius of 6 in. or less. The lamp-parts supply companies mentioned in the sidebar at right also sell preformed plastic cylinders in various sizes.

A nice trick Lasso showed me is the small wooden cord bracket shown in the drawing, top right. Lasso uses a heavily insulated vacuum-cleaner or pulley cord, which, when swagged through the bracket, will form an adjustable loop by which the fixture may be suspended. This type of fixture, when outfitted with a plug and pull chain switch, becomes fully portable. □

John Birchard is a professional woodworker in Mendocino, Calif.

Sources of supply

A couple of sources for lamp parts and lighting-fixture supplies are American Lamp Parts, Inc. (930 Belt Line Rd. #122, Irving, Tex. 75061) and Crystal Lamp Parts (Box 21814, 2050 E. 15th St., Los Angeles, Calif. 90021). If you plan to do a lot of fixtures, it will be worthwhile to send for their catalogs and check out the wide variety of supplies they sell. These are wholesale outlets, but if you don't have your own resale number, you can probably get your electrician or local building-supply store to order for you.

Building-supply stores usually stock a line of lighting supplies, but many of the specialty items needed for making your own fixtures are hard to find. The following examples of the kind of hardware you'll need are available through the two outlets mentioned above: steel and brass ⅜-in. nipples and locknuts; swivels for movable lamp fixtures; lamp sockets with various switches and dimmers; cluster sockets, fluorescent sockets, decorative sockets; wiring cords in bulk; ornamental stampings, castings, bases and shades; exterior lamp bases, globes, and bulbs; specialty tools, chain.

Building-supply stores usually stock a couple of different types of plastic diffusion panels. These are usually made of polypropylene, which works fine indoors if it isn't exposed to high temperatures. Acrylics and fiberglass, like the Syn Skyn mentioned in the article, are more durable and resist heat and sunlight better, but cost more. All the diffusion materials are somewhat flexible, and can be cut with a matte knife or a sawblade.

Stained-glass suppliers carry a wide variety of tinted and obscured glasses as well as crystals, bevels, and the like.

Two sources for Japanese rice paper are Soko Hardware (1698 Post, San Francisco, Calif. 94115) and J.C. Trading Co. (Mikado, Japanese Cultural Trade Center, 1737 Post St., San Francisco, Calif. 94115). Prices range from $1 to $10 a sq. ft., and it comes in 2-ft. by 3-ft. sheets. —J. B.

Classic Plumbing

A few years back I found myself settled in England with an opportunity to train as a plumber, courtesy of Her Majesty's Government. The town I was living in is called Bath, a city whose origins go back to Roman times. Most of what remains today is a Georgian city designed in 1770 by John Wood, the elder. As a result of the British passion for heritage, just about everything has a preservation order slapped on it. This makes rehabbing something of an exercise in archaeology. It's nothing to pull up floorboards in the course of an installation and find clay pipes, oyster shells and earthenware beer bottles left by the previous construction crew over 200 years earlier.

Unfortunately, traditional British plumbing hasn't significantly evolved since Sir Thomas Crapper invented the water closet in 1882. All systems are gravity fed, with yards of lead pipe snaking six floors up to the roof, where a 50-gal. zinc cistern, usually uninsulated and uncovered, provides water for drinking and washing.

Since wood-frame construction is practically unheard-of, running vents just simply isn't done. Everything discharges directly into an outside soil stack, usually but not always located at the back of the house. Pull the plug on the bathtub, and you can hear the kitchen sink gurgling 30 ft. away.

As for staying warm in Britain's notorious climate, don't expect anything so posh as American-style forced-air heating. Up until the last decade, the English version of central heating consisted of a second suit of tweed underwear. And if that wasn't comfortable enough, you could always run down six flights of stairs for a scuttleful of coal. That'll warm yer up, mate.

It was on one of the newfangled gas central-heating jobs that I almost set Anglo-American relations back 200 years. It was on elegant Northampton Row, just off Royal Crescent, where I rapped loudly on the front door with typical Yankee boorishness, deliberately ignoring the sign that directed tradesmen like myself around to the side entrance.

The lady of the house ushered me up the huge elegant stairway and showed me into the topmost room of the house, where she explained the job. It seemed simple enough. A stud-wall partition had to be moved 4 ft. to accommodate a new bathroom. That necessitated remounting a small hot-water radiator 4 ft. to the left. "Before you start, I want you to see the reading room below," she said. "You must be made aware of what you're working over."

The study turned out to be a set-piece of Neoclassical antique furniture arranged tastefully beneath shelves of leather-bound Latin grammars. Directly below the ceiling where I'd be working hung a gilt-framed landscape that looked alarmingly like a Constable, although I didn't ask. One doesn't discuss such things with plumbers.

"As you can see, young sir, these articles have considerable cultural value. Some of these books are destined for the Bodleian, so I really must urge you: do be careful." Explaining that she had another matter to attend to, she left the house and I got to work.

First I connected a hose to the wall-hung boiler in the kitchen and drained all the water from the radiators. Then I carefully traced the flow and return pipes floor by floor to the top of the house. The return from the radiator entered the stud wall and emerged out the other side, then turned down into the floorboards. No problem. I grabbed a hacksaw and started cutting. A jet of high-pressure water shot out.

I grabbed the pipe in disbelief, stanching the flow of water with a firm grip. Craning my neck, I peered into the ½-in. gap between the baseboard and the floor. Sure enough, the return entered the wall, but then it turned down into the space below, next to another copper line I hadn't seen before. I had cut through the supply line.

I thought quickly—the shutoff valve was in the kitchen, six flights down. That meant by the time I dashed down to turn it off, at least 30 gal. of water would have flooded the library below. I could yell for help, but the front door was locked and I was alone. There was only one thing to do: hang on.

If time flies when you're having fun, it's amazing how it slows down when you're not. By the time I had the wallpaper memorized, an all-too-rare ray of English sunshine had eased through the window and edged toward the opposite wall. Traffic murmured in the street below. Somewhere a fly buzzed. At one point I heard the noontime drinkers leaving the Rose & Crown across the street; that made it about 2:30, three hours after I had arrived. I was seriously beginning to wonder if my right hand would have to be amputated when I heard Lady Rutherford's footsteps on the stairs.

By the time she found the shutoff valve and stopped hyperventilating, I was trying to take some of the sting out of it by explaining that I'd held on for concern for Western Civilization, but no dice. "I wanted a plumber, not the Little Dutch Boy," she said.

Yes, travel broadens the mind, I told myself as I finished the job and packed up my tools. But only if you don't stay too long in one place. Where was it that I'd heard about a shortage of plumbers? Texas, wasn't it?

—Paul Penfield, Willoughby, Ohio

Drainage Systems

On sizing, laying out and choosing the right fittings for a residential waste system

by George Skaates

A residential drainage system is analogous to a watershed. Each fixture in the house, whether it's a lavatory, laundry sink or shower, is like a small creek that drains into a larger stream. These larger tributaries eventually merge with the building's drain, which conveys the household waste to the site's septic system or to the city sewer lines.

This article is about the procedures I use to size and lay out a residential drainage system. In the San Francisco Bay Area, where I do most of my work, plumbers and inspectors follow the guidelines set forth in the 1982 edition of the Uniform Plumbing Code ($28.95 from the International Association of Plumbing and Mechanical Officials, 5032 Alhambra Ave, Los Angeles, Calif. 90032). This code is widely respected within the plumbing industry, and the principles and definitions it lists are reflected in this article.

Drainage-system components—Any discussion of a drainage system has to start with a few definitions so we all know what we're talking about. Let's begin just outside the building's foundation, at the building sewer (drawing, right). The building sewer is a horizontal drain line that connects the *building drain* (photo right) with the sewage-disposal system—usually a public sewer line or a private septic tank. The code book defines *horizontal* as a piece of pipe that makes an angle of not more than 45° with the horizon.

The building drain extends 2 ft. outside the building's foundation. It is the lowest drainpipe in the building, and it receives the discharge from all the *soil pipes* and *waste pipes* within the structure. A waste pipe carries wastes that are free of fecal matter, while a soil pipe carries the discharge from toilets and urinals. A soil pipe may also carry waste from other fixtures.

A *branch line* is any drainpipe other than a stack feeding into the building drain—a *stack* is a primary *vertical* drain line. Vertical means that the pipe makes an angle less than 45° with the vertical, but a vertical pipe is usually as plumb as possible. An *offset stack* has to be bent to get around some obstacle. If you can bend it at 45° or less, the unit sizing is not affected.

Every fixture in a building has a *trap*. The trap is the U-shaped pipe that separates the fixture drain from the *trap arm*. The trap is always filled with water, which keeps sewer gases from in-

Plumbing contractor George Skaates lives in Alameda, Calif.

Drawings: Gary Williamson

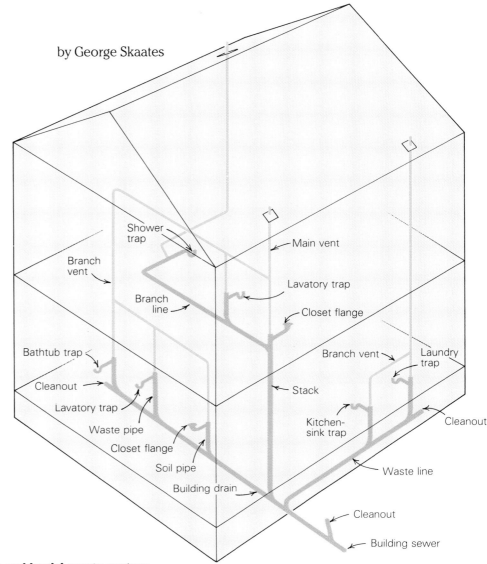

A residential waste system
The typical residential drainage system is a network of pipes that convey waterborne household wastes from fixtures such as sinks and toilets to the building drain and out to the building sewer. Each fixture is connected to a vent pipe, which equalizes the pressure in a drain line as water passes through it. In the drawings, vent pipes are blue; waste and soil lines are brown.

Right, a 4-in. building drain dives under a perimeter foundation on its way to link up with the building sewer. Just before the line descends into the earth, a 4-in. soil pipe rises above floor level, where it will be capped with a closet flange once the subfloor is in place. Just in front of the soil pipe, a 2-in. vent rises and then angles toward the wall that will eventually enclose it. At the bottom of the photo, a 1½-in. lavatory waste line is joined to the building drain by a combination tee and Y fitting.

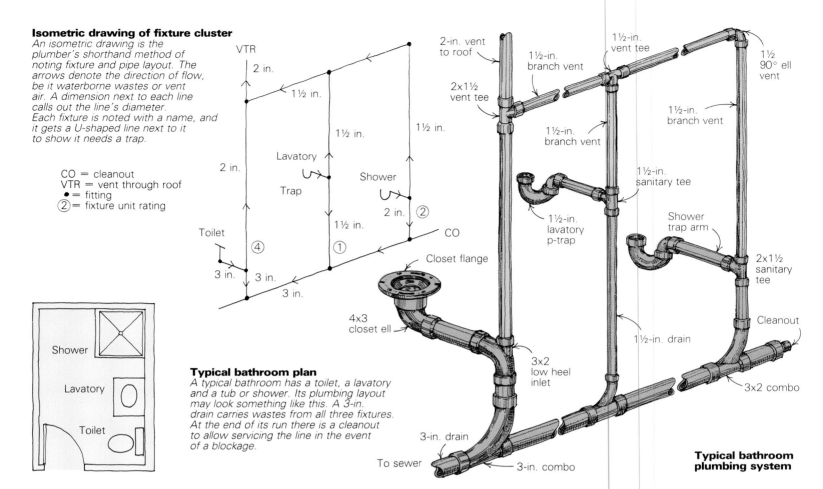

Isometric drawing of fixture cluster

An isometric drawing is the plumber's shorthand method of noting fixture and pipe layout. The arrows denote the direction of flow, be it waterborne wastes or vent air. A dimension next to each line calls out the line's diameter. Each fixture is noted with a name, and it gets a U-shaped line next to it to show it needs a trap.

CO = cleanout
VTR = vent through roof
● = fitting
② = fixture unit rating

VTR
2 in.
1½ in.
1½ in.
2 in.
Lavatory
Trap
1½ in.
Shower
2 in.
1½ in.
①
②
CO
Toilet
④
3 in.
3 in.
3 in.

2-in. vent to roof
1½-in. branch vent
1½-in. vent tee
1½ 90° ell vent
2x1½ vent tee
1½-in. branch vent
1½-in. branch vent
1½-in. sanitary tee
1½-in. lavatory p-trap
Shower trap arm
Closet flange
2x1½ sanitary tee
Cleanout
4x3 closet ell
1½-in. drain
3x2 low heel inlet
3-in. drain
To sewer
3-in. combo
3x2 combo

Typical bathroom plan

A typical bathroom has a toilet, a lavatory and a tub or shower. Its plumbing layout may look something like this. A 3-in. drain carries wastes from all three fixtures. At the end of its run there is a cleanout to allow servicing the line in the event of a blockage.

Shower
Lavatory
Toilet

Typical bathroom plumbing system

vading the house. The trap arm extends from the trap to the vent, and its maximum length is dependent upon its diameter.

A *main vent* (sometimes called a stack vent, or a vent stack) is the principal artery of the venting system. Its purpose is to provide an air supply to all parts of the drainage system. Without an air supply, waste water traveling to the building sewer could create a suction strong enough to pull the water out of the traps. A main vent extends upward through the building, eventually terminating above the roof. A house will occasionally have several main vents, but it's best to avoid penetrating the roof more often than necessary. Consequently, many fixtures are connected to main vents by *branch vents*. More on vents later in the article.

Pipes and fittings—The common materials for drainage systems are ABS plastic, PVC plastic, copper and cast iron. Pipes that are suitable for drains and vents are stamped with the letters DWV, which stands for drain, waste and vent. Typical pipe diameters for residential applications are 1½ in., 2 in., 3 in. and 4 in. Larger pipes are available, but are used primarily in commercial buildings.

ABS systems are less expensive to buy and less trouble to work with than copper or cast iron. ABS is easily cut and assembled, and its light weight enables one person to handle long sections of pipe. But there are some disadvantages to it. ABS expands and contracts a lot with changes in temperature, and it has to be supported with twice as many hangers as cast iron to keep it from bending. It gives off poisonous gases in a fire, and readily transmits the sound

of water running through it when the system is in use. Cast iron, on the other hand, dampens the sound of running water. It is quite durable, and less sensitive to temperature changes. I prefer to use 3-in. no-hub cast-iron drain lines in conjunction with 1½-in. and 2-in. copper branch drains and vents. The copper pipes are soldered together, while the no-hub cast-iron pipes are joined by stainless-steel bands over neoprene gaskets. But this sort of system costs my customers about 30% more than a plastic one. Most of my clients specify ABS to keep costs down.

Regardless of what material I'm using, I need a wide variety of fittings to join pipes and to make the changes of direction required in any plumbing system. No matter what the material, the shapes, functions and names of the fittings remain the same (see p. 77).

Layout preparation—Though most regions voluntarily follow one of the model codes, each town and county can institute additional code requirements. Before I begin a new job, I check with the district's chief plumbing inspector to find out what materials are approved for use in the area, and what code book is enforced.

Once I know what to expect from the building department, I visit the site to study any irregularities that may occur in the system. I locate the sewer hookup, and I check with the client to find out about any special fixtures that are to be included in the job. If a set of the building plans is available, I check them to make sure that the placement of the fixtures complies with code clearances. For instance, a toilet has to be centered in a space at least 30 in. wide, with 30 in. in front of the bowl. Does the location on the

blueprint take this into account? Then I find out what kind of toilet is to be installed, and I check the manufacturer's specs to find out where the center of the outlet is. This determines the placement of the closet flange. Typically, the centerline of a closet flange will be positioned 12 in. from the rough wall—11½ in. from the finished wall.

A lavatory drain line is typically 19 in. to 21 in. above the floor, while a kitchen-sink drain is usually 16 in. above the floor. This difference accounts for the depth of a garbage disposal. A bathtub drain is centered on the axis of the tub—usually 15 in. from the side wall. The placement of a washing-machine trap is between 6 in. and 18 in. above the floor—the stand pipe brings it up to the level of the machine's drain hose.

I also study the framing plans and consider the parts of the building that will affect the shape of the plumbing system. These are features such as windows, headers, medicine cabinets, offset walls and joists that want to run in contrary directions. All these factors affect the design of the system, and it's best to start thinking about them early on. I want the drains to run parallel to the joists wherever possible, and I need to know where the obstacles are so I can calculate the number of fittings that it will take to route the pipes around them.

The isometric drawing—This layout drawing is an isometric schematic of all the drains, vents and plumbing fixtures in a building. The plumbing for a small, one-story house can be shown on one drawing. But if the house is large or complex, I make detail drawings of fixture clusters, noting the drain connections with a heavy dot. The middle drawing on the facing page shows a typical isometric of a fixture cluster.

If there is an upstairs bathroom, I try to line the stack up so that it will fall in the same bay as the toilet drain. If it doesn't line up, I'll have to cut some large holes somewhere in order to install the drain line.

I begin my drawing at the approximate location of the sewer tie-in—about 2 ft. from the exterior of the house. As I work my way into the house I make a heavy dot at the intersections of the drain and vent lines to represent the fittings that I'll need, and I also mark arrows on the drains to show which way the waste goes, "CO" wherever a cleanout goes, and the note "VTR" to indicate where a vent goes through the roof. Although the isometric appears simple, it contains a lot of information. An expanded version of the same layout would look like the right-hand drawing on the facing page.

I don't make my isometric drawings to scale. Instead, I use the plan and section drawings of the building to take off the lengths of my plumbing runs and rises from floor to floor. I add these up and tack on 20% to get my pipe totals.

Sizing the drain and vent lines—Each
plumbing fixture requires a minimum-diameter drain. These dimensions are listed as "minimum trap and trap-arm sizes" in table 4-1 in the code book. For example, a toilet drain should be at least 3 in. in diameter, while showers should have a 2-in. trap arm and a 2-in. waste line. Lavatories, on the other hand, have a 1½-in. trap arm and a 1½-in. waste line. A toilet vent is 2 in., and vents to all other fixtures are 1½ in. for a typical house.

When I size the layout, I like to start at the end of the system—usually the bathroom farthest from the sewer hookup. I write a number next to the fixture's drain representing the pipe's diameter, and another one noting the diameter of its vent. Then I mark the unit rating for each fixture alongside its pipe diameter, as shown in the isometric drawing on the facing page.

To find the number of units assigned to each fixture, turn to the section in your code book on sizing drain lines (table 4-1). Notice that each fixture has a unit rating. These units represent the fixture's discharge in gallons per minute. One unit equals 0 to 7½ gallons, two units equal 8 to 15 gallons and so forth. Each fixture has a discharge rate based on this. For example, a kitchen sink has a unit rating of two units, a toilet is assigned four units and a lavatory is rated at one unit.

After I have completed the sizing for the bathroom, I make a note next to the branch line on the drawing that lists the total unit demand at that point. This tells me about how much more can be added to the drain line before its dimension needs to be increased. Table 4-3 in the code book lists maximum allowable units for any diameter pipe. For instance, a 2-in. pipe can handle up to eight units of flow if it's installed horizontally—sixteen units if it's vertical.

Now I go on to the fixtures that are the next farthest from the sewer hookup, and I repeat the same sequence, noting the diameter of each line and the unit load for each fixture. I continue this process until the entire plumbing system is designed. My finished drawing includes all cleanouts, changes of direction, vents, the unit total for each branch line, the diameters of the lines and a dot for every fitting that it will take to make the necessary directional changes.

Once I know the number of fixtures and their assigned units, I make a list of them and add them up to get the total number of units for all the fixtures in the building. Now I turn to the table on drainage systems in the code book (table 4-3), and I look for the section on pipe sizes. The table lists units on one scale, and pipe diameters on the other scale. Once I locate my unit number on the chart, it tells me what diameter building drain and sewer that the house will require. A 3-in. horizontal line can handle up to 35 units of flow, so it's usually plenty for a small house. On the other hand, if you're planning a big house with many bathrooms, a big kitchen, laundry and a spa, you'll need a 4-in. building drain. It can accommodate a whopping 216 units on a horizontal run.

While I'm sizing the building drain, I decide on how big my main vents have to be. Even though the vents to individual fixtures are either 1½ in. or 2 in. in diameter, the stacks to which they connect must be at least equal in cross section to the cross section of the building drain. For example, a 3-in. building drain would require a minimum of two 2-in. vents and one 1½-in. vent through the roof.

There are many ways to build a plumbing system that will work, but usually there is one way that will be easier than others. The alternatives you must weigh depend on types of construction, fixtures, proximity to vent stacks, crawl-space clearances, and clearances between floors.

Toilet layout—With a large crawl space and plenty of fall in your drainage system, a typical toilet layout might look like the drawing below left. The two key fittings here are a combo and a 3x2 low heel inlet. The combo is turned on its back, and the tee goes on top with the 2-in. outlet pointed vertically. The other fitting is a 4x3 closet ell. The 4-in. outlet goes through the floor and connects to the closet flange.

If the clearance is minimal—between floors is a good example—the toilet layout might look like the drawing below right. In this diagram, the 3x2 sanitary tee is turned so that the vent outlet is directed at an angle. This satisfies a code requirement that says that vents off a horizontal drain line must be directed at an angle that falls between 45° and 90°. The vent continues on

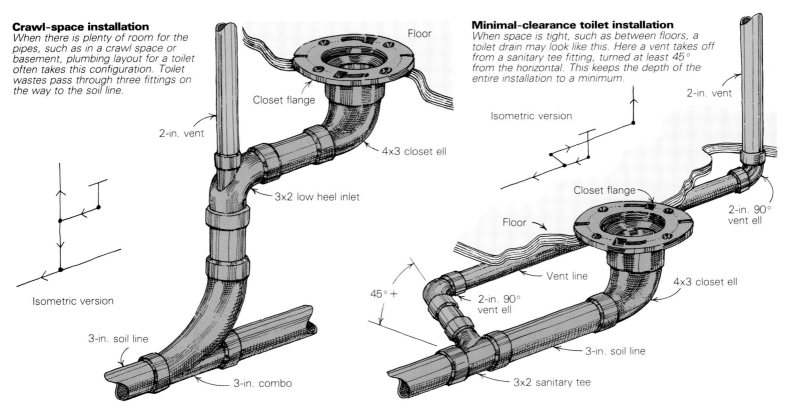

Crawl-space installation
When there is plenty of room for the pipes, such as in a crawl space or basement, plumbing layout for a toilet often takes this configuration. Toilet wastes pass through three fittings on the way to the soil line.

Floor

2-in. vent

Isometric version

3-in. soil line

3-in. combo

Closet flange

4x3 closet ell

3x2 low heel inlet

Minimal-clearance toilet installation
When space is tight, such as between floors, a toilet drain may look like this. Here a vent takes off from a sanitary tee fitting, turned at least 45° from the horizontal. This keeps the depth of the entire installation to a minimum.

Isometric version

2-in. vent

Closet flange

2-in. 90° vent ell

Floor

45° +

2-in. 90° vent ell

Vent line

4x3 closet ell

3-in. soil line

3x2 sanitary tee

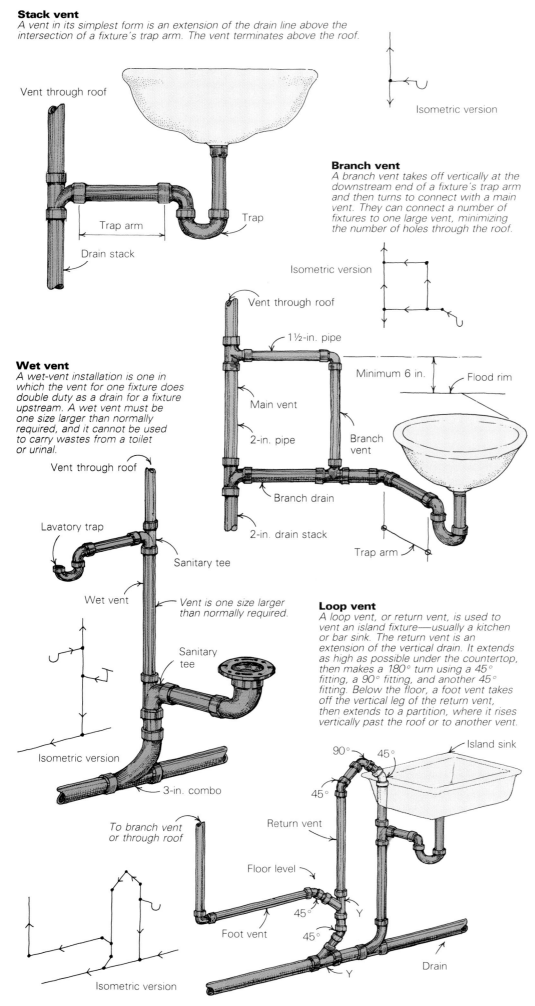

Stack vent
A vent in its simplest form is an extension of the drain line above the intersection of a fixture's trap arm. The vent terminates above the roof.

Vent through roof

Trap arm

Trap

Drain stack

Isometric version

Branch vent
A branch vent takes off vertically at the downstream end of a fixture's trap arm and then turns to connect with a main vent. They can connect a number of fixtures to one large vent, minimizing the number of holes through the roof.

Isometric version

Vent through roof

1½-in. pipe

Main vent

2-in. pipe

Minimum 6 in.

Flood rim

Branch vent

Branch drain

2-in. drain stack

Trap arm

Wet vent
A wet-vent installation is one in which the vent for one fixture does double duty as a drain for a fixture upstream. A wet vent must be one size larger than normally required, and it cannot be used to carry wastes from a toilet or urinal.

Vent through roof

Lavatory trap

Wet vent

Vent is one size larger than normally required.

Sanitary tee

Sanitary tee

Isometric version

3-in. combo

To branch vent or through roof

Loop vent
A loop vent, or return vent, is used to vent an island fixture—usually a kitchen or bar sink. The return vent is an extension of the vertical drain. It extends as high as possible under the countertop, then makes a 180° turn using a 45° fitting, a 90° fitting, and another 45° fitting. Below the floor, a foot vent takes off the vertical leg of the return vent, then extends to a partition, where it rises vertically past the roof or to another vent.

90° 45°

45°

Island sink

Return vent

Floor level

45°

Y

45°

Y

Foot vent

Drain

Isometric version

through the roof or ties into a branch vent at least 6 in. above the flood rim of the highest fixture on the line.

Vents—Every fixture needs a vent, but sometimes it's not immediately apparent how to tie the fixture's trap arm to a vent. The easiest solution is the stack vent (drawing, top left). This vent is an extension of the vertical drain, or stack, that carries waste to the building drain.

The stack vent is fine if your fixture is close to the drain stack, but if it isn't, you might want to tie into it with a branch vent. The branch vent takes off vertically from the trap arm, then makes a 90° turn toward the vent stack when it's at least 6 in. above the fixture's flood rim (drawing, second from top). The flood rim is the level at which the fixture begins to overflow.

The code allows wet vents in certain conditions—they can be especially handy in remodeling situations. A wet vent is a vertical vent that also serves as waste line—never a soil line. Each wet-vented section must be at least one pipe size larger than the required pipe under normal circumstances. The connection between the fixture's trap arm and the vent stack must be made with a sanitary tee (drawing, third from top).

If you want to vent an island sink, you'll need a loop vent (also known as a return vent). This system takes the vent as high as possible above the waste connection, and then back under the floor where it is tied by a pair of Y fittings to the branch line that carries the sink's discharge (bottom drawing). The vent then rises above the floor to connect with a vent stack. The connection between the drain and the foot vent makes it impossible for the low part of the vent to fill with condensation.

Trap-arm dimensions—Recall that the trap arm is that portion of a fixture drain between the trap and the vent. Table 7-1 in the code book lists the maximum lengths for trap arms of a given diameter. For instance, you can have a 3½-ft. trap arm with 1½-in. pipe, a 5-ft. trap arm with 2-in. pipe, and a 6-ft. trap arm with 3-in. pipe. In some cases you can save yourself some trouble by applying this rule. For example, I once had to tie a kitchen sink, centered beneath a large window, into a drain line about 5 ft. away. If I'd used the standard 1½-in. trap arm, I wouldn't have had enough length to get to my branch vent. So I went to 2-in. pipe, and gained the 1½ ft. needed to make a legal connection.

Cleanouts—A cleanout gives you access to the drainage system when something clogs one of the lines. You unscrew the threaded cap, insert a cable snake of some sort, and gnaw away at the blockage. A cleanout is required just outside the foundation, where the building drain meets the building sewer. Cleanouts are also required at the upper terminal of horizontal drain lines below the first floor, and there has to be plenty of clearance around each one so that you'll have room to maneuver maintenance equipment. There is a separate section in the code book that lists all the rules that apply to cleanouts—be sure to study this section carefully. Plumbing inspectors seem to like a lot of cleanouts. □

Common pipe fittings

Even though materials differ, the names and functions of the various pipe fittings used to join sections of drainpipe remain the same. The fittings in this list are the ones I use most often to assemble a residential drainage system. There are many more, but they are slight variations on the basic ones listed here.

Fittings are identified by numbers that designate the diameter of their outlets in inches, and an abbreviation of their shape. The size of the largest outlet is listed first. For instance, a reducing elbow with a 3-in. outlet and a 2-in. outlet is called a 3x2 ell. For a three-outlet fitting, such as a tee, Y and combo, the side-outlet diameter is the last number listed. For example, a tee with a 3-in. run and a 1½-in. side outlet is called a 3x1½ tee. If it's a reducing tee, three numbers describe the fitting and the side outlet is still listed last, such as a 3x2x1½ tee.

Most fittings have a socket at each outlet that accepts a piece of the nominal pipe. Fittings designed for cleanout plugs have a threaded female outlet. Adaptors can be either male or female, and nipples have threaded male ends. Street fittings have an outlet that's the same OD as the nominal pipe size.

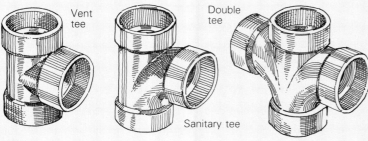

Vent tee
Double tee
Sanitary tee

Tees
Vent tee: A tee fitting used strictly for joining sections of vent pipe. It lacks the sweep of a sanitary tee, and shouldn't be used for waste or soil lines.
Sanitary tee: Unlike the vent tee, the sanitary tee has a sweep built into the intersecting line. This sweep has to be installed so the curve follows the direction taken by the waste. These fittings are used to connect trap arms to waste stacks, and to connect branch lines to waste stacks. They can be used in venting, and in horizontal to vertical drain applications.
Double tee: If you have two lavatories with the same flood rim on opposite sides of the same wall, you may connect them to the same stack and vent with this fitting. The vent stack continues upward from the top outlet.

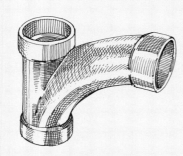

Ys
These fittings are used to join lines at a 45° angle, or to make a 45° change in direction while providing a cleanout outlet at the same time. The codebook requires this fitting for horizontal changes of direction. In a stud wall they can be difficult to use if a lot of angled holes have to be drilled in the framing to accommodate the angled line.

Combination tee and Y
Known as combos, this fitting is most often used for a 90° change in direction in the waste or soil lines where a cleanout is needed. It can be used in vertical or horizontal applications.

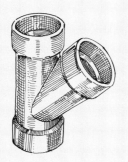

Bushings
For joining pipes of different diameters.

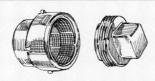

Cleanouts
These are watertight fittings with removable plugs. They consist of a threaded adaptor that inserts into a fitting or over a pipe. The adaptor accepts a threaded plug.

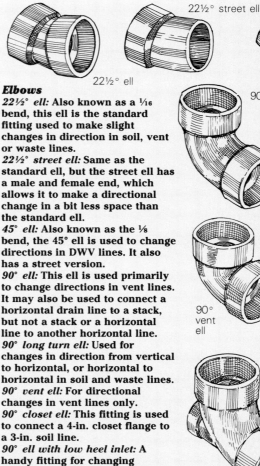
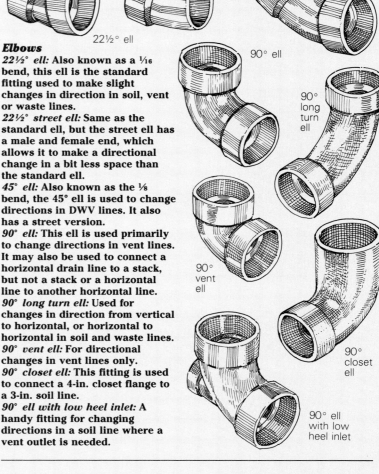

22½° ell
22½° street ell
45° ell
22½° ell
90° ell
90° long turn ell
90° vent ell
90° closet ell
90° ell with low heel inlet

Elbows
22½° ell: Also known as a 1/16 bend, this ell is the standard fitting used to make slight changes in direction in soil, vent or waste lines.
22½° street ell: Same as the standard ell, but the street ell has a male and female end, which allows it to make a directional change in a bit less space than the standard ell.
45° ell: Also known as the 1/8 bend, the 45° ell is used to change directions in DWV lines. It also has a street version.
90° ell: This ell is used primarily to change directions in vent lines. It may also be used to connect a horizontal drain line to a stack, but not a stack or a horizontal line to another horizontal line.
90° long turn ell: Used for changes in direction from vertical to horizontal, or horizontal to horizontal in soil and waste lines.
90° vent ell: For directional changes in vent lines only.
90° closet ell: This fitting is used to connect a 4-in. closet flange to a 3-in. soil line.
90° ell with low heel inlet: A handy fitting for changing directions in a soil line where a vent outlet is needed.

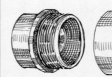

Trap adaptors
The trap adaptor is the transition fitting that connects the trap arm to the drain. There are two kinds: One is an adaptor that inserts into the side opening in a sanitary tee (left). The other fits over a pipe (center). Both have a slip-joint nut with a plastic washer that seals the trap arm (right). This links the fixture and the plumbing system. Trap adaptors are also used to connect a tub waste and overflow line to a p-trap.

Couplings
Coupling: A link between sections of waste, soil and vent lines.
Repair coupling: Same as the regular coupling, but it lacks the interior stop flanges, allowing it to slide onto a section of pipe while another pipe segment is brought alongside. Then the repair coupling is slid back to encompass the ends of both pipes. These are good for connecting pipes in tight spots.

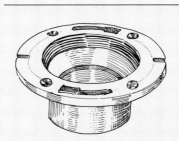

Closet flange
This is the transition coupling between a toilet and its soil line. The circular flange is screwed to the bathroom subfloor.

P-trap
The p-trap is the fitting that contains the water seal that keeps the sewer gases in the sewer. Toilets have built-in traps, but every other fixture requires some kind of p-trap. They are installed below the fixture drain.
—G. S.

Framing With The Plumber in Mind

A few tips to help you keep your sticks and nails out of my way

by Peter Hemp

Contrary to what you might believe, most plumbers, including yours truly, do not enjoy chopping a house to pieces in order to get plumbing systems in place. However, I do claim ownership of a carborundum-tipped chainsaw for just this purpose.

When cost estimating, whether I'm on a job site or working from a set of blueprints, I first start looking for the amount of chop time that's necessary to get the rough plumbing in place. The more wood that I can leave untouched, the cheaper my labor bill is going to be.

Many things will directly influence the labor cost of installing the rough plumbing, including the location of windows, medicine cabinets, let-in bracing, beams and the HVAC ductwork. But some of the most important factors are the direction and position of the floor joists and the availability of unobstructed pathways for vents.

Even minimal plan changes might need clearance from a higher authority, so I'd like to clue you in to those areas you can improve upon with little fuss, very little cost and all by yourself.

Laying down the joists—In the past, I have severed innumerable floor joists because they interfered with toilet wastes or tub and sink drains. Having done some time on framing crews myself, I remember how easy it was to lay joists from one end of the house to the other without thinking about the location of the walls until the subfloor was down. But in relation to plumbing costs, it's here that the greatest savings in labor (mine and yours) and the biggest gain in structural integrity can be realized.

On your next set of prints, look at the location of the bathroom wall behind the toilet. I call it the "tank wall." For standard toilets, the

measurement from the finished wall surface to the center of the toilet drain (or closet bend) in the floor is usually 12 in. I like to use 13 in., which gives more clearance behind the tank for future paint jobs (drawing below). I'll need a minimum 3 in. of clearance around this center point to rough in ABS plumbing (about 3½ in. for no-hub cast-iron pipe). This allows room for the pipe (typically 4½ in. in diameter), plus the added hub diameter of the closet flange (for more on toilet installation, see the article on pp. 98-101).

If there's a floor joist in that forbidden territory, I'm afraid it's recoil-starter time. When you plan to run joists 16 in. o. c. starting from the tank wall, center your first one about 8½ in. from the finished wall. You can then add a joist on the opposite side of the drain, again placing it at least 3 in. from the center, depending on the type of pipe used. Place an additional joist

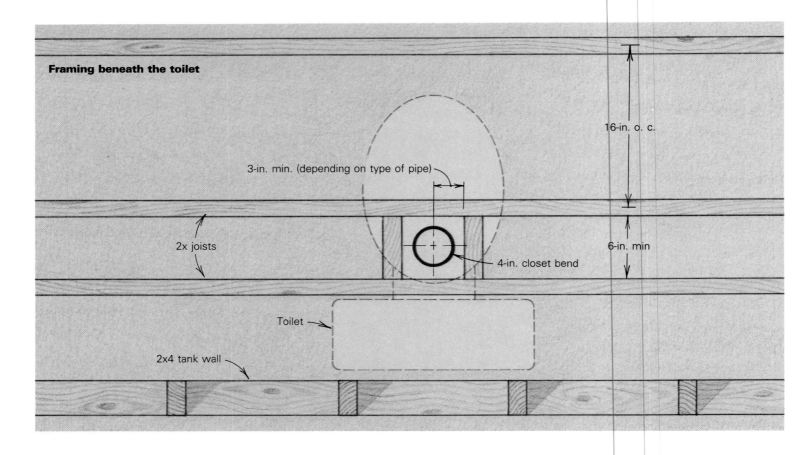

Framing beneath the toilet

16-in. o. c.

3-in. min. (depending on type of pipe)

2x joists

4-in. closet bend

6-in. min

Toilet

2x4 tank wall

wherever it's needed to satisfy the floor's structural needs.

If joists run perpendicular to the tank wall, I'll still need at least 3 in. of clearance around the center point of the closet flange. If there's a joist in the way, shift it over.

If you want to do a good deed for your customer after I've installed my drain, waste and vent system, and it has passed inspection, add some blocking around the closet drop. This blocking will stiffen the floor under the toilet, and that will help to prevent seepage from the toilet for the life of the structure. It will also save the owner lots of money later for the replacement of the subfloor and floor coverings.

Don't forget to take bathtubs into account when laying out the joists. Where joists run parallel to the length of the tub, I'd like a joist on either side of the drain hole, 6 in. from the center, with a block about 12 in. away from the shower-head (or valve) wall to support the pipe (drawing below). This distance will vary according to the type of tub and drain pipe, so check your tub before nailing up the block. When joists run perpendicular to the length of the tub, don't put a joist any closer than 12 in. to the valve wall if you can help it. If the toilet and shower head flank the same wall, you can't satisfy the requirements for both. In that case, leave a joist 8 ½ in. from the tank wall. I'll notch the top of the joist for the tub shoe (the drain fitting) if it's in the way and drill through the joist for the tub drain.

Again, you may have to add one or more joists to maintain proper joist spacing beneath the tub. But when you compare the cost of a couple extra joists to the cost of re-placing a severed joist in not-so-perfect working conditions (how would *you* like crawling around in the dark over moist, unidentifiable objects?) you'll find the cost of the extra joists a real bargain.

Framing for tubs—While we're on the subject of tubs, most residential tubs are between 30 and 32 in. wide. When carpenters frame the valve wall, they often put a stud about 16 in. from the adjoining wall. What a shame. How many times have you sat or stood in a tub and visually lined up the strainer in the bottom of the tub with the waste and overflow plate above it, the tub spout, the tub and shower valve and finally the shower arm and head? Did it bother you to see them all out of whack? Well, this all goes back to putting that stud in the middle of the valve wall. I have to carve up the stud to anchor my valve, spout and shower arm, and it never comes off looking professional.

Instead of that one stud in the center, please install two, dividing the width of the tub into three equal spaces. That way, I can add blocking between the two studs to anchor my plumbing fixtures. The blocking also makes it easy to line up the fixtures vertically.

Troubles at the perimeter—My final gripe about floor joists has to do with those lying beneath exterior 2x4 plumbing walls. When the joists run perpendicular to the plumbing wall, I have to contend with either a 2x rim joist or a rim joist with a row or two of 2x blocking. When the joists run parallel to the wall, I'll usually find a single joist toenailed to the mudsill.

When I have to bring 2-in. drain pipes (2½-in. O. D.) down through the bottom plate of the wall, the structure suffers. For the lines to stay completely inside the wall, (drywallers love you when they don't) I have to run a 2½-in. pipe through, at best, about a 2-in. space. If there's a fitting on the drain within the height of the joist, which is often the case, I need an additional ¼ in. to ⅜ in. of clearance. What does this mean? It means I have to remove ½ to ⅞ in. from the inside of the rim joist or block (if there's an inner block, I have to tear it out first). Worse, my drill makes a 2⅝-in. hole when it's sharp. When it's dull, it travels out-of-round and adds another ⅛ in. to that. So the joist or block can wind up being just ½ in. to 1 in. thick, give or take a few hairs. That's if my vertical cutting, done with the long rough-in blade in my reciprocating saw, is perfectly plumb, which it usually isn't. And that's before I chisel out between saw cuts.

You might be wondering why I don't use smaller pipes. If the same plumber who installed new pipes in a structure had to come back later to unclog them, there wouldn't be any drain lines smaller than 2 in. in a house. This happens to be my credo. Though our local building code calls for 1¼-in. drains for lavatories, 1½-in. drains for tubs and 2-in. drains for kitchens and laundries, I prefer to use 2-in. drains for all of them. If I do use a smaller diameter drain in a 2x4 wall, say 1½ in., it still means chewing away ¼ to ½-in of wood. I could reduce the diameter of the pipe by using DWV copper (which has half the wall thickness of supply-line copper) instead of ABS plastic or no-hub iron pipe, but

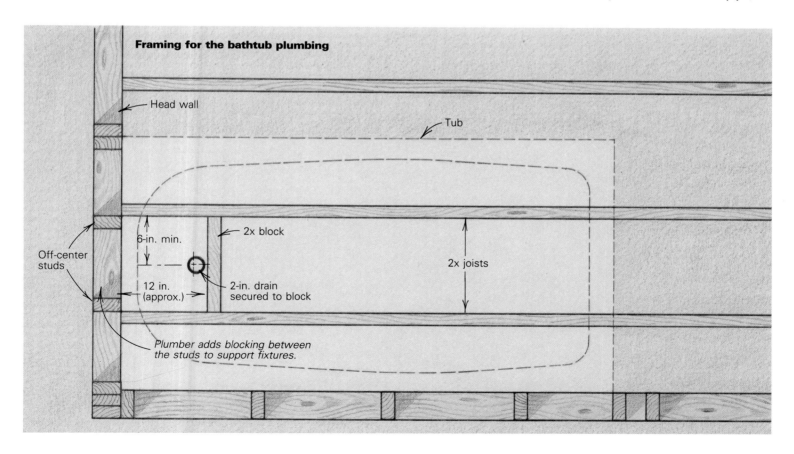

Framing for the bathtub plumbing

Head wall

Tub

Off-center studs

6-in. min.

2x block

12 in. (approx.)

2-in. drain secured to block

2x joists

Plumber adds blocking between the studs to support fixtures.

the cost of the copper pipe and fittings and of soldering the joints is considerable. Also, the torch I need for soldering could start a fire (if you don't think that plumbers are guilty of starting a few fires, think again).

So what is the remedy for all this? It's simple: furred walls. Nail 2x2s to the studs, and that extra 1⅝ in. will help me to stay clear of the rim joist or end blocks. You'll spend a few extra bucks for materials, but I'll bet in labor (yours and mine), furring the wall is cheaper than paying me to crawl and hack. And the structure of the house suffers less. If the rim joists parallel to the mudsill are doubled, which is sometimes the case, I'll still have to chew through the inner joist, but the furring will allow me to keep the outer joist intact. Of course, 2x6 walls would be even better than furring, or the designer can design the house to keep plumbing out of exterior walls in the first place.

Nails in the plumbing zone—A plumber spends most of his time boring holes. Unlike those "sparkies" who rarely have to drill any hole larger than a finger for their skinny little wires, we plumbers occasionally find ourselves boring 5-in. holes. And, the worst thing to encounter when boring big holes is a nail.

For fast drilling in wood, plumbers like to use self-feeding bits, which means we try to hang on to that powerful Milwaukee Hole Hawg, waiting to have it wrenched from our hands, pin our wrists, slap us in the face with the handle or spin us right off a ladder while the bit chews its own way through your masterwork. These drill bits can easily cost $25 or more and can be destroyed by nails the first day out of the box.

When I encounter a nail, I stop drilling immediately (as a safety feature, there is no trigger hold-down button on a Hawg; to have one would be suicide). I then have to remove the self-feed bit, replace it with a hole saw and continue drilling at a much slower rate, expending back-breaking energy. Now, if you were merely to stab your 16d sinkers a little differently, you would save me a lot of hassle and yourself some money.

Here's the program. Before you nail up a wall, consult your funny papers (some call 'em blueprints) to locate the plumbing fixtures. Next, mark the stud bays where the pipe is supposed to go, plus one bay on either side. Then, when you're nailing the bottom plates to the subfloor, start the nails in the middle of the marked bays, but don't sink them entirely. That way, if they interfere with my boring path, I can yank them out, move them over and set them myself. This also gives me the option of running the pipe through the adjacent bays if I have to. Do the same thing with the top plates; I'll sink all the nails when I'm through.

If the wall needs blocking, set the nails in the marked bays just enough to hold the blocks in place. I can bore the lower and upper plates, yank the blocks and bore them separately. Then I can slide them over my pipe (if there aren't any couplings in the way) and nail them in place myself. If the holes need to be bored near the ends of the blocks, the nails will usually split them. To avoid this, I use my cordless screw gun to predrill the blocks and screw them in place.

Backing the drywall—If you aren't asleep yet, hang on for the finale. My final suggestion deals with backing for the ceiling drywall. It used to be that a 1x6 was used for backing on top of a 2x4 wall, and a 1x8 backed a 2x6 wall. These days, two ceiling joists are often used instead, each slightly overlapping the opposite edges of the top plate (drawing below). This creates a U-channel, which can make it very tough for me to run my pipes.

If the plumbing wall is anywhere near the bottom slope of the roof, and the roof sheathing is already down, working in that location is almost impossible. The U-channel also makes it tough to tighten no-hub couplings, which are most often down in the channel. And there's more. Sometimes I try to avoid extra vents in the roof by back-venting several 2-in. vents into one 4-in. stack. The U-channels can end up getting so mauled that I have doubts as to their integrity.

On interior plumbing walls, I'd recommend using the 1x backing and avoiding center-span nailing in the plumbing bays. As I did for the plates and blocks, I'll finish the nailing for you after my pipe is through.

It may not be evident at first, but I think you'll find that my recommendations won't just save me labor, they'll save you some painful rehab activity that you would just as soon not experience. □

Peter Hemp is a plumber and writer from Albany, Calif., and author of The Straight Poop *(Ten Speed Press, P. O. Box 7123, Berkeley, Calif. 94707, 1986. $9.95, softcover; 176 pp.) a book on plumbing maintenance and repair.*

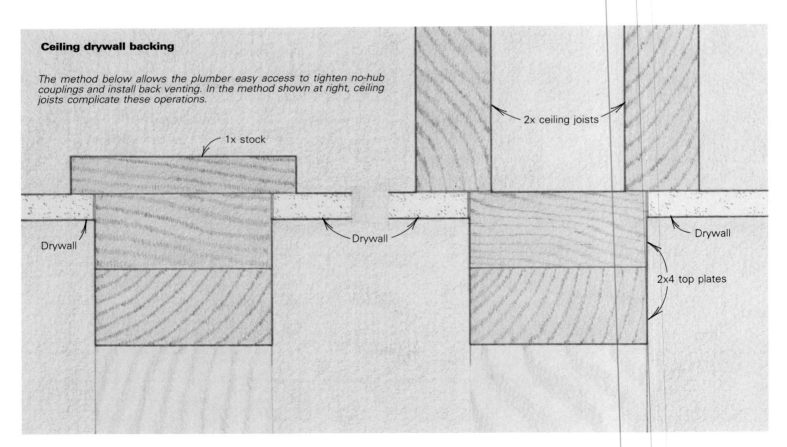

Ceiling drywall backing

The method below allows the plumber easy access to tighten no-hub couplings and install back venting. In the method shown at right, ceiling joists complicate these operations.

1x stock

2x ceiling joists

Drywall

Drywall

Drywall

2x4 top plates

Roughing in the Drain Lines

Advice on assembling a residential drainage system with plastic pipes

by George Skaates

When you've got a pad of yellow paper in your lap and a set of blueprints on the table, you can do a lot of plumbing without getting dirty. As I explained in my earlier article on designing and sizing drainage systems (see pp. 73-77), every well-organized job begins with isometric drawings of the various drain configurations, and lists of the fittings and pipes necessary to make the drawings a reality. Once you've got your drawings and lists figured out, you've got to get down to the nitty-gritty of plumbing, from squirming around in a crawl space with a glue pot in one hand to boring a vent hole in the roof sheathing with a Hole Hawg.

Although I install plenty of cast-iron drain lines for my customers, most of the systems that I put together are made out of ABS (acrylonitrile-butadiene-styrene) plastic. My clients often ask about the relative merits of cast-iron and plastic systems. Cast iron is better at absorbing the sounds made by running water, so if you'd rather not hear the system at work you should consider cast-iron pipes. Plastic pipes transmit sound, and they expand and contract at a rate roughly eight times that of cast iron. That means a plastic drain system requires a lot more anchoring devices to keep it from moving out of alignment. Still, plastic is a lot easier to work with than cast iron, and the fittings and pipe cost about one-third as much. Also, plastic weighs a fraction of what cast iron weighs, so one person can handle materials that traditionally took two.

Getting through the foundation—When I bid a plumbing job for a house, I make my calculations based on a drainage system that extends 2 ft. beyond the foundation. Tying into the sewer is a topic all by itself. Like my bids, this article will start just outside the foundation, and finish at the roof vents.

If you don't already know the location of the city sewer line, call the appropriate agency and ask them for the location of the sewer to which the drain will be connected. Under most conditions, the corner of the house that is closest to the sewer or the septic system is the point at which you will need a hole in the foundation for the building drain.

Before the foundation is poured, I get together with the contractor and we agree on the best spot for the plumbing penetration. Aesthetics and pragmatism are factors here—the drain should end up below grade after backfill, and it should be far enough below grade to ensure a

Under the floor. In the center of the photo, a 3-in. soil line leads to a 4x3 closet ell. A few feet in front of the ell, a 3x2 sanitary tee turned at a 45° angle leads to a vent for the water closet. At the plate line, the vent is extended upward with a 10-ft. mast for a water test. To its left, a branch line goes to a stub for a lavatory and an upstairs laundry. In the lower right, a stub protrudes for a bathtub. The drain line in the center is secured with a plastic hanger.

From *Fine Homebuilding* magazine (April 1987) 39:33-37

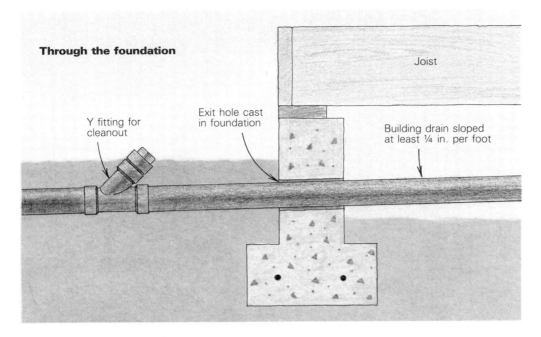

Through the foundation

Y fitting for cleanout

Exit hole cast in foundation

Joist

Building drain sloped at least ¼ in. per foot

---

fall of ¼ in. per linear foot of drain line from the plumbing fixture farthest from the foundation penetration (drawing, above). If the foundation is a stemwall and the drain is 3 in. in diameter, I use a piece of 4-in. plastic pipe as a form insert. The insert leaves enough space for the 3-in. pipe plus a little wiggle room for settling.

If the building drain is 4 in. in diameter, I still use a 4-in. form insert, but I build it up with a ½-in. layer of Flexwrap (Cal Western Supply, 1111A East Houston, Visalia, Calif. 93291). Flexwrap is ⅛-in. thick plastic foam that comes in 8-in. wide rolls. It's mostly used to wrap drain lines that will be entombed under slabs. When removed, the built-up form insert gives me enough room to run a 4-in. line.

I see more and more houses built on pier and grade-beam foundations these days. With these, the perimeter footings are usually shallow enough to tunnel under them, rather than running the line through the concrete.

In the crawl space—With a set of the plans in hand, I walk around the joisted subfloor and mark the locations of each fixture and vent with a crayon. If it's going to be a two-story house, I mark the location of the soil stack that will serve the upstairs bath. This line usually has to be installed with great accuracy because it's often in an interior wall.

Once I've determined how big the drain lines need to be to service the house, I begin my installation by laying out the unconnected lengths of pipe in their approximate locations. While the joists are in place, the subfloor is not, so it's easy to spread out the pipes and gain access to the crawl space. I start laying out the pipes near the exit point in the foundation, working each line toward the cluster of drains that it will serve. ABS pipe comes in 20-ft. lengths, and I try to use pieces that are full length wherever they will fit. Chances are I will be cutting into some of these long runs where drain lines intersect, but it's easier to align them initially if the pipes are as long as possible.

Once I have the pipes spread, I take another look at my isometric drawings, noting the intersections of the various drain lines and the fittings that it will take to join them. Then I lay the fittings next to the pipes, in the spots where they will be needed. This includes all my change-of-direction fittings, couplings and cleanouts. Getting all the parts spread out this way helps me to visualize the way the system will look when it's finished. Even with plenty of planning, I know that I'll have to tinker with the lines to get everything to fit. For making changes in the direction of the drain lines, I keep a good supply of 45° ells, Ys, 90° long-turn ells and combos on hand, in all the common pipe diameters.

Fittings distributed, I go back to where the building drain will exit through the foundation, and begin hanging the pipes with ABS pipe hangers. This type of hanger secures the pipe with a plastic ring that is affixed to a straight piece of plastic rod. When I've got the pipe at the right height, I drive a nail through the rod into a nearby block or joist (photo previous page). Then I snap the rod off flush with the tops of the joists.

As I hang the pipe near the exit point, I make sure that its centerline is close to that of the hole that passes through the foundation. Then I work toward the location of the fixtures that the line will serve, hanging each section of pipe so that it slopes toward the exit at ¼ in. per foot minimum. To calculate the slope, I use a plumber's torpedo level. It has graduations on it that show when a pipe is sloping at the proper angle.

At this stage I don't connect any of these pipes as I hang them. Instead, I butt them together. They will eventually be glued to one another, but for now I want to be able to move them around if need be. ABS pipes have to be anchored every 4 ft., but during this preliminary work I leave out half the hangers, and because I may want to adjust them, I don't drive the hanger nails in all the way.

Usually there is a water closet at the end of each one of these lines, so the pipes are at least 3 in. in diameter. I aim each of these horizontal lines to end up under the water closet, as shown

in the photo on the previous page. All the nearby fixtures will drain into this line by way of combination or Y fittings.

Getting through the floor—Once the horizontal lines are hung, it's time to install the fittings that get the pipes above the subfloor. Most of them will end up in walls. If the wall is to contain 3-in. or 4-in. pipes, it should be framed with 2x6s. Experienced contractors know this, but I have to remind owner-builders from time to time. The goal is to leave pipe stubs for each fixture and vent protruding at least 4 in. above the tops of the joists. This leaves enough pipe to glue to a coupling once the subfloor and wall plates are installed. When the pipe stubs are in place, each one is capped and the system is filled with water to check for any leaks. Then the inspector pays a visit. More on this in a bit.

Every plumbing job presents its own set of challenges, and the conditions I find influence the way I approach a job. There are plenty of ways to run pipes from the building drain to a water closet. The challenge is to do it with as few fittings and contortions as possible. I have to think about how I can install the system with a minimum of cutting into the framing, or getting in the way of other mechanicals still to come, such as heating ducts.

Some knowledge of framing carpentry is essential for a plumber. Sometimes the framing has to be changed, and I have to know what the options are. For instance, a floor joist may fall directly in the center of a closet flange. In a case like this, I've got to get the contractor to pull the joist and head it off.

Usually I begin final assembly of the horizontal lines by anchoring a fixture stub that requires accurate positioning to the framing, and then I work back toward the drain exit. For example, the center of the closet flange for most water closets has to be 12 in. to 12½ in. from the unfinished wall. After I mark the centerline on a nearby joist I nail a 2x4 block between the joists and strap the closet ell to the block (top photo, facing page). This way I've got the ell secured on the right centerline, and firmly supported from below. To strap plastic plumbing, I use ABS plumbers tape, with at least one full wrap around the pipe or fitting. Metal tape is not allowed by code because it will score the plastic as the pipes flex with temperature changes.

Cutting and gluing—When I first started plumbing with plastic pipe I used a crosscut saw to cut the stuff. This works okay, but it's hard to get a square cut with a handsaw, and the sawteeth leave burrs that have to be removed with a pocket knife. Now I use a big tubing cutter that is made specifically for plastic pipe. Both Reed (Reed Manufacturing Co., 1425 W. 8th St., Erie, Pa. 16512) and Ridgid (Ridge Tool Company, 400 Clark St., Elyria, Ohio 44036-2023) make good ones. The tubing cutter makes square cuts without burrs.

Glue specially formulated for ABS comes from your supplier in cans that range from half-pints to gallons, with applicator brushes affixed to the lids. I use pint cans for small-diameter pipes, and quart cans for 3 in. and up because the brushes are sized accordingly. To join a pipe and a fitting, both must be dry and clean. Fittings have hubs on their ends that taper inward toward flanges that restrict the travel of the pipe. When you are measuring the length of a pipe between two fittings, measure to the flanges.

To join a pipe and a fitting, generously swab the inside of the fitting with a glue-laden brush. Then quickly do the same to the end of the pipe—you want the glue to be wet when they go together. Now push the pipe into the fitting. When it bottoms out against the flange, twist it a quarter-turn. If you've used the right amount of glue, there should now be a wet bead of glue all the way around the pipe where it enters the fitting. When it dries (in a few minutes), the two are welded together and you can forget about trying to pull them apart, ever.

Unfortunately, ABS glue tends to stick not only to the pipes but to the plumber as well. It inevitably gets on my hands. If I have a lot of gluing to do and I have a helper handy, I sometimes wear cheap cloth gloves. Without a helper, it's difficult to get a good grip on the pipes while wearing gloves, so I end up using acetone to get the dried glue off my hands.

Assembly—Once I have a fitting such as the closet ell (photo top right) secured, I gather the pipes and fittings necessary to add a vent line and to connect it with the uphill end of my horizontal drain. Code requires a vent within 6 ft. of a water closet plumbed with 3-in. pipe and within 10 ft. with 4-in. pipe. So installing a vent is the next task. In this instance, I used a 3x2 sanitary tee turned at a 45° angle along with a 90° elbow to lead the 2-in. vent line toward the wall cavity. To make sure the sanitary tee ended up at 45° after I glued it in place, I dry-fit the tee on the pipe coming from the closet ell, and made registration marks with a crayon on the pipe and the hub of the tee. This way I could tell how far to twist the freshly glued fitting to have it end up at the right angle.

With this assembly, I next cut a short length of 2-in. pipe to connect a 90° elbow with the 2-in. outlet from the sanitary tee. Then I held another 90° elbow against the rim joist, and measured the flange-to-flange distance between the two ells. This measurement gave me the length of the horizontal vent. After cutting a piece of 2-in. pipe to that length, I glued a 90° ell onto one end of it. Then I glued the other end to the elbow coming from the sanitary tee, making sure the elbow at the opposite end pointed upward.

Because the location of the vent in the wall wasn't critical in this situation, I didn't have to secure the elbow next to the rim joist before connecting a pipe to it. In this manner, subassemblies of pipes can be glued together, then fitted into difficult-to-reach areas.

As I glue the pipes together, I pay attention to the labeling on the pipe. Once installed, the labels are required by code to be visible to the inspector. I like to see all labels on horizontal lines pointing straight up, aligned on high noon.

A rule of thumb for assembling ABS drain pipes is always to work away from fittings and pipes that have been secured. Sometimes though, you've got to link a couple of fastened fittings

Alignment is critical. The mark on the joist to the right of the water-closet drain stub in the photo above shows the closet flange centerline from the wall. Above it, the X marks the line of the wall. The tub p-trap (photo below) was positioned after the bathtub was in place. Most bathtubs have a skirt that conceals the floor behind them, so you can cut a fairly large hole in the floor to make it easier to align the fittings.

After enclosure. The same bathroom as the one on p. 81 with walls shows how the pipe stubs have been extended. A lavatory will connect to the branch drain feeding into the drain stack on the left. A vent rises from the branch drain, and turns right to connect with the toilet vent. A closet flange has been attached to the stub coming from the closet ell. Note the metal plates on the framing to protect the plumbing.

A recessed laundry box organizes the washing-machine supply lines and drain. The drain stack in the lower left corner is the extension from the downstairs bathroom in the photo at the top of the page. Urethane foam fills the gaps around the pipes at the plates, securing the pipes and cutting air infiltration.

with a section of pipe. In this case, a repair coupling can help. This coupling lacks the interior flanges of the regular coupling, which allows it to slide over a pipe. To use it, glue your pipes to their fixed locations so they end up butting one another—don't forget to slide the coupling on one of them first. Now swab the ends of the two adjoining pipes with glue, and slide the coupling back to where it overlaps the two pipes equally. This requires quick work.

As I do the final assembly of the pipes and fittings, I make sure everything that needs gluing in the immediate area gets glued. It is not pleasant to pull a system apart to glue the forgotten fitting. I also stress to all of my employees the importance of securing the pipes as you go. On horizontal runs, ABS has to be supported every 4 ft., and as I work my way toward the exit point I add any missing hangers. Plastic hangers are expensive, so instead of using more of them I use ABS tape wrapped around the pipe and screwed to a 2x4 block when the pipes are in a joist bay. Below the joists, I use sway braces. Sway braces are lengths of 2x4s with a wide V cut in one end (drawing, below). A double wrap of ABS tape secures the pipe at the V-cut end. The brace is nailed to a nearby joist or block. I install my sway braces at opposing angles—this way the pipes really stay put.

First rough inspection—The first visit from the inspector is to check the subfloor plumbing. All the horizontal drain lines in the crawl space have to be connected and secured, and the building drain taken beyond the foundation to a Y fitting. All the drain and vent lines have to extend above the subfloor, where they are capped for the first water test. There are exceptions to this. If I don't know the exact location of a shower or a tub p-trap I can cap the branch drain below subfloor height, and install the p-trap once the tub or shower is on site. Under these circumstances, I usually cut a big hole in the subfloor behind the tub surround (bottom photo, previous page), giving me enough room to work.

There are three kinds of caps that can tempo-

rarily seal ABS pipe for water tests. Two are glued in place, one clamps on. One of the glue-ons fits inside a pipe, while the other fits over a pipe like a jar lid. Of the two, I prefer the former—it's easier to remove and less likely to leak. I like the clamp-on kind the best of all. It's a rubber cap with a metal band that can be tightened. Clamp-on caps rarely leak, and they can be reused.

Once the glue has had a chance to dry for 24 hours, you have to pressurize the system to check for leaks. To do so, attach a vertical length of pipe to an uncapped vent or drain, as shown in the photo on p. 81. It has to extend 10 ft. above the highest fitting in the system. It will eventually be filled with water, so brace it with a stud. Now plug the Y fitting outside the foundation with a mechanical test plug or an inflatable rubber test ball. If you don't own one of these, a contractor's rental yard will have one. I prefer the mechanical plug. In a pinch, a cap backed by a stake driven into the ground will also work.

If a system is going to leak, it usually does so around the threaded cleanout plugs. I've found that wrapping the plug's threads with Teflon tape and then coating the wrapped threads with a liberal application of pipe dope will keep these leaks to a minimum. (Make sure the pipe dope is compatible with ABS pipes.)

When you're sure everything is capped and plugged, stick a hose down the pipe mast and fill up the system. When it overflows, turn it off and let it sit while the air bubbles come to the surface. Then top it off, and let it sit overnight. The 10-ft. head is enough to put about 5 lb. of pressure on the system. This will make unglued joints quite evident. If you're losing water and can't see it, the test bulb is leaking.

Cutting into the frame—Once the inspector signs off the subfloor rough, I pull the plug on the exterior Y fitting and drain the system. Now the carpenters go to work, and I don't return until all the studwalls are in place, the roof sheathing is nailed down and the pipe stubs are

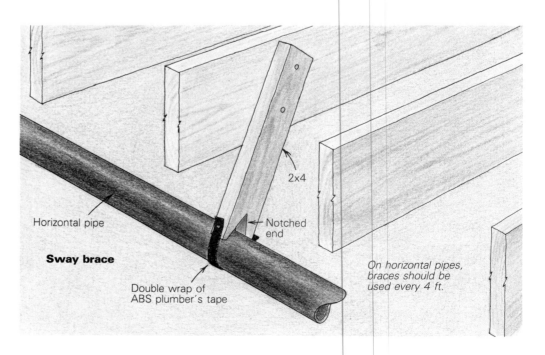

Horizontal pipe

Sway brace

Double wrap of ABS plumber's tape

2x4

Notched end

On horizontal pipes, braces should be used every 4 ft.

protruding through the bottom plates. Then it's my turn to cut wood.

I carry a skillsaw, a Sawzall and a Hole Hawg in my tool box for modifying the framing. They are all indispensable, but the Hole Hawg gets used the most. Along with the Hole Hawg, I bought Milwaukee's plumber's kit, which includes self-feeding bits that are sized for pipes. They cut holes that are about ⅜ in. oversize for each diameter pipe.

Like all high-torque drills, the Hole Hawg has to be used with caution. If you hit a knot or a nail with the bit, the bit stops but the tool wants to continue in the opposite direction. Be aware

of this. Always position yourself so that the tool won't smash your hand into a stud or whack you in the face if the bit binds. Try to rest the tool against something solid while operating it. Because nails are common obstacles in wall drilling, I keep a cat's paw in my kit.

Sometimes cutting holes in plates and studs that are large enough for pipes leaves very little wood in some parts of the frame, so the pipes have to be protected by metal plates where the remaining wood isn't thick enough to take the length of a drywall nail (top photo, facing page).

Sometimes you have to cut through a floor joist to get a drain into the right location. When

this happens, never remove wood from the tops or bottoms of the joists. To do so would destroy the loadbearing, compression/tension properties of the joist. You can however, cut a hole in the center of a joist to accommodate a pipe. The largest allowable hole is equal to a third of the depth of the joist.

Washing machines and sinks—In addition to water closets, kitchen sinks and lavatories, a typical residential plumbing system will have a drain for a washing machine. I like to run its fouling chamber (the drain line above the p-trap) into a recessed laundry box (bottom photo, facing page). The box fits flush with the drywall, and includes space for the water supply valves.

Typically a sink will drain into a sanitary tee. The drain will go straight down, and the vent straight up (photo left). The top photo on the facing page shows a variation on this. Here the sink will drain into a 90° long-turn ell, which is connected to a trap arm. The vent comes off the trap arm, rises and makes a turn to the right where it links up with the water closet vent.

There are a lot of ways to handle the various conditions you find in a plumbing job. The best way to find out about what works and what is legal is to get a copy of the Uniform Plumbing Code ($34.00 plus applicable tax from the International Assn. of Plumbing and Mechanical Officials, 5032 Alhambra Ave., Los Angeles, Calif. 90032) and scrutinize the pertinent sections.

Vents—In the walls or in the attic space, a vent line can be at any angle from horizontal to vertical. It cannot, however, slope downward. Vents leave the building vertically through the roof, where they pass through a flashing. They have to extend at least 6 in. above the roof. Horizontally, they have to be at least 10 ft. away from a window, and at least 1 ft. from a vertical wall such as a dormer or a parapet. According to ABS pipe manufacturers, the carbon pigment that turns the plastic black will protect it from the sun, so you don't have to paint it.

When I install an ABS system, I use roof flashings made by the Oatey Co. (6600 Smith Ave., Newark, Calif. 94560). They have neoprene collars that are sized for the common pipe diameters. The neoprene fits tightly around the pipe, preventing leaks while still allowing the pipe to move up and down as it expands and contracts with temperature swings. Since I'm usually not around when the roof gets shingled, I ask the contractor about the roof finish. For composition shingles I leave the standard flashings— shake roofs need larger ones.

When the vents are through the roof, it's time for another inspection. I plug the Y outside the foundation again, and I make sure that any open drain lines are closed with glue-on plugs or threaded caps. Then I stick the hose in one of the vents, and fill the system until the lowest vent on the roof overflows. If I can't find any leaks, I call the inspector. I don't return to hook up the fixtures until the walls have been painted, but that's another story. □

This basic lavatory drain is secured to a 2x4 block. The outlet from a sanitary tee atop a vertical drain is capped with a threaded plug. The plug is screwed to a threaded trap adaptor that is glued to the tee. When the sink is installed, its tailpiece will fit into the trap adaptor, where it will be sealed with a compression ring.

George Skaates is a partner in Skaates Canepa Inc. Plumbing Contractors in Alameda, Calif.

The Septic Tank Revealed

How to install a new system, and keep it working

by John Wetzler

One of the primary tasks in planning a new home in rural America is laying out a private sewage-disposal system. The homeowner who lacks access to any centralized collection and processing complex is responsible for waste management on the property. Unfortunately, there is currently only one method of disposal that county health and building departments will approve without a fight: the common septic tank. Used throughout rural America for more than 100 years, this simple mechanical system treats wastewater through a natural biological process. A properly installed septic system will be well worth the careful planning it entails. Trouble-free service is the most important goal —few things are worse than a troublesome septic system.

The components—The four basic components of a septic system, diagrammed below, are the main drain line from the house plumbing facilities, the septic tank (also called the holding or storage tank), the distribution box and the leach lines and leach field. These work together to return flushed water safely to the aquifer from which it came. It is very important to note that only the water is treated and returned to Nature. Solids and other particulate wastes are stored and digested into a heavy, compact sludge at the bottom of the storage tank. Thus the septic system is not a closed or complete sewage-disposal system. After a period of time the tank sludge must be pumped and taken away from your property. It is usually trucked and dumped into the sewer system of a modern treatment plant, where it is dried and hauled away to a special landfill dump. In some rural counties, there now exists considerable controversy over where septic effluent may be hauled and dumped. This question will have to be resolved if the septic system is to continue as the principal acceptable wastewater system in rural areas.

The leach field—Let's assume you select the septic system as the waste-disposal system for your property. From a planning standpoint, the leach field is by far the system's most important component, and deciding where to put it will be your most time-consuming task. First, you must determine the location of your house and its water source. In doing so, consider the general lay of the land. It is best to place a leach field downhill from your home and at least 100 ft. away from any water source. Uphill leach fields can be used but require pumps and electrical controls. During the power outages so frequent in rural America, owners of uphill leach fields may be plagued by more than just no lights.

One of the first ground probes done on a newly purchased piece of raw property is the perco-

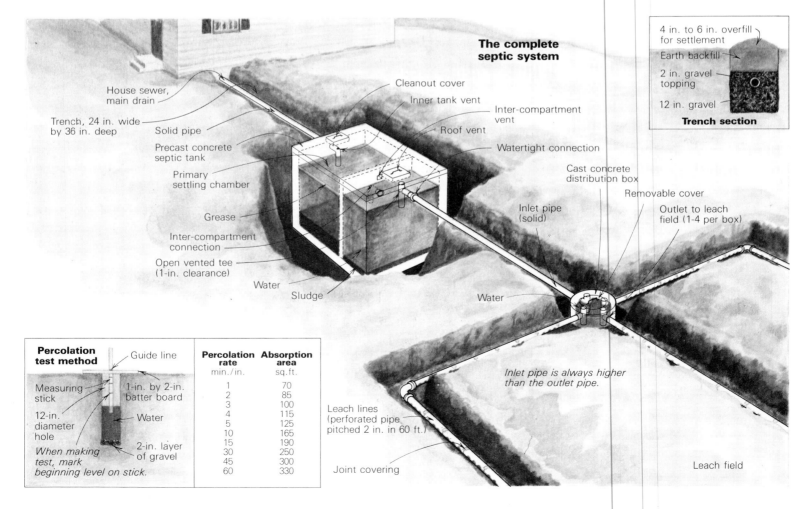

The complete septic system

House sewer, main drain

Trench, 24 in. wide by 36 in. deep

Solid pipe

Precast concrete septic tank

Primary settling chamber

Grease

Inter-compartment connection

Open vented tee (1-in. clearance)

Water

Sludge

Cleanout cover

Inner tank vent

Inter-compartment vent

Roof vent

Watertight connection

Cast concrete distribution box

Inlet pipe (solid)

Removable cover

Outlet to leach field (1-4 per box)

Water

Inlet pipe is always higher than the outlet pipe.

Leach lines (perforated pipe pitched 2 in. in 60 ft.)

Joint covering

Leach field

4 in. to 6 in. overfill for settlement

Earth backfill

2 in. gravel topping

12 in. gravel

Trench section

Percolation test method

Guide line

Measuring stick

1-in. by 2-in. batter board

12-in. diameter hole

Water

2-in. layer of gravel

When making test, mark beginning level on stick.

Percolation rate min./in.	Absorption area sq.ft.
1	70
2	85
3	100
4	115
5	125
10	165
15	190
30	250
45	300
60	330

lation test. Its purpose is to discover how quickly your ground can absorb water. The speed of absorption determines the required size of the leach field. Most counties require that an engineer, percolation contractor or county sanitarian perform the test. The procedure is relatively simple but very exacting. A series of 12-in. diameter holes is dug or bored into the ground of the proposed drain field (inset drawing, facing page). These holes are of uniform depth and spacing. The depth of the holes should equal the depth of the proposed leach trenches, which must be at least four feet above the maximum seasonal groundwater level. Your present groundwater level can usually be determined by boring with a hand auger until you hit water. You can case this mini-well with perforated pipe to prevent a cave-in, and check the water level throughout the year.

If you don't have a year to determine maximum groundwater level, you can get a qualified engineer to evaluate soil mottling. The engineer will look for soil discoloration caused by waterborne chemicals that flood the soil, leaving a traceable residue. This residue identifies the maximum groundwater level. Other ways to determine this level include consulting local hydrology reports; noting decomposition of vegetable material, such as roots; noting soil color in general; and observing general topography, since the presence of swales (lowlands) and bogs indicate areas of groundwater collection.

Once you have decided on a location for your field, you are ready to drill percolation test holes and begin the test.

In the percolation test, the bottoms of the test holes are covered with 2 in. of gravel and then continuously filled with water (usually over a 4-hour period) to reach a point of saturation. After a 12-hour interval, or the next day, the holes are again continuously filled with water until a constant level is maintained. The holes are now well saturated and ready for percolation measurements. The hole is filled once more then all filling is stopped. The time it takes the water to drop one inch is measured. This percolation rate is then applied to the county sanitarian's table of standards in order to determine the square footage of leach-field absorption area needed per planned bedroom. Yes, per bedroom. Sanitarians are well aware that people flush toilets and that toilets in good repair don't normally flush themselves. So it is not as important how many toilets one may have as how many people will be using them.

Once you know the size and location of your leach field, you determine the number, length and configuration of the leach lines. Various slope and soil conditions affect these decisions. You can satisfy the sanitarian's determination of leach-field area by combining one to four lines in whatever lengths will give the required total square footage. For example, if the leach-line trench is 2 ft. wide, a 60-ft. line will have 120 sq. ft. of absorption area. There are many different methods of dealing with adverse conditions of slope and soil, including the problem of subsurface erosion, to ensure equal water distribution throughout the field. Again, complicated leach-field installations are best considered individually by engineers and county sanitarians. The variations are mind-boggling.

Let's assume your parcel is a gently sloping to flat area, with a good percolation rate suitable for the installation of leach lines. Leach line trenches normally are flat bottomed, no more than 60 ft. long, 24 in. wide, and 30 in. to 36 in. deep. They usually run in parallel lines along a level contour of land, at 10 ft. intervals. Viewed in cross section, the trench bottoms are filled with 12 in. of leach gravel, which is smooth, round rock, 1 in. to 2 in. in diameter (photo, below). Leach line pipe is then laid on top of the gravel. This pipe is 4-in. round Orangeburg perforated pipe, or drain tile (2 ft. sections of vitrified clay), or thin-walled ABS plastic pipe. Prior to filling, each pipe is plugged at the downhill end, and its uphill end is connected to the distribution box. Another 2 in. of gravel is packed around the top of the pipe. This is topped with a suitable permeable barrier, such as straw or newspaper, to allow evaporation. Finally, the trench is backfilled, hand compacted, and crowned 4 in. to 6 in. to allow for settling.

Correct grading of the leach field is of course essential. Before pipe is put into the trench, the rock surface should be smoothly pitched over the run of each leach line: 2 in. in 60 ft. is a standard pitch. Thus, the capped end of the leach pipe should be 2 in. lower than its beginning. A word of caution: Should the pipes be incorrectly positioned, an overabundance of water from the distribution box will be concentrated at low points along the way, saturating them while leaving the rest of the leach field dry. Roots that normally grow in the leach gravel bed will grow up into these spots, find their way into the leach pipes, clog the lines, create more flooding, and in turn attract more roots. Root-bound leach lines will quickly disable any septic system and clog the main sewer line from the house. By the time this happens, the only good remedy is to replace the root-bound section of pipe and regrade the entire run of leach line. If careful grading can be maintained during installation, a leach field should last 20 to 25 years, flooding septic water equally throughout its lines.

The distribution box—To distribute water equally throughout a leach field, each leach line must receive the same amount of water. This is the job of the distribution box. Usually made of concrete, and the size of a large truck tire, the distribution box sits between the septic tank and the leach field. It is part of the water-tight end of

Photos: Nan Motolinsky

Leach-line trenches are generally about 3 ft. deep and 2 ft. wide. This trench bottom is being filled with 12 in. of leach gravel—round stones 1 in. to 2 in. in diameter.

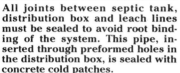

All joints between septic tank, distribution box and leach lines must be sealed to avoid root binding of the system. This pipe, inserted through preformed holes in the distribution box, is sealed with concrete cold patches.

Solid pipe

Serial distribution (flat land)

Perforated pipe

Gravel-filled absorption trench

Watertight joints at bend

Serial distribution (sloped land)

Solid pipe from septic tank

Perforated pipe

Tight joints

6 ft. min.

Undisturbed earth

Trench

Capped end

Undisturbed earth cut away to show pipe resting on gravel-filled trenches.

Tee connector   Ell connector

Backfill 12 in. min. to surface

Stone

a septic system. The box is designed to receive direct discharge of septic effluent from the septic tank and distribute that effluent into each leach-line outlet at an equal rate. The inlet to the distribution box is always higher than its outlet holes. Most standard boxes come with an inspection cover, an inlet hole preformed and open, and three or four outlet holes formed and sealed but easily knocked out with a hammer and cold chisel. Thus, the standard distribution box readily adapts to systems with one to four leach lines. The outlets are formed level so that the flooding of the box will be carried away equally to all lines. It is very important to set the distribution box level on firm ground. Problems can arise if a distribution box settles out of level, and floods more water into one side of the leach field, setting up the over-saturation syndrome.

The distribution box almost always connects to the septic tank on one side and the leach lines on the other by means of concrete cold patches (photo, above). These can be rather clumsy connections. The connecting pipes must be inserted into the tank outlets and patched with mortar. Cold joints such as these are prone to problems. They may misalign, due to settling and even early backfilling, thereby breaking the watertight integrity of the connection. Some tanks and distribution boxes come with pipes and receiving devices preformed in them. With these tanks and boxes, the standard mechanical plumbing connections can be made to ensure a watertight joint that is easily repaired.

Whichever method you use, a watertight connection must be made at all points uphill from the leach field. These points include leach lines to distribution box, distribution box to septic tank,

and septic tank to main building sewer. Any leaks at these points will immediately encourage the growth of roots into the septic-system passageways with the usual results. Here again, careful installation will secure your system and increase its longevity.

Although it is still commonly used, the distribution box may have seen its day. Some tests have shown that equal distribution to an entire drainage field may not be advantageous or possible. Varying rates of soil absorption can adversely affect the drain field, and there is some doubt that equal distribution of water can be maintained throughout the life of the system.

One alternative to the distribution box may be serial distribution of leach water. Serial distribution foregoes the use of the distribution box and pitched leach lines. In their place a series of level leach lines is successively flooded to saturation through the use of water-tight connection pipes. The drawings above show configurations used for flat and sloping land. On flat land the entire field is laid out on a level plane and is flooded simultaneously by interconnected leach lines. On sloping land a series of horizontal leach lines across the hill is joined by sloping pipes.

Both the distribution box and serial distribution lines receive effluent from the septic tank. This effluent should always be relatively clear water emanating from the middle to upper level of the septic tank. You should make periodic inspections, using the distribution box inspection cover or the cleanout on the pipe leading from the tank to the first serial trench. If solids or sludge flood the box or lines during a flush cycle from the house, the tank should be pumped immediately. The presence of sludge indicates

the tank's holding capacity has been reached and that clogging of the leach pipes will soon render the system inoperative.

The septic tank—The purpose of the septic tank is to provide a watertight settling basin for heavier-than-water solids and a semi-solid scum trap for lighter-than-water grease and fat, thus allowing only clarified, digested effluent to reach the leach field. The cross section of an operating septic tank should reveal three distinct layers of gravity settling. Raw sewage entering the holding tank liquid quickly separates into heavy solids, water and lighter-than-water grease and fat. The septic tank provides an anaerobic environment, in which there is no free oxygen. Special anaerobic bacteria digest the solids that enter the tank into a thick sludge, and give off methane gas bubbles. These gases rise to the top of the liquid level and help suspend the floating grease and fat above the water level until they are partially decomposed. These smaller particles can then sink back down through the liquid into a heavier sludge. The word "septic" refers to this anaerobic digestion of human waste.

For most homes a 750-gal. tank is adequate. Most codes allow from 1 to 7 people for a tank of this size, but require a 1,000-gal. tank for 8 to 10 people. If your household contains 11 to 15 people, you'll need a 1,500-gal. tank.

The modern, common septic tank is usually made of precast reinforced concrete (photo, facing page). Concrete is a perfect material for this use because it is strong, can be made watertight, and is non-corrosive. Other tanks presently being installed are built of hardened brick or solid concrete blocks, vitrified clay, or the increasingly popular thick-walled fiberglass. Fiberglass tanks can be used in difficult terrain where a large truck would be unable to deliver a very heavy, precast unit.

The inlet to all septic tanks from the building sewer line should be 3 in. above the waterline of the holding tank. The tank waterline is determined by the level of the tank outlet. Its level must be low enough to provide room for a 5-in. to 6-in. scum layer and a clear area at the top for gas travel between compartments. While many single-compartment tanks have performed well for many years, the general drift in septic-tank manufacture has been to two-compartment tanks. A baffle separates the two tank sections. The primary settling chamber is attached to the sewer line and receives all waste from the plumbing system of the house. The primary compartment is usually $\frac{2}{3}$ to $\frac{1}{2}$ of the total volume of the tank. This configuration is supposed to do a better job of digesting and precipitating surface scum, thus preventing it from traveling into the leach field. The inner tank baffle has a 4-in. flood pipe installed above the sludge level, to allow clear water to enter the second compartment, and a gas vent on top of the separation wall, to allow back-venting to the house sewer vents. The baffle holds the floating scum and grease in the primary settling chamber for a longer time, and should hold the sludge deposit in the first half of the tank until periodic pumping takes place. The second chamber should pass relatively clear water to the distribution box or primary leach trench.

Wastewater from the main sewer line should enter the septic tank through an open, vented tee drainage fitting. This configuration has two functions: to direct sewage to the bottom of the tank, and to release gases and displaced air back into the house venting system. The proper venting of all house drains connected to any septic tank is a must (see article "Venting the Plumbing System," pp. 96-97). These vents have a definite function. Every time the drain system is used, some water and solids quickly enter the septic tank. This added volume compresses the upper gas layer in the tank, and the excess pressure must be relieved back through the sewer line and into the building vents. If the venting system is improperly installed, or if there are no vents, the pressurized methane gas will vent back through the house plumbing fixtures.

While leach-line location is crucial and is dictated by the health department, you have more choice over placement of your septic tank. You should locate the tank as near the house as you can to minimize the length of the sewer line. The building sewer should travel in a straight line from the foundation to the septic tank inlet, and the tank should be placed with its inlet facing the building sewer as it comes from the house. A 12-in. minimum earth cover is required over this sewer line, which is generally 3-in. or 4-in. ABS plastic pipe. Finally, the tank position must conform to county building codes, which normally require a 10-ft. offset from the house foundation, a 10-ft. offset from any property line, and a 100-ft. offset from any water supply.

For proper maintenance of the septic system, you should install cleanouts where the building sewer leaves the house, at the junction of the building sewer and the septic tank (to facilitate location of the septic tank later), and at the outfall of the tank into the distribution box or primary leach trench.

An experienced backhoe operator should be able to install any standard septic system in a few days. A standard septic-system installation will cost between $1,000 and $2,500, including material and labor.

Maintenance—Care of a new septic system, or maintenance of an old one, requires knowing the location of its various components. With a new system, all the junctions, inspection covers and cleanouts should either be staked out or mapped. Maintenance of an existing system, buried long ago, can involve much more work. First, you must find the system. If you haven't any idea where your septic system was laid out, a good place to start the search is the main sewer outlet from your house. Observe the lay of the drain system under the house to determine the approximate location of the main sewer line; then use a soil probe to pinpoint the line. If your house is on a slab, try the exterior walls near the main bathroom. The septic tank should be at the end of the main drain. Be careful—many old tanks had wooden or light-gauge sheet metal lids. I am told you never forget falling into a septic tank.

Once you find the tank, check the condition of the lid and outfall piping. Mark the tank and inspection cover. If the septic system has been installed properly, only a few duties performed periodically will ensure its long life. Once or twice a year, depending on the size of the tank and the last time it was pumped, check the tank outlet to the leach field for passage of sludge. Use and tank size also will determine the appropriate pumping schedule: every two or three years, or at even longer intervals. Finally, an annual treatment of about 3 lb. of copper sulfate will discourage root growth. Flush it in late in the evening so maximum dilution can occur in the tank before the solution is flooded into the leach lines the next day.

Any discussion of septic systems has to be general. No two septic systems are alike; nor can any set of standards be applied to septic system installations nationwide. This is why local public-health officials have the final say on waterwaste disposal. It is their duty to protect the natural water source for us all. As long as most Americans use pure drinking water as the medium for waste disposal, while desiring pure water for other household uses, local sanitarians will have their work cut out for them. □

John Wetzler, a plumber, owns Wetzler Water Works in Little River, California.

A 1,200-gal. precast concrete septic tank is lowered into the ground. The white spot on the top of the tank is a cleanout cover. The hole will receive the 4-in. unperforated pipe that carries clear effluent to the distribution box.

Soldering Copper Pipe

A veteran plumber explains the art of copper joinery

by Niles T. Powell

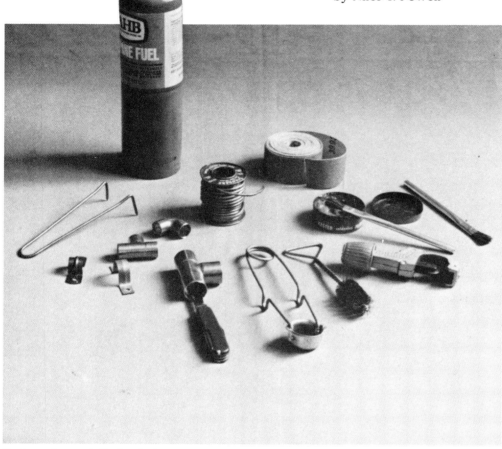

Tools and materials. Clockwise from back: propane gas canister with torch tip, wire solder, roll of emery paper, paste flux with flux brushes, tubing cutter, wire brush for cleaning inside fittings, spark igniter, different fittings and pipe supports (hangers).

If you know how to soft-solder a joint between a copper tube and its fitting, you can assemble most residential hot and cold-water supply lines. Sweating a joint, or soldering, is a technique for joining two metals by melting a third, softer metal between them. This third metal is called solder. A properly soldered joint looks neat and shiny, will not leak, and is nearly as strong as the materials it joins. The goal is to fill the narrow gap between the tube and fitting with solder so that there are no voids and the solder bonds well to both surfaces.

Materials and tools—The contents of a plumber's toolbox are pretty standard, as is the choice of materials if you're working with copper pipe (photo above). I'll cover these basics first, and then discuss soldering, step by step.

Tubing. Copper tubing, sometimes just called pipe, is sold hard-drawn in 10-ft. and 20-ft. lengths, or soft-drawn (malleable) in 30-ft., 60-ft. and 100-ft. rolls. For residential use, ⅝-in. or ⅞-in. outside-diameter tube is normally used. Hard-drawn tubing costs about half as much as malleable, and is more durable. But it takes longer to install because it can't be bent around corners, as the softer stuff can. Once installed, malleable tubing needs to be protected because it can easily be deformed by bumps or blows.

With both types of tubing, you have a choice of wall thickness. Hard-drawn tube is designated M, L or K, with M denoting the thinnest wall. Malleable tube comes only in L and K thicknesses. Type M is acceptable for most above-ground residential work, but it's best to check with your local building inspector for specific requirements. Manufacturers are required to mark approved copper water tube at frequent intervals with the appropriate letter as well as with a continuous color-coded stripe; type M is marked with a red stripe, type L with a blue stripe and type K with a green stripe.

Fittings. You need fittings for two purposes: to connect lengths of tubing and to make changes in direction. Fittings are made of cast brass or wrought copper and have a socket into which the tubing fits. At the bottom of each socket is a small bump or stop to prevent the tubing from penetrating too far into the fitting. There are fittings to make all kinds of intersections and changes in direction, and fittings that adapt to threads for valves, water heaters, faucets and other fixtures. Plumbing supply dealers have these items in stock.

Torch fuel. Propane, butane, Mapp gas and acetylene (also called Presto-lite) can be used as fuel for soldering work. The first three types of gas are sold in small, hand-held canisters that will accept an inexpensive torch tip.

Solder. The most common soft solders are mixtures of tin and lead that melt somewhere between 250°F and 550°F. Hard solders, which melt above 750°F, aren't required for most residential work, and a 50/50 mixture of tin and lead should be adequate for most jobs. Solder is available as bars and as rolled wire; most plumbers find the wire easier to use. It's best to get solid rather than hollow-core wire if you're soldering water supply lines.

Flux. Spread over the joint area before the solder is melted, flux prevents rapid oxidation on the mating surfaces, allowing the solder to flow freely into the joint for a good bond.

Pipe supports. These hangers secure runs of pipe under floor joists and against walls. The most common supports are simple metal straps that hook under the pipe and are nailed to a joist, but I prefer the newer plastic supports that fully enclose the pipe. Especially in long runs, they do a lot more to isolate pipe noise.

Tools. Don't cut tubing with a hacksaw; it usually leaves a ragged, out-of-square edge that is far more difficult to solder. Buy the best tubing cutter you can find, and make sure it is fitted with a copper-cutting wheel. This tool will adjust to any small tube diameter and make the required square cut quickly and easily. Most tubing cutters have a deburring tool attached, and you can use this to remove the burr on the inside of the tube that is left by the cutter. Some plumbers use a jackknife or a small round file for deburring.

Buff the outside of the tubing and the inside of the fitting socket with emery paper. This removes any foreign material adhering to the

From *Fine Homebuilding* magazine (August 1982) 10:40-41

copper and also gets rid of the oxidized surface layer around the joint so the solder will bond well. I have found that wet/dry 150-grit emery cloth in 1½-in. wide rolls works best; you just tear off a length and use it until it's worn out. Steel wool will also work. If you have a lot of joints to prepare, there are several sizes of circular wire brushes designed for cleaning tubing and inside different-sized fittings. These tools definitely save time on big jobs.

The flux brush is a small, inexpensive tool used for spreading the paste flux. It doesn't cost much, so buy several. If you burn one or drop it in the dirt, don't bother trying to clean it; just replace it with a new one.

For soldering the smaller sizes of copper water tube used in most residential water-supply systems, the least expensive type of torch is more than adequate. If you plan to solder larger sizes of tube or to work in cold weather, then you'll need a torch that produces more heat. You can switch either to a fuel gas that burns hotter or use a specialized torch tip that produces a hotter flame from any given gas. These tips cost more than standard screw-tip units, but they fit the same gas canisters and work well. Propane burns at the lowest temperature, and butane, Mapp gas and acetylene burn increasingly hotter.

To light your torch you'll need a striker, an inexpensive spark igniter that is far safer and quicker to use than matches. Turn the valve knob on your torch tip until you hear gas rushing out, hold the striker right beside the torch tip and squeeze its handle so that sparks shoot into the stream of gas. Once the torch is lit, adjust the gas flow to produce a steady flame that appears to be connected to the tip. If the flame drifts away from the tip, turn down the flow of gas. Every torch behaves differently, so it's a good idea to spend some time with your tool until you know its idiosyncrasies.

Cut, clean and join—These are the first steps in any joint-sweating job. To cut a length of copper tubing, adjust the knob on your tubing cutter so that the tube is held between the cutting wheel and the two rollers that oppose it. Slide the cutter along the tube until the cutting wheel lines up over the cut line. Turn the knob to seat the wheel slightly in the copper, and then rotate the entire unit around the tube. If you start to score a spiral, guide the cutter back onto the cut line so you get a groove that meets itself. Keep moving the cutter around the tube, tightening the knob gradually to deepen the groove. Soon you will have cut all the way through the wall. Developing the right touch with the tightening knob takes time. If you tighten too much, you'll distort the tube, break through its wall unevenly or make a large burr that's tough to remove. If you tighten too little, the job will just take a bit longer.

Now deburr the inside of the tube you've just cut. Whether you use a round file, a pocket knife, or a deburring tool, the goal here is the same: to produce a shiny, beveled inner edge to reduce the sound of rushing water when the system is on. If you're using a deburring tool, don't press the pointed blade into the tube with

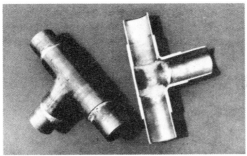

*A **well-made joint** has a solid, even solder bead on the outside and a smooth band of solder inside. The tube has been deburred and beveled.*

Sweating a T-joint. Heat the joint until the flux boils, then feed the solder wire into the joint until a bead of melted solder forms around it. Sheet metal protects the nearby wood.

so much pressure that the tube end flares. Just keep tooling the inside edge until you can't detect a ridge with your finger.

Buff the outside surface of the tube that will go into the fitting, plus an extra ¼ in. of length for good measure. You can use emery cloth or steel wool, but keep at it until the copper is clean and uniformly shiny. This step is critical to the strength of the soldered joint, so do it carefully. Perform the same operation on the inside of the fitting, and then coat the buffed parts with a thin film of paste flux. If you miss fluxing a spot, the solder may not flow there, but if you use too much flux it will harden in the tube and eventually wash out. While flux is not considered toxic, it will impart a greasy taste to the water. Achieve a happy medium between these two extremes by brushing on a light but thorough coat. Now you're ready to solder. Almost. If you're joining new tube to an existing system, make sure that you drain the line you're working on. Also, to protect them from heat change, remove the rubber or synthetic packing from any fittings to be soldered.

Insert the tubing into the fitting until it bottoms against the stop. All tubes joining a particular fitting should be prepared, assembled and soldered at once unless prohibited by special circumstances. It's difficult to solder one end of a fitting without heating the other end to the melting point and disturbing the previously soldered joint. Support the joint where it is to be installed and protect any nearby combustible materials from the torch with a scrap of sheet metal or asbestos-cement board. I prefer to use the sheet metal since it can be bent into tight spots where the rigid board won't fit. If you are prefabricating a joint (soldering it in one location to be installed in another), you should still set it up so that all parts are supported. All joints should be kept motionless while they are cooling. Always try to solder soon after fluxing, because after a few minutes the flux will start to oxidize the copper, and this can contaminate the joint.

Turn on the heat—The torch flame is composed of an outer mantle of yellow, an approximately conical blue core, and an invisible inner core of unburned gases. The hottest part of the

flame is at the tip of the blue cone. Use it to warm the tube first, but be careful not to burn the flux. I usually direct the flame away from the exposed flux. Then heat the socket of the fitting. When the flux begins to boil, direct the flame more toward the center of the fitting; this maintains an even level of heat in the joint area without overheating the joint. Now touch the tip of your wire solder to the intersection of the tube and fitting. If it flows readily into the joint, take the heat away and continue feeding solder into the joint until it flows around the tube. If the solder doesn't flow, keep heating the fitting until it does.

Finally, after the fitting has cooled enough for the solder to harden but while it is still warm, wipe the joint thoroughly with a soft, dry cloth. This removes the corrosive flux residue and produces a clean, shiny surface. Don't try to hasten cooling with a wet rag, because this can cause tiny fractures that will weaken the joint. Before you turn the water on, examine the finished joint carefully for flaws.

Practice makes perfect—Solder is carried into the joint by capillary action. It will flow uphill into a properly heated fitting as well as downhill. But in most cases you can't see where the solder is going, so determining if it has flowed properly is a sense that you'll gain by experience. If you haven't soldered before, do a few practice joints before trying your hand at water supply lines. Try soldering a short length of tube to one end of a straight coupling fitting; then you can look inside the fitting and see where the solder has gotten to. What you should see inside and outside the fitting is a tight, even bead of solder at both junctures of tube and fitting. If solder has run down inside the fitting or if it has been sucked inside the fitting and no bead appears on the outside, then the joint was too hot when you applied the solder. Holes or bubbles in the solder bead also indicate excess heat. If no solder appears inside the fitting, the joint wasn't hot enough. A smooth, even coat of solder in the joint means you've done everything right. □

Niles Powell is a general, electrical and plumbing contractor based in Oakland, Calif.

Remodel Plumbing

How to connect the new pipes to the old ones

by Steve Larson

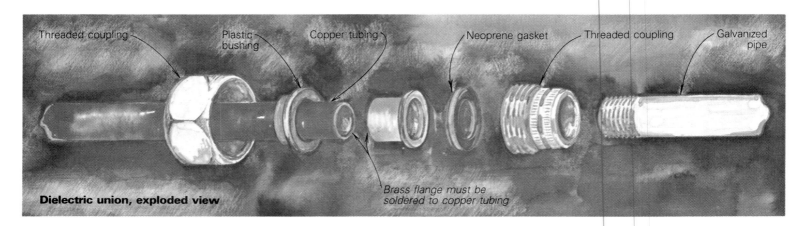

Threaded coupling · Plastic bushing · Copper tubing · Neoprene gasket · Threaded coupling · Galvanized pipe

Brass flange must be soldered to copper tubing

Dielectric union, exploded view

Sound connections. **New copper lines can't be joined directly to old galvanized supply lines, or the metal will corrode. Therefore building codes often specify use of a dielectric union (drawing, top). In the center of the photo, a dielectric union-to-steel nipple screws into the leg of a galvanized tee. Coming off the same tee is a brass nipple/brass union/copper tubing transition. New galvanized pipe is tied into an existing galvanized line with a tee fitting, nipples and union (drawing, right).**

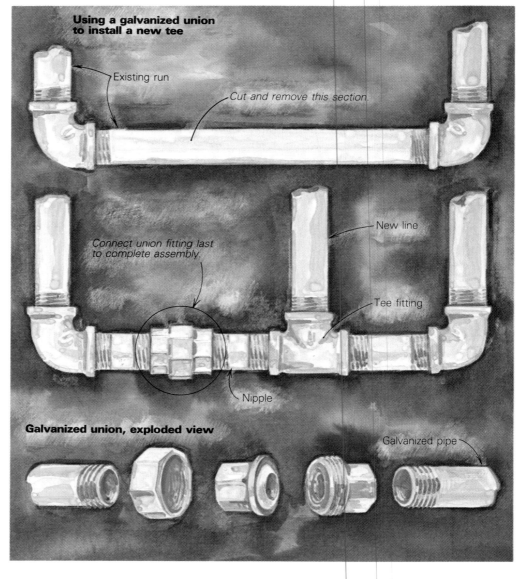

Using a galvanized union to install a new tee

Existing run

Cut and remove this section.

New line

Connect union fitting last to complete assembly.

Tee fitting

Nipple

Galvanized union, exploded view

Galvanized pipe

At some time in just about every remodeling job, new plumbing has to be joined with the old. You might be replacing a corroded supply line, plumbing a bathroom addition or relocating the lines for a remodeled kitchen. Most plumbers agree that remodel plumbing is far different from doing new work. Sometimes it's as simple as connecting new fixtures to the old lines, but often it's an excruciating exercise in Murphy's Law. The old-pipe diameters aren't the same as the new ones, the pipes aren't made of the same materials and your workspace is ideal for a dwarf contortionist. Fortunately, these are common problems, and those who have been down this road before have figured out some good solutions. This article is a stew of advice, products and tools that can make your remodel plumbing connections work out for the best.

Checking out the old system—Before hooking into the old system, you have to look at what's really there. Check for obvious leaks and look for traces of rust or corrosion on the outside of galvanized fittings. Reduced water flow and rusty tap water are signs that the water-supply system may be ready to rupture. A rust-weakened pipe that might otherwise last for years will often break apart with the first torque of the pipe wrench.

Restricted flow can be caused not only by rust buildup but also by non-corrosive mineral deposits. But in either case, when you start knocking around the old pipes you will often dislodge enough crud to clog things up somewhere else. Make sure that the existing drain lines are working well and that they are properly vented and sloped before you tie into them. Your new work may be fine, but if it overloads a dying system, you'll be the one to inherit the problems.

Tapping into supply lines—If the old supply lines are in good shape, choose a place to tap into them that's close to your new fixtures. You'll also want to make sure that your tap-in location is easy to get at so that you won't lose time working in cramped quarters.

Most older homes have galvanized water-supply pipes, but I recommend using copper tubing for all new supply lines because it will last longer than galvanized and it's easier to cut and assemble (see article on pp. 90-91). Some plumbers have switched completely to plastic pipe and fittings, since two new materials—chlorinated polyvinyl chloride (CPVC) and polybutylene (PB) can even be used for hot-water supply lines. But plastic supply lines haven't been approved by many local building codes, so you'll have to check your municipal regulations before using them. For drain, waste and vent (DWV) lines, I always use plastic for economy and ease of work, and there's little code resistance to this.

If the old line is galvanized pipe, you'll have to cut into it with a hacksaw or a reciprocating saw. If the line is copper, use a tubing cutter. In a tight space, a compact tubing cutter is indispensable for breaking into a copper line. Lacking this, you'll have to use a hacksaw

blade. In any case, make sure the water is turned off before you cut the line, and have a bucket handy to catch the drain-off.

If you're joining new copper tube to existing galvanized supply lines, the dissimilar metals will corrode each other unless you use a dielectric union. This special fitting separates the two types of pipe with a non-metallic gasket (drawing, facing page, top). For the same reason, support copper tubing with brass, copper, plastic or plastic-coated hangers.

A dielectric union in a grounded water pipe will break the ground circuit—the gasket inside the union won't conduct electricity. So this circuit must be reconnected by bridging the dielectric union with clamps and ground wire. Some local codes require a continuous ground wire, so it's important to check with your building inspector.

Another way to join copper and galvanized supply lines is with a brass union and nipple (photo facing page). The brass doesn't corrode in contact with copper or galvanized steel, so it's a good transitional material. Again, codes vary, so check with your inspector for the preferred coupling.

Dielectric unions have a flange that must be soldered to the copper tubing. So that you don't overheat the gaskets, remove them before soldering. And when you solder tubing in place, always keep a spray bottle of water within reach in case something starts to smolder. Otherwise, by the time you crawl out from under the house, you might need a fire truck to put out what one quick squirt could have quenched—and the water is probably turned off too.

If you choose to continue using galvanized pipe, a galvanized union will allow you to insert a tee with minimum dismantling of the old lines (drawing, facing page, bottom). You'll have to cut a small section from an existing straight run of pipe using a hacksaw or reciprocating saw. Again, pick a location that's accessible. Ideally there should be some play in the old pipe so that you will be able to push or pull the line slightly to get your final fit. If the old line is rigidly held in place, you'll have to be more exact in fitting nipples and tees into the section you've cut from the old pipe. Remember to add ⅜ in. to ½ in. for each threaded connection. The last connection will be the two halves of the union itself.

Threading pipe in place—If you're working on galvanized supply lines, you'll probably have to cut and thread pipe in place. The alternative is to remove an entire existing section to alter or replace it. If your workspace is cramped, or if the old pipe is too corroded to take new threads, you'll save time and aggravation by simply replacing it. But in many cases cut or broken galvanized pipe can be threaded in place using a ratcheted pipe threader (photo right). It holds the die in a ratchet assembly and requires only 1¼ in. of clearance around the pipe.

Most plumbers own several pipe threaders, but they're expensive, so you might want to rent one from a contractor's tool yard. Even

with the best tool, threading a pipe in place can be a knuckle-busting proposition. Apart from working in cramped quarters, you have to keep the pipe from wiggling around, as it usually wants to. The best way to do this is to clamp or block the pipe against nearby framing members, or to hold it in place with a pipe wrench. Another trick in tight spaces is to replace the threader's standard handle with a shorter section of ¾-in. threaded pipe.

Flexible connectors—When a new house is being plumbed, water heaters are normally joined to the hot and cold lines by means of rigid pipe and standard unions, but I find it a timesaver to use flexible water-heater connectors. They easily bend to reach a repositioned heater, or one with an intake line in a different location. Where I live, in earthquake country, I strap the water heater to the frame of the house, especially when I'm using flexible connectors. And if the heater doesn't have a temperature/pressure-relief valve, install one in the hot line at the top of the heater or at the specifically marked outlet on the heater itself.

The offset closet flange is another helpful fitting for remodel plumbers. It allows you to change the mounting position of the toilet slightly by rotating the flange. If you need to move a toilet a few inches one way or another to gain some clearance, if you're installing a new unit with different wall-to-flange dimensions, or if you want to avoid chopping into a floor joist, this is the fitting to use.

Tying into the DWV system—The traditional way of plumbing drain, waste and vent lines is with cast-iron pipe. Pipe sections have a bell-shaped hub at one end, and a small ridge called a spigot at the other. The spigot fits into the hub, leaving a small gap that is packed with oakum (an oily, rope-like material) and sealed with molten lead (photos p. 95, left and bottom right). Working with cast-iron pipe is difficult under the best of circumstances, but dragging it around under a house or through a hot and dusty attic while remodeling can be a nightmare.

Fortunately, plastic pipe (ABS schedule 40

A ratcheted pipe threader needs only 1¼ in. of clearance around the pipe, making it ideal for threading pipe in place. For extremely tight spaces, the handle can be replaced with a short section of ¾-in. threaded pipe.

Photo this page: Steve Larson; Illustrations: Barbara Smolover

A snap cutter is used for cutting cast-iron drain, waste and vent (DWV) pipe or clay-tile sewer pipe. Integral cutters break through the pipe as the chain is tightened. In this photo, a plumber is adjusting the tension of the chain before snapping the pipe by bringing the scissor handles together.

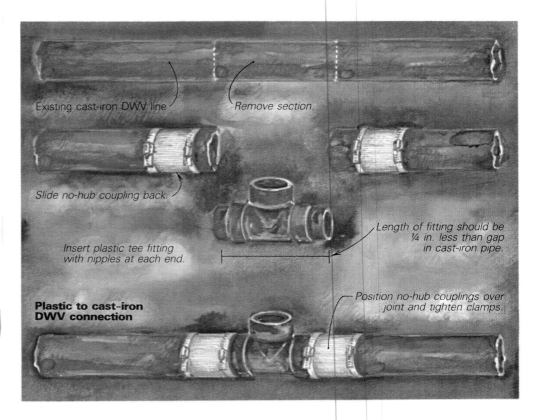

Existing cast-iron DWV line

Remove section.

Slide no-hub coupling back.

Insert plastic tee fitting with nipples at each end.

Length of fitting should be ¼ in. less than gap in cast-iron pipe.

Position no-hub couplings over joint and tighten clamps.

Plastic to cast-iron DWV connection

or PVC-DWV) can be substituted for cast iron in nearly all residential applications (check with your building inspector). Runs of exterior DWV line are an important exception. Sunlight can cause the plastic to decompose, and extreme temperature changes can cause it to expand and contract enough to break its seal with the roof flashing or with horizontal branch lines. Our local codes allow plastic vent lines on the exterior of the house if they are coated with two coats of latex paint.

If you're joining new plastic waste lines to an existing cast-iron system, you'll probably have to cut the metal pipe at some point. I know plumbers who have used a hammer and cold chisel for this job, but I don't recommend this approach. The best tool to use for cutting cast-iron or clay sewer pipe is the soil-pipe cutter, also called the snap cutter. You can usually rent one at the tool yard or plumbing-supply store.

Most snap cutters have a heavy chain that you tighten around the pipe until the cutting discs in the chain snap the pipe in two (photo above). The snap cutter almost always makes a clean cut, but occasionally old pipe will break unevenly. Another snap usually solves the problem. Whenever I can't afford a mistake, I use a reciprocating saw with a metal-cutting blade. A masonry blade will cut clay sewer pipe in similar fashion.

New plastic pipe can be joined to old cast-iron pipe with the no-hub coupling, a neoprene sleeve that is clamped around the plastic and iron pipes with adjustable, stainless-steel collars, as shown in the drawing above. The collars are just larger versions of the hose clamps used on auto radiators. You tighten them with a nut driver or a screwdriver (the former tool does a faster job). The neoprene sleeve fits over the ends of both pipes, and

tightening the collars makes the connection watertight. Because the seal on a no-hub coupling relies completely on the compression of the neoprene sleeve, it's important to clean or file the outside of the old pipe to remove rust, dirt or other projections.

The outside diameter of 3-in. or 4-in. cast-iron DWV pipes will usually be about ¼ in. smaller than the outside diameter of plastic DWV pipes. You can often deal with this discrepancy by cranking down tighter on the cast-iron side of the collar, but in some jurisdictions the building inspector will want you to use Mission couplings. These are identical to the no-hub coupling except that they have a stepped sleeve that accommodates the slight difference in pipe diameter.

Pipes with substantially different wall thicknesses, such as clay to cast iron, are often joined with a Calder coupling (photo facing page, top right). This connector is similar to the no-hub coupling, but is used with adapter bushings, or donuts, of different sizes.

If you run into a situation where you need a Calder coupling but can't lay your hands on one right away, you can wrap a strip of inner tube around the smaller pipe until you've bushed it out to the diameter of the larger one; then join the pipes with a standard no-hub fitting. If the pipes are roughly horizontal, make sure that the strip of inner tube starts and stops at the top of the pipe. This trick isn't sanctioned by code, so you should use it only as a temporary measure.

Plastic pipe has been around long enough so that you may come across an existing plastic DWV system in renovation work. An easy way to tie into such a system is with a glue-on saddle tee. Just cut a hole in the existing pipe (make sure it's the same size as the inside pipe diameter of the tee), swab the tee fitting

with glue and then temporarily hose-clamp it in place until the glue sets.

Testing your work—A thorough inspection of any remodel plumbing is essential, since a leak can damage the home and ruin the furnishings. Once, in the middle of an upstairs remodeling job, I learned a lesson that I won't soon forget. I'd installed some new copper supply lines, and before heading home for the evening, I turned on the water and checked them thoroughly for leaks. There weren't any, so I left the supply system on. But an overheated solder joint let loose a few hours later, and several hundred gallons of water spewed out all night long. Luckily, it flowed into an area we were planning to remodel anyway.

Now whenever I'm plumbing upstairs, I use air pressure instead of water to test new lines. The idea is to isolate the new plumbing from the old, cap off any openings, attach an air-pressure gauge and pump up the system with an air compressor or a bicycle pump. Pressure test gauges are available at plumbing-supply outlets, and they accept a ¾-in. nipple. I leave the gauge on for a few hours (local code says 15 minutes). If the system loses pressure, I know I've got a leak. I locate it by squirting a detergent/water solution on each pipe joint. Instead of spewing a stream of water, a leak will blow bubbles. This lets me find leaks without producing puddles. If a joint leaks, I don't have to drain water out of the lines to resolder.

For final hookups between new fixtures and the old system, you'll have to rely on the standard test of running water through the lines and watching for leaks. □

Steve Larson is a building and remodeling contractor in Santa Cruz, Calif.

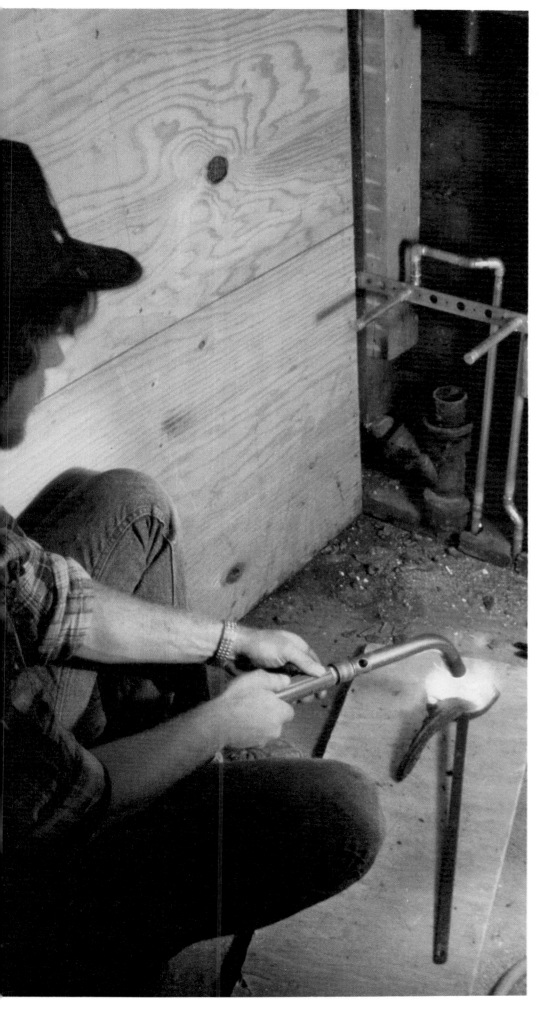

Cast-iron and clay waste lines are connected with a Calder coupling. A thick bushing fits over the smaller pipe to equalize the different outside diameters.

Adding drain, waste and vent lines. Most new DWV lines are plastic, but in old houses, they need to be joined to existing cast-iron pipe. At left, lead is melted with a torch, then poured around the oakum-packed joint between the cast-iron bell housing and nipple of the waste line, above, to seal it. Then a plastic sanitary tee fitting will be plumbed onto the cast-iron nipple with a no-hub coupling. A neoprene sleeve will seal the joint.

Venting the Plumbing System

Unvented fixtures are dangerous; understanding how the system works will help avoid health hazards

by Michael Litchfield

When Americans brought the privy indoors in the late 19th century, they also brought potential health hazards into their homes. Indoor plumbing was first developed in large urban areas where, following epidemics of diptheria and cholera, the importance of venting the plumbing system was discovered.

The first indoor toilets did have water traps to keep the smell of sewage at bay, but these water seals were often broken by falling wastes that created a partial vacuum in drainage pipes; air was sucked through fixture openings and water was siphoned from the traps. A source of air independent from fixture-drain openings was needed to maintain atmospheric pressure so wastes would fall freely and siphoning would not occur. Vent pipes linking fixture traps to outside air solved this problem, and were incorporated into sanitary plumbing systems.

This venting primer will help you to understand accepted practices and evaluate your venting system. Before remodeling or planning a new installation, consult your local plumbing code for specific requirements in your area.

A typical residential vent system (shown in the drawing) consists of a network of pipes ultimately connected to a source of fresh air. Air for venting is drawn into the *stack vent*, which rises above roof level and runs vertically through the house until it connects to the upper end of the *building main*. The nearly-horizontal building main carries all house wastes to the sewer or septic tank. The *soil stack* receives wastes from all plumbing fixtures, including toilets, and acts as a vent for those fixture drain pipes located close enough to be directly connected to it. The *vent stack* joins the soil stack above the highest (and sometimes below the lowest) drain pipe emptying into the soil stack. Vent stacks don't carry any wastes; rather, they supply air to the *branch vents* of individual fixture traps. Where plumbing fixtures are inconveniently located for a branch-vent or vent-stack connection, a separate stack vent can run from the fixture through the roof. Stack vents that vent toilets are also called *soil vents*.

Knowing what a vent system looks like makes planning a layout easier, but there is also an important distinction between vent types that affects planning decisions. If a vent is sometimes used as a drain for fixtures placed above it on a pipe run, it is a *wet vent*; if it carries no wastes, it is a *dry vent*. Some building codes require dry venting to ensure that no vent will clog due to wastes entering the pipe higher up. If some wet venting is allowed, you can save money by using less piping and fewer connectors. In practice, many venting hookups are combinations of wet and dry venting, with toilets clustered at the soil stacks (wet venting) and other fixtures venting into a vent stack (dry venting).

Clustering plumbing fixtures around a soil stack is probably the oldest method of venting. This technique, also known as *stack venting*, employs the soil stack as both a waste drain and a vent pipe. It's the easiest, most direct and most effective venting method. It offers little flexibility in arranging plumbing fixtures, yet the savings on plumbing supplies are considerable, and cuts through wall studs and floor joists are kept to a minimum.

In stack venting, a toilet should not be installed above any other fixtures on the stack because its discharge could break the water seals in the traps of the smaller fixtures below. (To add fixtures below those already stack-vented, use a vent stack and branch vents.)

The maximum allowable distance from stack-vented fixtures to the soil stack depends on the size of the pipe servicing each fixture:

Waste-pipe inside dia. (in.)	Max. distance to soil stack (ft.)
1¼	2½
1½	3½
2	5
3	6
4	10

Although you can increase the waste-pipe diameter to bridge longer distances to the soil stack, in reality, this may be impractical. While the chart above indicates a maximum distance of 6 ft. for a 3-in. waste pipe, a stack-vented toilet is more commonly located 3 ft. to 5 ft. from the soil stack. The 10-ft. distance given for a 4-in. diameter pipe is theoretically possible, but can also cause problems: The difficulty in routing so long a pipe and the hazards involved in cutting through floor joists often make back venting a better choice.

Continuous venting, or *back venting*, consists of a vent stack and several branch vents. It's more complex and more expensive than stack venting, but it satisfies the most stringent plumbing codes. Although the small-diameter vent pipes (2 in. or less) used in back venting are not difficult to hide inside walls, routing the maze of pipes can be tricky, especially in renovations.

The angle at which a branch vent leaves a waste pipe is crucial: It may go straight up or, to work around an awkward spot, at 45° to the waste pipe's take-off, but the branch must never exit off the side of the waste pipe, since it could become clogged with waste.

Branch vents must rise to at least 42 in. above the floor before beginning their "horizontal" run to vent stacks. This measurement adds a safety margin of 6 in. to the height of the highest fixture in the room, usually a kitchen sink set at 36 in. The horizontal run to the vent stack is, in fact, always pitched at least ⅛ in. per foot upward toward the source of fresh air.

When fixtures are too distant for vent-stack connection, as when a laundry room and bathroom are at opposite ends of a house, a separate vent can be run from the fixture through the roof. Avoid such individual stack vents if you can, for they are expensive, unsightly and create another place where the roof could leak.

In areas where plumbing codes are lax or not enforced, one occasionally sees separate stack vents piercing exterior house siding and running up the side to the roof. Such vents look terrible, even if they are boxed in, and are virtually illegal in the United States, being allowed only in areas where there is no danger of frost, which could build up inside the pipe and reduce its diameter or clog it completely.

Before deciding on a venting method and layout, you must size the vent system. This can be complicated, and plumbers often consult a number of tables that interrelate fixture discharge, the number of fixtures per horizontal waste pipe, vent-pipe lengths and pipe diameters. If you are unsure about the capacity of your system, by all means have a professional calculate it for you; in fact, many building codes require this.

Pipe sizes required for residential applications vary according to local codes, but some are fairly

From *Fine Homebuilding* magazine (February 1981) 1:34-35

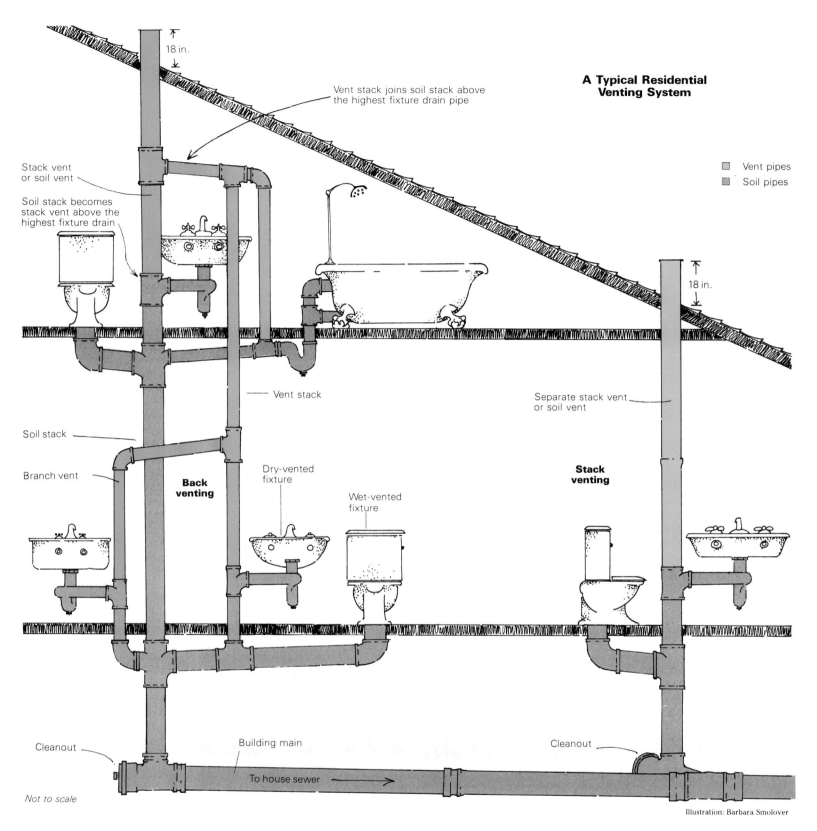

18 in.

Vent stack joins soil stack above
the highest fixture drain pipe

**A Typical Residential
Venting System**

Stack vent
or soil vent

Soil stack becomes
stack vent above the
highest fixture drain

Vent pipes
Soil pipes

18 in.

Vent stack

Separate stack vent
or soil vent

Soil stack

Branch vent

Dry-vented
fixture

**Back
venting**

Wet-vented
fixture

**Stack
venting**

Cleanout

Building main

Cleanout

To house sewer

Not to scale

Illustration: Barbara Smolover

standard. (All pipe sizes refer to interior diameters.) The soil stack is commonly 3 in., but the greater carrying capacity of a 4-in. stack makes it a prudent choice if future renovation is likely and you intend to add more fixtures. Further, codes in some colder regions specify a 4-in. enlarger on the soil stack just before that stack pierces the roof; this prevents a buildup of frost from clogging the pipe. All stacks must extend 1½ ft. to 2 ft. above the roof, depending on local codes. Other sizes include 4-in. building mains and 1½-in. branch vents. Waste pipes for most

fixtures are 1½ in., except for toilets (3 in.), kitchen sinks and shower stalls (2 in. each).

When you begin laying out and executing a venting system, make it as simple and compact as codes will allow. Plumbing supplies are expensive—especially copper pipe—and you don't want to buy more than you need for an efficient system. The fewer jogs and bends you include, the fewer fittings you'll need for the job; each fitting is costly and a potential source of leaks. Try to cluster fixtures around vent and soil stacks; run vertical pipes inside walls and hori-

zontal ones between joists, and don't cut into the structure any more than you must. Where studs and joists don't allow your hiding pipes between them, you can box out individual pipes, build elevated floor sections, and resort to lowered ceilings to gain the space you need. ☐

Michael Litchfield is Fine Homebuilding's *founding managing editor. Technical assistance was supplied by licensed plumbers Nate Dembowitz of Cheshire, Conn., and Frank Petrone of Rocky Hill, Conn.*

Installing a Toilet

It's mostly in the flange

by George Skaates

Plumbing fixtures like sinks and toilets are among the last items to be installed in a bathroom. By the time the room is ready for them, the finished counters are atop their cabinets, the floors are down and the baseboards and walls are painted. Ordinarily, there is an extra measure of satisfaction for a plumber as these fixtures are put in place because they signal the end of the job. I say ordinarily because if the drain and supply lines aren't in the right place for these fixtures, this last phase can be a nightmare for the plumber—especially if the toilet connections are misplaced. With a lavatory, the hookups are usually made inside a cabinet, and adjustments are hidden from view. But it's hard to hide a toilet that is too far from the wall or off center in its bay because the flange was carelessly affixed to the subfloor in the wrong place. And if the position of the water supply isn't correct for the type of toilet that's being installed, you might have to tear out part of a finished wall in order to make things fit.

Layout—Most toilets are roughed in at 12 in. from the finished wall. This means that the centerline of the closet flange, the fitting to which the toilet is attached, should be 12 in. from whatever wall surface will eventually cover the framing behind the toilet. Since most houses are finished with ½-in. drywall, the centerline of the flange ends up 12 ½ in. from the framing. If the wall surface is to be thicker, for instance a layer of drywall followed by mortar and tile, you have to allow for the additional thickness as you position the closet flange. Finished walls to the side of the toilet should be at least 15 in. away from the centerline of the closet flange.

All is not lost if you put the flange a bit too close or too far from the back wall. Toilets are available for 10-in. and 14-in. flange positions. But like other oddball orders, you pay a premium for these special fixtures.

The water supply for most toilets should leave the wall about 6 in. to the left of the center of the closet flange and about 6 in.

above the level of the finished floor (drawing below). This position is correct for all the two-piece toilets (where the tank and bowl are separate) I've ever installed, but not for the one-piece, integral tank-and-bowl toilets known as lowboys. They need a supply line about 2 ½ in. to 3 in. above the floor. If you are at all in doubt about the supply-line and flange positions for a toilet, check the manufacturer's spec sheet for the location.

Closet-bend anchorage—When I rough in the drain for the toilet, I make sure the closet bend is secured to the framing with strapping (photo 1). The importance of this step cannot be overemphasized. If you ignore it, the coupling between the toilet and the drain line will flex over a period of time, and that will lead to a broken seal. Eventually the toilet will leak. To anchor cast-iron drain systems, our crew uses 20-ga. galvanized steel strapping called band iron. Most often, I'll place a 2x4 block under the closet bend to

1. In wood-frame construction, a closet bend should be supported from below with a 2x4 block and held in place with strapping.

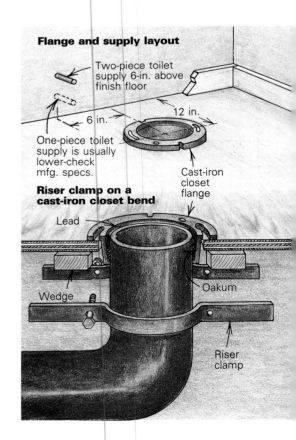

Flange and supply layout

Two-piece toilet supply 6-in. above finish floor

6 in.

12 in.

One-piece toilet supply is usually lower-check mfg. specs.

Cast-iron closet flange

Riser clamp on a cast-iron closet bend

Lead

Wedge

Oakum

Riser clamp

Drawings by Michael Mandarano

provide solid bearing and a place to attach the band iron.

If the floor construction is such that I can't easily install a block, I'll use a riser clamp on a cast-iron drain. A riser clamp is composed of two steel bars. Each one is deformed in the middle to form a U-shaped cradle. In use, the bars are bolted together to encircle the pipe near the point where the closet bend passes through the subfloor. As shown in the drawing (left), the riser clamp should be far enough away from the subfloor to allow room for the closet flange. Wedges driven between the subfloor and the riser clamp complete the assembly.

Plastic closet bends should be secured with plastic strapping. Don't use steel strapping for this as the constant expansion and contraction of the plastic pipes will work the fitting against the steel straps' sharp edges.

Another way to anchor a plastic closet bend is with a fitting called a Stay Put Stabilizer (drawing below). Made by Specialty Products Company (P.O. Box 186, Stanton, Calif. 90631), the stabilizer is cemented to the closet bend, then nailed through the flange and into the subfloor.

For eliminating closet-bend movement in slab floors, Specialty Products makes another stabilizer that is installed prior to the pour (drawing below). On slabs, you've got to wrap the pipe stub where it emerges from the concrete to allow room for the closet flange. This goes for plastic or cast iron. I use Flexwrap for this (Cal Western Supply, 1111A East Houston, Visalia, Calif. 93291). It is a pliable foam, about ⅛-in. thick, that comes in 8-in. wide rolls. I build it up around the pipe until I've got

a layer ⅝-in. or so thick. When the foam is removed after the slab has cured, I've got the necessary cavity to accept the flange.

Flange to plastic drain line—About two-thirds of my customers want plastic drain lines—the others ask for cast iron. With plastic pipe, the flange is installed after the pipe stub protruding above the level of the floor has been trimmed (photo 2). For this operation, I use a flexible handsaw made just for cutting plastic pipe. It bends enough to make a cut that's flush with the level of the floor.

A closet flange for a plastic drain line has a plastic collar coupled with a painted steel ring that bears on the floor (photo 3). The collar fits over the pipe stub, and once the fit is right, it is glued to the stub with the same solvent-type cement used to assemble the pipes and their fittings. When a floor has been tiled (or, as in this case, covered with marble), tilesetters will sometimes let their

mortar and thinset get a little too close to the pipe to allow room for the flange. If this happens, bust out a groove for the flange with a cold chisel, or use a reciprocating saw with a masonry blade to cut a channel (photo 4).

Once you've got the flange cemented to the stub, secure the ring with galvanized screws. Use a masonry bit to drill through any tile between the ring and the substrate. If I'm affixing the ring to a slab floor, I will use concrete screws or lag screws driven into plastic shields.

A closet flange for plastic drain pipe has a pair of slots in the metal ring that accept closet bolts (photo 5). The slots allow the bolts, which have T-shaped heads, to be slid around for adjustment.

Flange to cast-iron drain line—A cast-iron closet flange is a beefier version of the one used for plastic drains, and it has slots and a pair of notches for locating the closet bolts. I

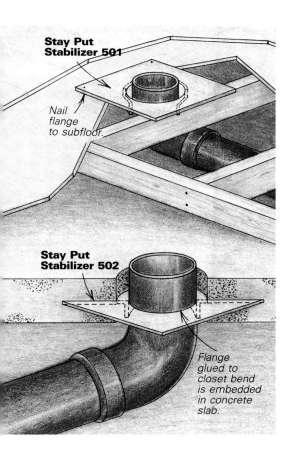

2. **Before installing a closet flange, cut the plastic pipe flush with the floor.**

3. **Slots in the steel ring of a closet flange accept closet bolts. They will protrude through holes in the base of the toilet.**

4. **Sometimes tile or stone floor coverings will crowd the pipe stub, making it difficult to install the closet flange. When this happens, use a cold chisel or a reciprocating saw to make room for the flange.**

5. **Closet bolts are made of brass and have machine threads and a T-shaped head. The head fits into the slot in the flange ring, and the bolt slides into position. Then, the head is turned 90°, and the bolt is tightened in place.**

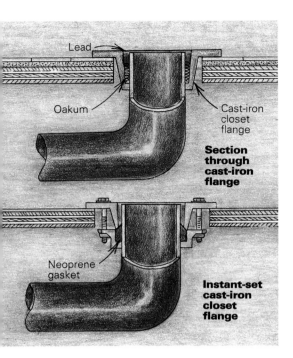

Lead

Oakum

Cast-iron
closet
flange

**Section
through
cast-iron
flange**

Neoprene
gasket

**Instant-set
cast-iron
closet
flange**

6. Skaates uses a yarning iron to push the oakum into the space between the cast iron closet flange and the drain. Next he will use a packing iron (the right-hand tool in the trio above) to press it home.

7. A bent-handled ladle, anchored by a box full of pipe nipples, makes a handy basin in which to catch molten lead.

don't use the slots because the iron is very thin at this point in the casting, and I've seen it break under the stress of tightening the closet bolts. Stick with the notches and you'll avoid this problem.

Unlike the installation of a closet flange in a plastic drain system, you trim the cast-iron stub after the flange has been installed. The flange hub, which is slightly tapered, fits over the pipe, leaving a gap of about ¼ in. all the way around (above drawing). I make the seal between the two with lead and oakum.

Oakum is a sticky material made of hemp fibers that have been treated with tar. Plumbers use yarning irons and packing irons to stuff the oakum into the space between the closet flange and the drain (photo 6). I pack the oakum down until there is a space about 1 in. deep for the lead.

I have a small acetylene torch that I use for sweat-soldering copper pipes. It also comes in handy for melting lead for small jobs like this. Holding a lead ingot with a pair of pliers, I can fill a ladle in a hurry by heating the side of the ingot (photo 7). A word of caution: If you need to melt lead in quantity with a setup like a cast-iron pot atop a burner, don't add cold or wet pieces of lead to a batch that has already melted. To do so runs the risk of a nasty explosion that can send molten lead flying through the air.

When I've got enough molten lead, I use my ladle to pour it into the joint between the flange and the drain line (photo 8). When it hits the cold iron, it sets up immediately, shrinking slightly in the process. To make up for the shrinkage, the lead has to be driven downward slightly with caulking irons. Caulking irons resemble cold chisels, but they have blunt, radiused ends matching the curvature of the pipe and the fitting. I use one iron to set the outside edge of the lead (photo 9), and another to tap home the inside edge where it meets the drain line. This

isn't a bone-crusher operation—a couple of light taps in each spot will do, but be sure to cover the entire surface of the lead.

I finish up a cast-iron closet-flange installation by trimming off any excess drain line with an internal pipe cutter, (photo 10)which scores the inside of the pipe until it snaps. If you don't have access to one of these cutters, use a grinder to cut a shallow groove around the outside of the drainpipe where it meets the flange. Then use a crescent wrench as a lever to bust off the unwanted stub. Clean up the ragged edges with a grinder (make sure to protect the walls), and you're ready to screw the flange to the floor.

While a closet flange for a plastic drain will likely have half a dozen screw holes in the steel ring, a cast-iron flange has only two. This is because of the inherent rigidity of a cast-iron system. If you've got the cast-iron closet bend secured, a properly installed flange isn't going to move either, so a couple of screws into the subfloor will anchor it.

An alternative to the leaded-flange installation for cast iron is a device called the instant-set flange. It is a two-piece casting that sandwiches a neoprene gasket between the drainpipe and a metal collar (above drawing). As you tighten the four bolts, the gasket swells to create a seal. Instant-set seals install quickly, but don't work any better than the leaded variety and they cost much more. Consequently, I don't use them. But for those lacking the tools for working with lead and oakum, they can be worth the extra money.

Installing the toilet—The toilet's outlet is connected to the closet flange by way of a wax and plastic gasket (photo 11). The plastic portion of the gasket is a funnel that fits into the the drainpipe. The wax, which is soft and sticky, conforms to the spigot as the toilet is positioned. Some plumbers will press the wax onto the spigot, then lower the toilet

onto the closet flange. I prefer to set the wax gasket in the flange and lower the toilet onto it. Either method works fine.

Once you've got the closet bolts through the holes in the base of the toilet, gently rock the bowl back and forth until it comes in complete contact with the floor. Then use the nuts and washers supplied with the closet bolts to secure the bowl to the floor. Tighten them very carefully—the toilet is porcelain, and you can break it with too much torque.

If you are installing a two-piece toilet, insert the bolts through the bottom of the tank and place all washers in their respective positions (photo 12). Set the tank on the bowl, making sure the bolts go through the corresponding holes on the bowl. Now carefully tighten the nuts, alternating between bolts to spread out the compression, until the tank

11. The transition between the toilet outlet and the closet flange is made with a wax and plastic gasket.

8. With the oakum in place, the gap between the drain and the flange is filled with lead.

9. The hardened ring of lead is packed into the joint with a caulking iron.

10. An internal pipe cutter will quickly trim a cast-iron stub to the desired length.

comes in contact with the bowl. This prevents the tank from moving around.

Now that the toilet is in place, you can connect the water. The chances are that the supply tube coming out of the wall is encrusted with paint. Use the escutcheon plate to scrape it off by installing the plate backwards, then moving it in and out until the tube is clean. The supply-tube stub will have to be trimmed back to about 1 ½ in.

A compression-fit valve called an angle stop fits over the supply stub. I connect the valve to the tank with ⅜-in. rigid copper supply tube designed for toilets (photo 13). It makes a clean installation accepted by every plumbing inspector I've ever met. To bend the tube, I use a tool made for the job (Ridge Tool Co., 400 Clark St., Elyria, Oh. 44036-2023). But some supply tubes are easier to

install—especially the new flexible stainless steel hoses. Before your inspector nixes one, make sure they're legal in your area.

When the water has been connected, re-tighten the nuts, if necessary, that secure the bowl to the floor, trim the bolts with a hacksaw and snap the plastic bolt caps in place. The installation is complete. Turn the angle stop on and fill the tank.

Flange too low?—Regardless of whether you're working with plastic or cast iron, the closet flange is supposed to end up atop the finished floor surface (photo 3). But they often don't. Sometimes they are even with the floor, and sometimes below it. Why? Because people change their minds and decide on different floor finishes. For instance, the floor in photo 14 was to be vinyl, but the clients

decided to put in marble instead. The thickness of the mortar and the marble put the flange about an inch below the finished floor. This can create a problem because the toilet spigot won't fully engage the wax ring, which means a leak. In this situation, cut the wax portion away from a second gasket and stack it on top of the gasket already in place. The added wax should make up for the low position of the closet flange.

Finally, caulk the toilet to the floor. I use a bead of DAP tub and tile seal all around the base of the toilet where it meets the floor. It prevents the accumulation of noxious grunge and prevents roaches from taking up residence under the toilet. □

George Skaates is a partner in Skaates, Canapa Plumbing, in San Francisco, Calif.

12. Two-piece, or close-coupled, toilets have separate bowls and tanks that must be bolted together carefully.

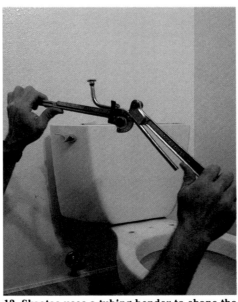

13. Skaates uses a tubing bender to shape the supply tube leading from the angle stop valve (lower left) to the toilet tank.

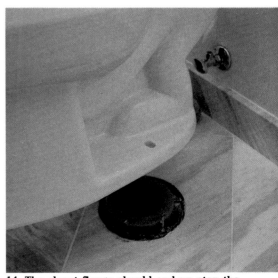

14. The closet flange should end up atop the finished floor surface, but it doesn't always work out that way. In the installation shown here, another wax ring has been added to the gasket to make up the difference.

Mosaic Tile
For restoration and decoration

by William Palanza

In 1918, Count Arnaud Cazenave purchased the small Creole cottage in New Orleans that was to become the basis for a great restaurant. As his success grew, he purchased one house after another between Bourbon Street and Dauphine Street, in the French Quarter of New Orleans. Today, Arnaud's consists of eleven adjacent houses, connected by a maze of corridors and covered patios. It's a restaurant in the tradition that has made New Orleans famous. Tall, slender Corinthian columns, cypress wainscoting, hammered tin ceilings, lazy ceiling fans and ornate mosaic floors blend Art Nouveau with the French Quarter interiors typical of the 1920s. Although the Count's daughter later turned some of the interiors into rooms reminiscent of a dark German pub, Arnaud's now stands restored.

Restoration of the Cardinal Room posed a unique problem. Construction of newer restrooms elsewhere in the building eliminated the need for the two old restrooms that occupied a 14-ft. by 9-ft. corner of the room, and so they were removed. Once the walls were down, though, the decorative mosaic floor of the dining room ran headlong into the black and white tile of the former bathrooms. Since the same mosaic pattern extended into other rooms near-

by, the new floor had to match. My sister Dorothy and I moved temporarily to New Orleans to produce and install a floor that would match the intricate pattern of the original.

Thousands of tiles—The first step was to figure out how much tile we were going to need. The best way to do this is to find the repeat of the tile pattern, and calculate from that. We found that the individual rows of tiles repeated in one direction every 24 in., and in the other every 12 inches. Once we counted the tiles in this block, it was easy to figure what we needed for the entire floor. I soon realized that we'd need about 32,000 tiles to complete the job.

Now, 32,000 tiles would be an awful lot to set one by one, and even smaller mosaic jobs aren't usually laid that way. Instead, various techniques can be used to prefabricate sheets of tiles by attaching them to a backing. Since the repeat of the pattern on this floor was 1 ft. by 2 ft., we decided that this would also be the size of each prefabricated sheet. I drew a full-scale pattern (including grout lines) on non-reproducing blue grid vellum to the precise dimensions of the floor repeat—figuring on ⅝-in. tiles and a ⅟₁₆-in. wide grout joint. Since this grid would eventual-

ly become the guide for assembling the sheets of tile, I shaded in the appropriate areas to help us keep track of the colors.

And one shall become many—Since the five colors used in the existing floor matched perfectly with five colors in the American Olean mosaic-tile line (Mosaic Tile Division, Olean, N. Y. 14760), I checked with them to see if they had any tiles of the exact size used in the original floor. Olean has a mural department, and my local distributor sent them some samples of the tiles we were trying to match. But the closest that American Olean could come to the original ⅝-in. size of the tiles was 1 in. square, a common size these days.

However, the color match was so close that we decided to cut ⅝-in. tiles out of American Olean's vitreous 2-in. square tile (a vitreous tile is harder than a glazed tile, and the color goes clear through, so it's ideal for floors). We had cut a lot of tiles by hand before, but we weren't about to cut thousands of them that way. Instead, we decided to use a pair of Target wet saws (Federal Mogul, Target Products Div., Kansas City, Mo. 64130), each mounted with an 8-in. diamond blade to slice up the larger tiles into

From *Fine Homebuilding* magazine (December 1986) 36:64-67

smaller ones. A wet saw looks something like a power miter saw, but instead of the blade pivoting down onto the work, the saw table slides into the blade. It's noisy work, so we wore hearing protection.

The wet saw uses water pumped from a reservoir tray to cool the blade as it grinds through the tile. It's important to maintain a good strong flow of water on the blade in order to keep it from heating up and becoming glazed by the clay. The heat of cutting actually can melt a slight bit of the tile around the cut, particularly on glazed tiles, and this melted material collects on the blade to slow cutting. Some blade manufacturers say that it's a good idea to cut a brick now and then to clean the blade of accumulated deposits—the relatively soft brick does the same thing that a gum-rubber bar does for cleaning sanding belts.

Figuring on about ⅛ in. of saw kerf, we were able to get four ⅝-in. tiles out of each 2x2 tile. To speed the work, we made two stacks of tiles, three high, held them against the saw fence and cut through all six tiles with one pass. We kept cutting the pieces until we ended up with twenty-four ⅝-in. tiles. Then we'd stack new tiles on the saw and repeat the process. In a day, using both saws simultaneously, we could cut about 3,200 tiles. The saws never missed a beat, but the work wasn't easy on our sawblades. We went through eight blades on the job, and at $80 apiece, it's a good thing we included this expense on our bid.

Prefabricating the sheets—We planned to reproduce the existing pattern by using a mosaic fabrication technique known as the reciprocal, or double-reverse, method. Using the full-size pattern of the repeat that I'd worked up, copies of the pattern were made at the printer's (the 1-ft. by 2-ft. patterns were too large to photocopy) as guides for laying out the tiles. Using a spray adhesive (and working in a well-ventilated area), each pattern was lightly fastened to ¼-in. corrugated cardboard—large sheets can be salvaged from boxes or purchased from a manufacturer of cardboard boxes. The cardboard provided a smooth, sturdy yet lightweight surface to work on. Since the pattern boards can be used more than once during the fabrication of the floor, we didn't need to make more than 10 or 12 of them for the job.

We began the mounting process by first spraying the pattern with an extremely light covering of adhesive; a two or three-second burst of the aerosol was enough to keep the tiles from sliding on the surface. I laid tiles one by one on the pattern, face up, and worked diagonally across the pattern until the whole thing was filled with tiles. The tiles were then covered with a sheet of lightweight kraft paper (photo above right) that had been liberally covered with a water-soluble paste (the paper would later be removed after the tiles were on the floor). When the paste dried, the tiles were carefully peeled away from the pattern board, leaving the back of the tiles exposed. When all 63 sheets were complete, they were packaged in boxes, with sheets of kraft paper between the tile sheets to keep them from sticking to each other. Since

Nearly all of the 32,000 tiles needed for the floor were fabricated into sheets, rather than being set in the floor one by one. Each sheet was covered with kraft paper coated with water-soluble paste, which would hold the tiles together as they were later set into place.

the floor had a tile border in a different pattern, we followed the same procedure for fabricating 12 border sheets.

Laying the tile—When all the sheets were complete, we began to remove the old bathroom floor. Traditionally, mosaic (and marble) floors were installed over a layer of concrete upon which a 2-in. thick layer of packed sand and cement was applied. After the two were mixed dry in a mortar box, water was added a little at a time until the mix began to ball up—just wet enough so that a fistful would maintain a shape when squeezed. This kind of tile base isn't as hard as concrete, and the material can be chiseled away fairly easily even after it cures. But its advantage is that it maintains a slight resiliency during the installation of tiles, allowing the tilesetter to adjust the setting bed to accommodate differences in the thickness of tiles. After two or three days, the packed base gets quite hard, but never as hard or stiff as concrete. The original floors at Arnaud's, for example, had few cracks because of this slight resiliency, even though the foundation had settled somewhat. We had a fairly easy time of removing it. A 90-lb. jackhammer driven by a portable air com-

pressor broke through without damaging the concrete beneath.

Once the original base had been broken up and removed, we cut or chiseled out any adjacent original tiles that had been damaged in the earlier remodeling, and vacuumed the area to remove all dust and loose material. We began immediately to lay down a new packed sand and cement base. Dorothy did the mixing—about one part portland cement to three parts fine brick sand—and carefully monitored the consistency. The proper mix is crucial because slight variations make it tough to screed when you dump it on the floor. But the right consistency is tough to describe. Like barbecuing a chicken, you know when it's ready if you've burned a few.

When a batch was ready, the concrete slab was dampened to keep it from sucking moisture from the mix, and we dumped small batches, spreading each with a plastering trowel. The mix was then tamped down firmly with a wooden float, and screeded with an aluminum straightedge to a height ⅜ in. below the top of the old mosaic tiles. This would accommodate the new tiles and about ⅛ in. of thinset mortar. After screeding, the bed was floated using a wooden

To prepare the base for the new floor, clean fine sand, cement and a small amount of water were thoroughly mixed together, spread over the sub-base of concrete, and then compacted, screeded and floated to a fairly smooth finish. This base provided a uniform, durable setting surface—an important consideration when using small tiles.

The Palanzas set small sections of the floor at a time, and gently removed the kraft paper as the base set up. In the photo above, the bright white of the new tile is all that distinguishes it from the old. Note the translucency of the kraft paper—this allowed the setters to see through it as they aligned the sheets. A section of the finished floor is shown below.

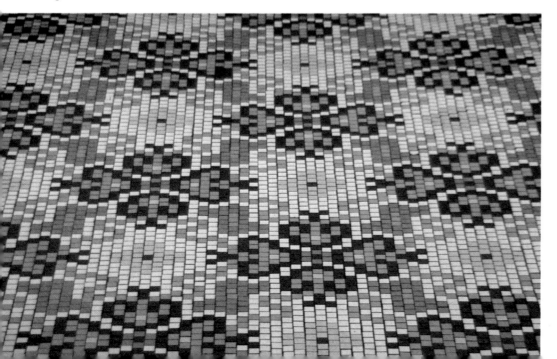

float, and any holes were filled with additional gobs of mix. We filled and screeded sections of the floor until the entire area was prepared. The edges were then trimmed up to make a clean connection with the existing tilework (photo top left). Since the concrete subfloor was slightly uneven, the final thickness of the new base ranged from 2½ in. to 3 in. We let it cure overnight before we began to lay the mosaic.

Starting at the edges of the old floor, we first spread a thinset wall mortar mix on small areas of the floor—the heavier-bodied, grittier mix generally used on floors would have interfered with the bond between the small tiles and the concrete base. The thinset was mixed with water to a creamy consistency and spread on the bed with ⅛-in. notched trowels. Dorothy went over the area with a flat trowel and forced the thinset into the minute crevices in the base to improve the mechanical bond between the two materials. While this layer was still wet, a second layer was added and smoothed out.

Compared to preparing the bed, laying the sheets of mosaic was fairly straightforward. After each sheet was laid and aligned with adjoining surfaces, I tapped it lightly into the mortar bed with a wooden block to ensure that the tiles were set. I like to work on a diagonal across the floor because it allows me to work simultaneously on a horizontal and vertical axis to align the tile sheets. It also keeps error from accumulating at one side of the floor or another. The kraft paper on the face of the tiles (photo middle left) was dampened and gently pulled away once the sheets had begun to set up, and any excess thinset that had squeezed up between the tiles was removed to provide enough depth for a grout joint.

Our grouting mix was 3-to-1 portland cement to sand, with a dash of black masonry color added to darken the grout so it would match the aged grout of the old floor. We mixed the grout with water to a soupy consistency, and spread it over the tiles with a rubber grouting trowel. The soupy mix filled in the small grout joints better than a thicker mix would have. Before the grout could cure, we dusted the floor with a dry mix of the same grout. This filled any areas where the soupy mix had settled, and also helped to clean the tiles—the sand acts as a mild abrasive to remove any residues of thinset.

The grout cured in about 72 hours. We rubbed the floor with pieces of burlap to remove excess grout, and then cleaned the tile further by rubbing it with dampened sawdust. Sawdust makes a wonderful cleaner because it absorbs the residues of grouting, and is enough of an abrasive so you can trim down heavy joints to even them up. As the final step, the floor was swept and allowed to cure for another three days before we let anyone walk on it.

The results were wonderful (photo bottom left). Except for the new white areas being brighter than the old ones, there was very little difference between the two floors. The total cost of the restoration worked out to be roughly $63 per sq. ft.   □

William Palanza and his sister Dorothy are mosaic-tile artisans in Staten Island, N. Y.

Installing decorative mosaic

Decorative mosaic work is among the oldest of all crafts. In the ancient civilizations of the Middle East, mosaics were constructed by embedding conical clay pegs into surfaces of wet mud. The ends of the pegs were individually colored in red, white or black, and portions of these mosaics are still intact today, nearly 3,000 years later. The ancient Greeks used pebbles embedded in mortar to make floors they called *pavimenta.* Early Roman mosaic work was done with stone pieces known as *tessera,* and later the great European cathedrals were decorated with mosaics made from bits of colored glass. This later process reached a peak in the late Renaissance, with the development of *micro-mosaic,* an extremely tedious technique in which pinhead-sized bits of glass were embedded in mortar, ground flat and then polished to a high gloss finish.

Decorative mosaic work is characterized by bold texture and bright colors. Bright colors are possible because decorative mosaics needn't withstand heavy traffic, so they don't have to be made from vitreous tiles (vitreous tiles are fired to very high temperatures, which tends to "burn out" the colors). The tile work we did on a shower surround in Manhattan provides a good look at how decorative mosaics can be done.

Fabrication—We prefabricated the mosaic at our studio using the direct method of mosaic construction, which is similar to the method we used at Arnaud's. The important difference, however, is that no kraft-paper sheet obscures the face of the tiles. Since decorative mosaic patterns are less predictable and more artistic than the rigid geometry of standard mosaics, we wanted to be able to see the face of the tiles at all times. We drew a few different repeating designs on 10x10 non-reproducing blue grid vellum, photocopied each design and mounted them on sheets of cardboard for presentation to the client. After selecting a pattern, our clients picked out a basic color scheme, and we decided how and where to use the colors. We were then ready to fabricate the tile panels.

The cardboard pattern board was covered with a self-sticking clear plastic—shelf paper from a hardware store works fine. This kept later work from sticking to the boards, and protected the pattern from smudging or other damage. Next, we sprayed a light coat of spray adhesive over the plastic, and an open-weave fiberglass mesh was laid over this. The adhesive held the mesh in place, but not too tightly; mesh and pattern board would later have to be separated. The mesh provides a flexible backing for the mosaic tiles.

Cutting and installing the tiles—When the pattern board was complete, we used a wet saw to cut tiles into strips varying in width from 1⁄16 in. (red accent strips) to 3⁄8 in. (blue background tiles). To get the exact length of tile we wanted, all we had to do was snip off what we needed with a pair of tile nippers—a pliers-like device with sharpened jaws. With acrylic craft glue, each bit of tile was fastened to the mesh

Decorative mosaic tile allows for a less rigid design, more texture and brighter colors than standard mosaics. It also involves a somewhat different fabrication technique. For this shower surround, a pattern of the design was made on cardboard, fiberglass mesh was lightly glued to it, and then squares and slivers of tile were glued to the mesh using an acrylic craft glue (above). The completed mosaic (below) contrasts with the rigid geometry of the surrounding glazed tiles, and adds a splash of color to the room. Decorative mosaics are particularly appropriate for walls.

on the pattern board, as shown in the photo at top.

We let the panels set up overnight, and then separated them from the pattern board by first removing the cardboard, and then peeling the plastic sheet away from the fiberglass mesh. This was a time for great care and patience because only the plastic mesh and the tile cement held the tiles together after the pattern board was gone. The panel was set aside to dry completely, and a new panel was started. It's not a good idea to make panels over 36 in. long because they're tricky to transport to the site and awkward to lift into place on a wall.

Mosaic panels can be installed over any clean, stable surface, like gypsum or Wonderboard. My sister Dorothy and I think mortared walls are about the most durable surface, however, and prefer to work with this base. On this job, we affixed the panels to a mortar base with thinset mortar spread with 1⁄8-in. notched trowels. We tapped each panel lightly with a rubber grouting trowel to ensure a good bond with the thinset.

After the thinset had cured, the tiles were grouted with a mixture of cement, marble dust and mason's lime. We used marble dust because of its light color and very fine texture. You can buy it from lapidary-supply stores (it's used to polish stones) or from a marble supplier, but we make our own. When we use the wet saw to cut marble for a job, the mix of water and dust forms a slurry that we strain through cheesecloth into a bucket of water. Once it has settled, the water is poured off and any moisture allowed to evaporate—the remaining marble dust is collected for future use.

The completed mosaic at this job catches the eye and enlivens the room (photo above), but bathroom decoration isn't the only place where mosaic tile can add a splash of color. As it did in Renaissance times, fine mosaic work can once again flourish as an important element of interior design. Foyers, countertops and backsplashes are excellent for decorative mosaic work. For example, a floor done in solid ceramic or marble can be highlighted with a decorative mosaic made, in part, from the same material used in the larger area. The cost for decorative mosaic work varies according to the size and complexity of the job. A border like the one in this apartment can be fabricated for about $80.00 per linear foot.   —*W. P.*

Tiling a Mortar-Bed Counter

How one tile setter builds the classic kitchen work surface

by Michael Byrne

I think the best part of being a tile setter is that my work doesn't get covered up by someone else's labors. On the other hand, setting tile is tough, physical work—especially large floors, where my knees cry out for a desk job and my back creaks from all the bending. So it's no wonder that I enjoy tiling countertops.

Ceramic tile offers many advantages as a finish material in the kitchen. A hot pot won't damage a tile surface, and a properly waterproofed installation can stand up to all of the splashes and spills that cooks can dish out.

The best tile countertops are done on a thick bed of mortar called a *float*. The float is usually ¾ in. to 1 in. thick, and the solid base it provides for the tile isn't affected by moisture. I'll be describing the most common type of counter that I do. It has V-cap face trim and a single row of tiles for the backsplash. To make cleanup easier for the cook, the sink is recessed beneath the surface of the counter and is trimmed with quarter-round tiles (drawing, facing page).

Choosing the tile—Kitchen-counter tiles should be either impervious or fully vitrified (see sidebar on p. 116). These ratings mean that the tile will absorb almost no water, a property that increases the life expectancy of the installation.

Many tiles are designed to decorate rather than protect. You should be able to find a tile that does both. But you need to be careful even with heavy glazes since some of these are easily marked by metal cooking utensils. I urge my customers to get samples of their favorite tiles, and to rub them with a stainless-steel pan, an aluminum pot and a copper penny. Some tiles can be cleaned up after this kind of abuse—others can't. The surface is important in another way, too. Because most appliances need a flat surface to work efficiently, tiles with irregular faces, such as Mexican pavers, make beautiful backsplashes but lousy work surfaces.

Layout—The goal here is to keep tile cuts to a minimum, to locate them in the least conspicuous places, and to eliminate tiles that are less than half-size. On a straight-run counter, this usually means beginning the layout halfway

Tile layout. **Byrne has used a ³⁄₁₆-in. trowel to spread thinset mortar over the float, and he now aligns the rows of tile with a straightedge. The chalklines at the inside corner of the counter mark the position of the V-cap trim, and the starting point for the first full sheet of tile.**

From *Fine Homebuilding* magazine (February 1985) 25:32-37

along its length or at the centerline of the sink. If you take a close look at sink installations, you'll find that there is often a trimmed tile in the center of the front edge, in line with the spout. This trimmed tile keeps things symmetrical, and it allows full tiles along the edges of the sink. I begin the layout on an L-shaped counter at the intersection of the two wings (photo facing page).

Once I have the tiles in hand, I use the direct method of measurement to help lay out the job. I unpack some of the tiles and move them around the cabinet top. Sometimes, shifting the tiles an inch this way or that can make a substantial improvement in the finished appearance. Small tiles are more forgiving, allowing you to adjust the width of the grout lines to make things fit. But unless the counter has been meticulously designed with the tiles as modules, cuts are inevitable.

The substrate—The substrate should be at least ¾-in. plywood rated for exterior use. Particleboard won't do. The waterproofing on most counters consists of a layer of 15-lb. asphalt-saturated felt or a similar protective paper. I take this a step further and laminate the felt to the plywood with wet-patch fibered roofing cement.

Tiling a counter is a messy, gritty project. To keep the asphalt (and later the mortar and grout) from soiling the cabinets, I first drape kraft paper or plastic film over the face of the cabinets, and staple it to the counter plywood. I also protect the floors with canvas dropcloths.

I use a ⅛-in. V-notched trowel to spread a thin layer of roofing cement onto the plywood around the sink and about 3 ft. to each side. This helps to protect the vulnerable areas under the dish drainers. Ideally, the asphalt should cover the exposed plywood end grain in the sink cutout (drawing, below). If the sink is already in place, I squeeze the asphalt into the junction between the sink and the plywood. At the backsplash I make a tight crease in the felt and lap it up the wall about 3 in. Later this flap will be trimmed to about ¾ in. above the finished counter. Combined with the backsplash tiles, it makes an effective water barrier, keeping moisture out of the rear of the cabinets.

Screeds and rails—Once the waterproofing is completed, I set the sink rail. This rigid galvanized sheet-metal channel reinforces the mortar bed down the entire front edge of the counter and makes it easier to level the bed. The rail has narrow vertical slots every 3 in. for nails or screws (photo below left). Along its top edge are ⅝-in. dia. holes. Mortar will ooze through these holes, linking the mortar that faces the counter edge with the countertop float. This helps to anchor the V-cap finish on the edge.

I start screwing the rail in front of the sink, adjusting it to suit the height of the quarter-round trim in relation to the top of the sink. Once all the rail is in place, I use ½-in. thick pine to box in any openings in the substrate that have been cut for the cooktop, chopping block or other built-ins. These are installed at the exact height of the finished float. Attaching the sink rail and boxing the openings is a lot like setting up the forms for a slab floor.

Metal reinforcing—My experience has taught me that metal reinforcing in a counter float reduces or eliminates cracked tiles and grout. Consequently, I use plenty of it. First, I cut 20-ga. 1-in. wire mesh (chicken wire) and secure it to the plywood substrate with ½-in. staples, overlapping neighboring pieces at least 4 in. The mesh (photo below right) extends from the sink rail to the back wall and covers the entire substrate. Rather than cut the mesh a little short to make an easy fit between the sink rail and the wall, I cut it a bit long and bend the excess back over itself.

Finally, I use 9-ga. galvanized wire like rebar to strengthen those parts of the mortar bed that will be narrow in cross section. This prevents the cracks that often appear in the tiles close to the front or back corners of sinks and cooktops. I center the wire and run it parallel to these narrow sections, and I anchor it with ¼-in. or ⅜-in. furring nails. Then I bend it at about a 45° angle where the counter broadens, and extend it at least 6 in. toward the center of the field. At first, I used the wire rather sparingly. But now I use it all over the countertop—at inside and outside corners and across peninsulas—and I've found cracking problems a thing of the past. When all the reinforcing is in place, I check to make sure none of it protrudes above the top level of the sink rail. This can be done either with a 2-ft. level or by sighting the top of the sink rail.

Deck mud—Most of my jobs are in the San Francisco Bay Area, where the adobe soil swells during the winter rains and shrinks in the long

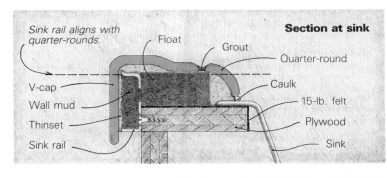

Section at sink

Sink rail aligns with quarter-rounds. — Float — Grout — Quarter-round — Caulk — 15-lb. felt — Plywood — Sink
V-cap — Wall mud — Thinset — Sink rail

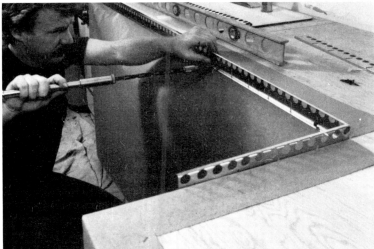

Sink rail. **Before floating the mortar bed, Byrne screws a galvanized strip called a sink rail to the edge of the plywood substrate. It serves as a screed, edge reinforcement and a framework to anchor the thin layer of mortar that will face the edge of the countertop.**

Reinforcement. **Chicken wire stapled to the plywood substrate covers the area to be tiled. If a mortar counter cracks, it usually does so in the narrows around the sink, or at inside corners. These areas are reinforced with 9-ga. galvanized wire held in place by furring nails.**

A. **Float strips** are the key to controlling the thickness of the mortar countertop. Here the author beds a float strip in a mortar pad, getting the strip's relationship to the sink rail right with a level. The float strips will guide the screed board while the mortar is leveled. Later, the strips will be removed and the resulting voids filled with mortar.

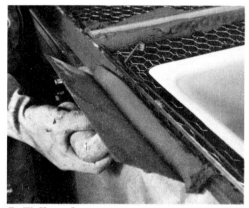

B. **Wall mud**—a special mortar blend that includes masonry lime and latex additive, which help the mortar to cling to vertical surfaces—fills the sink rail before the counter is floated. Some of this wall mud squeezes through the holes in the rail, keying it into the deck mortar.

C. **Deck mud** is loosely spread across the counter with a wood float after the sink rail is filled with mortar. Because the mortar in the rail is still fragile, it has to be supported by a steel trowel so it won't break away.

D. **Leveling the deck mud.** Byrne uses an aluminum straightedge as a screed board, and he moves it in a side-to-side motion as he gradually pulls it forward. Here both ends of the screed are resting on float strips. Note the difference in texture between the crumbly deck mud and the smoother wall mud used on the rail and around the sink.

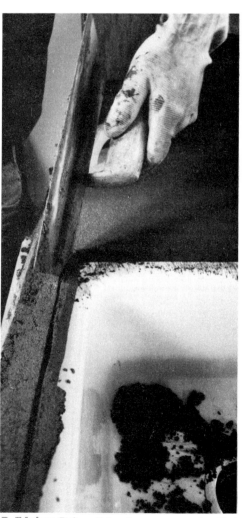

E. **Edging.** Before it hardens, any mortar that overlaps the sink rim is trimmed away. This allows the sink to be removed later if necessary, without damaging the mortar bed. The open edge will be trimmed with quarter-round tiles.

hot summer. Add to this the occasional earthquake tremors, and you have mortar beds that tend to move around quite a bit. I use 3701, a mortar-and-grout admix made by Laticrete International (1 Laticrete Park North, Bethany, Conn. 06525) that allows my floats to flex a little without cracking. Other companies, like Custom Building Materials (6511 Salt Lake Ave., Bell, Calif. 90201) and Upco (3101 Euclid Ave., Cleveland, Ohio 44115), make similar products.

The amount of admix I need depends on the weather and how wet the sand is (see the sidebar, facing page). This deck mud, as it is called, is considerably drier than brick-type mortars—it has just enough moisture to bind the ingredients and no more. This means that the mix can be compacted into a uniformly dense slab.

Floating the counter—Before I can start spreading the mortar around the countertop, I have to install float strips along any edges that aren't boxed or that don't have a sink rail. Float strips are ¼ in. thick and 1¼ in. wide pine or fir rippings that will sit temporarily atop a layer of mud as I level the mortar. Each float strip begins on a mound of loose deck mud piled slightly higher (about 1 in.) than the height of the finished float. Then I take a level and, placing one end of it on the sink rail for a reference and the rest of it on the float strip, I tap the strip with a hammer until the strip is leveled, as shown in photo A, top left.

Floating begins with filling the front edge of the counter. The channel formed by the sink rail must be filled with what's called wall mud. To make the wall mud, I take a small portion of deck mud (for this job about 2½ gallons), add about a quart (dry measure) of masonry lime, and enough Laticrete 3701 to make a thick, heavy paste. Then, using a flat trowel, I press the mix onto the face of the sink rail until the mud is forced through the ⅝-in. holes (photo B). The resulting extruded lumps of mortar will key into the deck mud.

Once the sink-rail face is filled, I use the remaining wall mud to surround the sink. Then I dump the deck mud onto the countertop and spread it around with a wooden float while I keep the rail and its wall mud steady with my steel trowel (photo C). By this time, the mud in the sink rail has begun to harden, but if it is not supported, it will be pushed off the rail when the nearby deck mud is compacted.

To level the deck mud, I use a straightedge as a screed board (photo D). Using a side-to-side motion, I pull it toward me, gradually removing the excess mud until the straightedge makes contact with the float strips or sink rail. I apply a horizontal rather than vertical pressure on the straightedge to avoid mashing the strips out of position. Smoothing out one area at a time, I gradually work my way around the countertop until the screeding is done. The surface is now flat, but not all the mud is compacted. The float strips also have to be removed, and the resulting voids have to be filled.

I take a lot of pride in my finished floats—they are my pieces of sculpture, and the wood float is my finishing tool. First, I scoop some deck mud onto the flattened top and ram it into the voids where the strips sat with the float. Then with the edge of the tool, I gradually slice off the excess. Experience allows me to "feel" my way across the surface by the way the float sits in my hand. I scour the top until it feels right. With all the voids filled, the top is an unbroken expanse of grey.

The last two areas of mortar to clean up are the sink rail and the sink perimeter. The top and bottom edges of the metal sink rail provide a good surface for the float to trim off the excess mud. Around the sink, I square up the mortar with a trowel, trimming it back far enough to expose the edges of the sink (photo E, facing page). Although it is no picnic, this makes it possible to remove the sink without having to rip up the field tiles. These edges are covered later with quarter-rounds.

Inevitably, some mud will fall away from the rail, or the screed will knock a float strip out of position. Fortunately, the material is very forgiving, and problems are easy to fix. I skip over these minor accidents until the initial work is done, then I go back and fill in dings with fresh mortar before everything sets up.

Setting the tiles—Instead of laying the tiles as soon as I finish the float, I let it harden overnight. This way most of the shrinkage likely to occur will happen before the tiles are in place and grouted, and I can be less concerned about deforming the float as I set the tiles.

The next day, the first order of business is to vacuum loose sand and cement particles from the top to increase the grip of the thinset mortar that bonds the tiles to the float. Then I snap chalklines along the edges to mark the layout for the V-cap trim. I usually spread a few sheets of tile around to confirm my earlier layout; then I mix up enough thinset mortar to last through a couple of hours of setting.

Thinset is a portland-cement based mortar that contains very fine sand. The bond it forms is unaffected by moisture, and it is ideal for applying ceramic tiles to a mortar base. On this job I used Bon-Don (Garland-White & Co., P.O. Box 365, Union City, Calif. 94587). I mix the stuff with water to the consistency of toothpaste, using a drill and a mixing paddle.

The sheet-mounted tiles going on this counter are a little less than ¼ in. thick, so I used a ³⁄₁₆-in. V-notched trowel to comb out the thinset. Spreading too thick a layer will cause the adhesive to ooze up between the tiles. On the other hand, the backs of the tiles must be completely covered. These 12-in. by 12-in. sheets covered the top quickly. I used a short straightedge to help align them.

Everything went smoothly on this job until I reached the open side of the L. There I realized that the tiles were falling short of the V-cap layout line by about ⁷⁄₁₆ in. Checking back, I found that the sheets in one box were all undersized. Adding a narrow row of tiles that have been trimmed to make up for a mistake like this never looks right, so before the thinset dried I quickly widened the grout lines between the rows of tile. The string backing prevents the tiles from being spread apart, so I cut through it with a utility knife, and used a long straightedge to

Mixing the mortar

Of all the skills necessary to produce durable tile installations, none is more perplexing to the novice than mixing mud. There is no substitute for experience, but having a good recipe, the right tools, and knowing a few good mixing techniques can produce workable deck mud. The recipe I use comes from instructions printed on the bucket of latex admix (when using various mortar additives, always follow the manufacturer's recommendations). With Laticrete 3701, the mix is 1 part portland cement, 3 parts mason's sand, and about 4½ to 5 gal. of the admix per sack of cement. To help keep the batches consistent, I measure the dry ingredients in 3-gal. or 5-gal. buckets instead of counting shovelfuls. A full 5-gal. bucket holds ¾ cu. ft. of sand, and when I calculate the volume of mortar for a job, I disregard the cement. It fills the spaces between the sand particles. The sand I use comes damp from the yard, although occasionally I use dry sand shipped in paper sacks. With the dry sand, I measure out the amount I need and mix it with just enough water to dampen it.

I use a steel mixing box and a slotted mason's hoe rather than a rotary mixer, which can cause the mix to form marble-sized lumps. I layer the sand and water evenly in the box and chop them three times back and forth with the hoe. Each time, I take lots of small bites with the hoe, and I pull the ingredients toward me to form a pile at one end of the box. Before any liquid can be added, the sand and cement must be thoroughly blended to prevent lumps from forming.

Next I level the dry ingredients and use the handle of my hoe to punch holes in the mix (photo above right). This allows the liquid to distribute itself more evenly instead of just sitting on top. Then I repeat the mixing procedure, chopping back and forth three times. At this point, I pick up a handful and squeeze it. If the moisture content is right, the deck mud will form a tight ball that sticks together without cracking apart (photo below right). If it oozes through my fingers, the mix is too wet and must be adjusted by adding some dry sand with the right proportions of cement. If the ball falls apart, I need to add more liquid.

The direct rays of the sun can ruin the mud at this point, so I pack it into buckets and get it inside the house. If it's above 90°F, I'll have only about a half-hour to work the mortar. If it's 65°F to 75°F, I may have as long as two hours.   —M. B.

A steel mixing box (top) is the place to prepare a batch of deck mud. Byrne blends the dry ingredients with his hoe, then pokes holes in the mix with its handle to help spread the latex admix. Properly blended mud is fairly dry, but it will cling together in a ball when you squeeze a handful of it (above).

open up the joints, as shown in the photo at left. For getting out of a jam, nothing beats a good set of straightedges.

Cutting the tiles—The narrow tiles in front of and behind the sink can be cut with a snap cutter (p. 112 and pp. 113-114), but I prefer to use a diamond-bladed wet saw for the accuracy and smoothness of cut I get in one step. The saw is set up outside the house, and running back and forth for each cut eats up time, so I accumulate a stack of tiles to be cut for each trip. You can use a ruler to take measurements and then set the saw fence to these, but that leaves a lot more room for error than just marking the tile directly. The water jet on the saw can sometimes blast away a pencil mark while cutting, so I cover the tile with masking tape and make my mark on the tape.

V-cap, backsplash and quarter-rounds— After all the field tiles are positioned, I set the V-cap. Complicated trim tiles like these often distort a bit in the kiln, so they must be set with extra care. I usually butter each piece with thinset and then tap it into place, controlling the amount of thinset I use to suit the alignment (photo facing page, top left). At inside and outside corners, the V-cap tiles are mitered, and I cut them a bit short to allow for a grout line.

Before I can set the single row of backsplash tiles, I trim the excess tar paper down to about ½ in. to ¾ in. above the deck tiles (drawing, facing page). The joint between the backsplash and the deck must allow for free movement, so later, when the grout is dry, I seal it with a bead of silicone caulk. I allow a full-width joint here rather than have the splash tiles rest directly on the deck tiles. Bon-Don is especially sticky thinset, allowing me to hang these relatively light tiles on the wall without any support from below. Heavier tiles usually require wood or plastic shims between the last course of deck tiles and the bottom edge of the backsplash tiles.

The last tiles to go down are the small radiused tiles that trim the sink. Unlike the other tiles, these quarter-round trim pieces are set on a bed of grout. This grout is the same used to pack the joints, only it is mixed stiffer. To make sure that the quarter-rounds adhere to the float mud around the sink, I coat both the float and the back of each quarter-round with thinset for a stronger bond between the tile and the grout.

Factory-made inside corner pieces look and feel better than the miter cuts you can make on a tile saw. They are set before the straight sections of quarter-round. With quarter-rounds, it's important to apply more grout than is actually needed to set each piece. As the tile is slowly pushed home (photo facing page, below left), the excess grout is squeezed out of the joint. Once the piece is in the right position, I support it with my fingers for a few seconds to prevent it from moving. When all the pieces are set, I

Adjusting the courses. **Instead of adding an unsightly row of narrow tiles, the distance between courses can be slightly increased. This strategy can spread out a discrepancy so it can't be seen, and save tedious tile-trimming.**

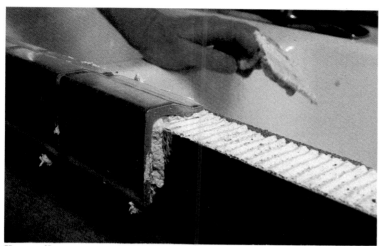

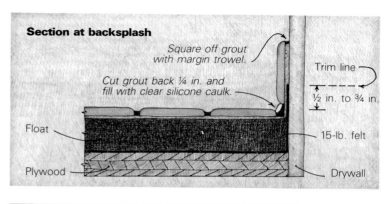

Section at backsplash

Square off grout with margin trowel.

Cut grout back ¼ in. and fill with clear silicone caulk.

Trim line

½ in. to ¾ in.

Float

15-lb. felt

Plywood

Drywall

V-cap tiles, which trim the leading edge of the counter, receive a lot of contact. It's important that they be securely anchored to the mortar bed—any voids between them are unacceptable. Byrne butters the back of each trim piece with a generous helping of thinset, and presses it in place until it's in the same plane as its neighbor.

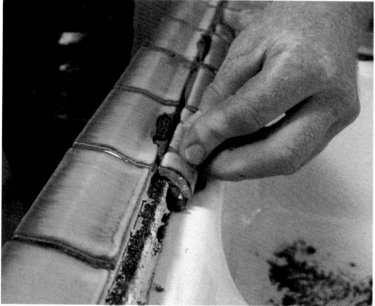

Quarter-round tiles, which trim the edge of the sink, are the last tiles to be placed. They are set on a bed of stiff grout. Before bedding them, Byrne applies a thin layer of thinset mortar to the tiles and to the float. The thinset mortar helps to strengthen the bond between the two.

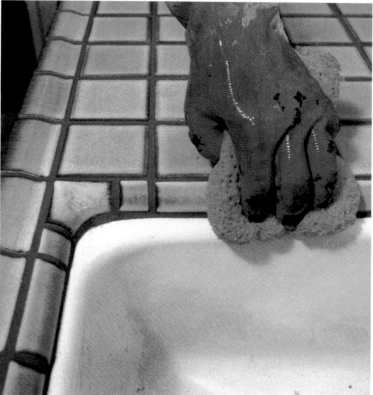

Finish. The entire counter has been grouted and sponged. Residual cement is cleaned up with a damp sponge. The corner of the sink is trimmed with a factory-made inside-corner piece. Next to it, the quarter-rounds have been trimmed to align with the V-cap edge trim and the field tiles. The last step will be to undercut the grout around the sink, and fill it with silicone caulk once the grout dries.

leave them alone for about a half hour or so to allow the grout to set up. Meanwhile, I prepare another batch of grout.

Grouting—I prefer a grout made with a latex admix because it is a lot stickier than regular grout. This allows it to adhere tenaciously to the slick edges of glazed tiles—an important advantage on a tile work surface that gets constant use. Also, grout with admix is far more resistant to liquids, and to the erosion they can cause.

To prepare the grout, I follow the directions on the sack, which usually recommend combining the dry ingredients with water or a latex admix to the proper consistency, and then allowing the mix to sit for five or ten minutes. The grout is then mixed again and it's ready for use. During this wait, I trim the excess grout from the sink quarter-rounds.

There is no single method for grouting, and the techniques for grouting floor tiles (see p. 117)

can also be applied to a counter. The porosity of the tiles, the moisture content of the setting bed, the addition of admixes, temperature and humidity levels are all factors that determine how much grout can be spread before it's time to clean off the excess. Usually, I begin by spreading about 8 to 10 square feet. I hold the rubber trowel at an angle between 30° to 40° as I force the grout into the joints. I work the grout from different directions until I'm satisfied that the joints are packed solid.

I start the cleaning by scraping away loose grout with the edge of my rubber trowel. Then I take a wet sponge and wring out as much water as possible. This is important because any excess moisture will weaken the grout. I work the sponge across the counter, gradually lowering the level of the grout until it is slightly below the plane of the tile, with a concave surface. During this process, the pores of the sponge quickly fill with grout and must be flushed constantly. Once

the entire counter has undergone this step, I go back over it with a clean sponge to remove most of the cement haze (photo above right).

The last step is to trim the grout in a few places. At the sink, I undercut the grout below the quarter-rounds about ⅛ in. so the joint can be caulked with clear silicone. This allows the sink to move a little, without breaking the waterproof seal, and lets the color of the grout show through the caulk. Because the counter and the wall will move slightly in relation to one another, I use the same technique to seal the joint between the deck tiles and the backsplash. At the top of the backsplash, I square up the grout line with my margin trowel. This makes it easier to paint or paper the wall.

Finally, I remove any grout haze with cheesecloth or fine steel wool, followed by a thorough vacuuming to take away the loose particles. □

Michael Byrne lives in Walnut Creek, Calif.

Laying a Tile Floor

Epoxy mastic on a plywood subfloor is a durable alternative to the traditional mortar-bed method

by Michael Byrne

Of all the finish floors available to the builder, none is more permanent than ceramic tile. Tile floors hundreds of years old attest to the durability of the materials, and today ceramic tiles are available in almost limitless colors and patterns. Because ceramic tile can resist the ravages of water (see p. 116), it is often chosen as the finish floor in wet locations like bathrooms, kitchens and mudrooms. But regardless of how durable and pretty the tile is on top, its useful life depends on things that can't be seen: a sturdy subfloor, high-quality mastics or mortar, an accurate layout and sound installation.

This article describes a typical tile installation in a small bathroom. The job was a remodel, but the procedures are the same for new construction. The tools are the same, too (photo below left). Except for the snap cutter, which you can rent from most tool-rental centers, tile-laying equipment isn't expensive.

Preparing the subfloor—The floor in this bathroom had been covered by wall-to-wall carpeting that extended from the neighboring living room. Years of careless splashing in the shower had rotted a corner of the rug, and the subfloor was about to follow. Fortunately the joists weren't damaged, so I didn't have to perform any framing surgery. I just had to remove the toilet and tear out a rotten rug.

The original subfloor was 1x6 T&G planking over joists 16 in. o. c. This is a satisfactory substrate for a finish floor that can flex, like vinyl or carpet, but a tile floor requires a stiffer base, or it will crack. I won't install a tile floor unless the subfloor and the underlayment are at least 1¼ in. thick, so I covered

the planking with ⅝-in. CDX plywood and fastened it down with 2-in. ring-shank nails driven into the joists every 6 in. At the walls, I left a ¼-in. expansion gap.

I never use particleboard as an underlayment because it's not as strong as plywood and it swells if it gets wet. Exterior grades of plywood, when properly fastened, can stand up to the occasional tub oveflow without swelling and popping the tiles loose.

I left a gap of about 1⁄16 in. to ⅛ in. between the pieces of plywood for a glue joint. By edge-gluing the plywood sheets with the epoxy thinset, the underlayment becomes an integral layer that won't move in isolated spots as a result of a water spill. If individual pieces are allowed to move, the result can be cracked tiles or broken grout lines. Unless the subfloor needs a lot of surface preparation, glue the plywood edges as the tiles are set. Adjacent pieces of plywood shouldn't be more than 1⁄32 in. above or below each other, and for a larger floor, the edges of the plywood sheets should be staggered.

Traditionally, floor tiles are set in a 1-in. thick bed of mortar. This is still the best method for wet locations, but it's also messier and trickier than using epoxy tile adhesives. The epoxy thinset used on this job (Latapoxy 210, manufactured by Laticrete International, 1 Laticrete Park North, Bethany, Conn. 06525) is acceptable for use in wet locations. Epoxy is really the best choice where raising the level of the floor with a layer of mortar is out of the question. Its water resistance, compressive strength and holding power allow it to stand up to daily bathroom use.

I would never use an organic mastic for this

installation for two reasons. (Organic mastics were originally made from rubber-tree extracts. The term now describes a general class of ready-to-use thinset mastics that cure by evaporation.) First, water will eventually get through it to the subfloor and the tiles will loosen. Second, organic mastics don't get hard enough to support floor tiles, so the tiles in the high-traffic area will eventually move, and the grout will crack.

To make sure that the tiles will sit on a flat plane, I knock down any high spots in the subfloor with a disc sander and I fill in the low spots with epoxy mastic. Even slight irregularities can make for wavy grout lines once the tiles are in place. Small tiles look especially bad on uneven surfaces.

To find the low spots, I use a straightedge. I make pencil marks at the edges of the depression just where the light begins to appear under the straightedge. I draw around each depression until an outline defines the low spot. I thoroughly vacuum the floor so that a layer of dust doesn't prevent adhesion between the mastic filler and the subfloor. Then I mix a batch of mastic and trowel it into each low spot with a side-to-side motion of the trowel (this will pick up any remaining dust on the floor), and I screed off excess mastic with a straightedge. Once the mastic has set up, I remove ridges with an abrasive stone.

Laying out the tile—Rather than provide a line for each sheet or piece of tile, it's more convenient to divide a small floor like this one into workable parts. By projecting the location of a few grout lines onto the floor with chalkline or a pencil, I can visualize the alignment

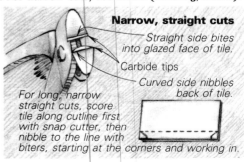

Narrow, straight cuts

Straight side bites into glazed face of tile.

Carbide tips

Curved side nibbles back of tile.

For long, narrow straight cuts, score tile along cutline first with snap cutter, then nibble to the line with biters, starting at the corners and working in.

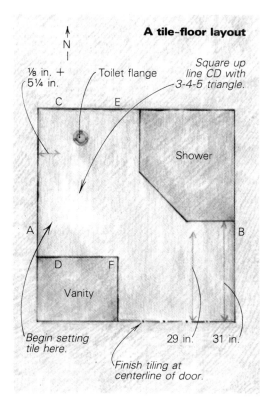

A tile-floor layout

⅛ in. + 5¼ in.

Toilet flange

Square up line CD with 3-4-5 triangle.

Shower

Vanity

Begin setting tile here.

Finish tiling at centerline of door.

29 in.   31 in.

Layout. After the newly laid plywood subfloor has been leveled, it is divided by layout lines into sections that will be set in sequence, beginning with the quadrant farthest from the door and ending with the section around the door. As shown in the drawing above, the layout is square to the door opening, emphasizing the most visible lines in the room.

of the finished floor. I make each section large enough to give me space for my tools and materials, yet small enough so that I can reach the entire area without straining—it's surprising how easy it is to lose one's balance and fall onto the finished work.

To establish the layout, I usually start at the centerline of the door, directly over the threshold. The most visible portion of the floor is usually just inside the door, so it's important to make sure that the grout lines are straight, and parallel or perpendicular to the threshold. The centerline of the closed door marks the edge of the tile.

The distance between the door centerline and the shower in this bathroom is 31 in. Since the tiles for this job measure 3 in. by 6 in. including the grout lines, there's enough room for 10 full rows of tile plus one row made from pieces about 1 in. wide. But a row of 1-in. wide tiles among 3-in. wide neighbors wouldn't look very good, so I decided to cover the 31-in. width with nine rows of full tiles and two rows of tile trimmed to 2 in. This meant that a grout line would fall at 29 in. from the threshold, so I marked line AB on the subfloor (drawing above).

The distance from A to B is 64½ in. Since 11 rows of tile set lengthwise take up 66 in., I had to trim away 1½ in. from the total. Again, I split the difference by trimming ¾ in. from the tiles that fall at the margins. Whenever possible, plan your layout so that the snap-cut edges of the tiles face the wall. This way,

they'll be covered by the trim tiles. On line AB, I measured out 5¼ in. from the edge of the subfloor to allow for the trimmed margin tiles, and then added another ⅛ in. for a grout line. Then I laid my carpenter's square along line AB, and drew line CD. I checked it with the 3-4-5 triangle method to make sure that line CD was perpendicular to line AB. From line CD, I measured over another 18 in. to mark the grout line for another three rows of tile, and scribed line EF on the plywood. These three lines gave me workable sections that were square to the threshold, and took the most visible tile cuts into consideration. The subfloor was ready (photo above).

Because my epoxy adhesive has such a short pot life (about 30 to 40 minutes, depending on the weather), I like to have all my tools, a sponge and a bucket of clean water nearby before I start setting the tiles. I also cut the first row of tiles to size before I mix up the goo. From experience, I've learned that in spite of everyone's best intentions, walls run out of square and out of parallel a little here and there, and bathroom fixtures like tubs and shower stalls frequently have slightly irregular surfaces. So even though I've allowed 5¼ in. for the first row of tiles, chances are that the actual measurement will vary a bit. Cutting the first row before I mix the adhesive lets me check the tiles in place for fit without having to think about $40 worth of epoxy turning to stone in my best bucket while I'm fiddling with the tile cuts.

The snap cutter—This is the tool you'll need to make straight cuts in tiles. A snap cutter costs about $40, but most tile shops or tool-rental shops rent them out. The cutter (photo facing page, center) consists of a metal base covered with a rubber pad that helps to hold the tile in place while it's scored. An adjustable fence braces the tile for 90° and 45° cuts, and a track over the base holds and guides the cutter wheel.

To make a cut, mark the cutline on the tile (I use a fine-point, felt-tip pen for this) and line it up with the cutter wheel. Hold the tile in place with one hand and the cutter handle in the other. Lift up on the handle so that the wheel touches the glazed surface of the tile, and pull the handle toward you. Try to score the glaze along the cutline in a single pass with the cutters. Making more than one pass will usually result in a bad break.

To break the tile, hold it in place with one hand, position the cutter handle over the tile and hit the handle firmly with the heel of your other hand. If you've done it right, the wings at the base of the handle will push down on the tile, causing it to break along the scored line. If you haven't ever used a snap cutter before, practice on a few scrap pieces of tile to get the technique right.

It's difficult to snap-cut strips narrower than about ¾ in. Usually the tile breaks in the wrong place. Instead, score the tile with the snap cutter, then nibble to the line with a pair of biters (drawing, facing page), specialized

Illustrations: Barbara Smolover

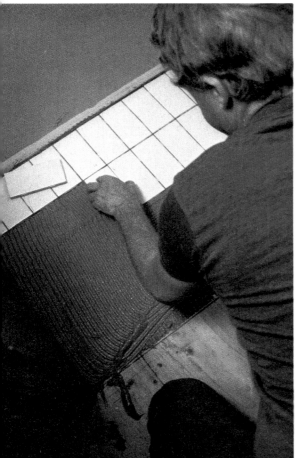

Epoxy mastic mixed to a stiff consistency is spread out along the first layout line (top photo) with a notched trowel. Notch depth should be about two-thirds the thickness of the tile. Frequently checking alignment with a straightedge, Byrne seats each tile with firm hand pressure (left). A light tap with the wooden handle of the trowel will seat the occasional proud edge. Pull up a freshly set tile occasionally to make sure the mastic coverage is correct, as in the photo above.

cutters that have a straight cutting edge on one jaw and a curved one on the other. Use the straight jaw on the glazed side, or face, of the tile.

Epoxy mastics—These adhesives were originally developed for industrial applications that required high bonding strength and resistance to chemicals. A tile-setting epoxy is composed of three separate components that are mixed together just before use. Part A is a resin of oxygen, carbon and hydrogen molecules suspended in a water solution. When combined with a hardener (part B) the resin molecules polymerize into long chains that form a resistant skin with high bonding strength. Part C is a mixture of portland cement and very fine sand. It is blended into the concoction of parts A and B to add body and compressive strength.

There are several brands of epoxy mastic, and they all do basically the same thing. They are sold by the unit, half-unit or in bulk. A full unit, enough to do a floor of about 50 sq. ft., costs about $40. I use Latapoxy 210 chiefly because the liquids are packaged in wide-mouthed containers that are easy to use, and they're mixed at a one-to-one ratio.

The two liquids have to be thoroughly mixed in their own containers before they are blended together. Although it's tempting to use a beater mounted on a drill for mixing, don't do so unless you have a very slow drill. High-speed mixing will whip air bubbles into the liquid, and they will weaken the mastic's bonding and compressive strength. I use a stick or a margin trowel for mixing.

Once the individual liquids are homogenized, pour them into a bucket in the proportions specified by the manufacturer, mix thoroughly, and slowly add the cement and sand while you keep stirring. I like to use my margin trowel for this because I can scrape the sides and bottom of the bucket with the trowel's straight sides and broad nose. There should be no lumps in the final mix, and it should be the consistency of very thick syrup. Never add water to thin the blend; it will render the bond useless.

I've found that the ideal temperature for working with epoxy mastics is between 70°F and 85°F. On hot days, the epoxy sets up faster. Conversely, a cold day slows the stuff down. I've laid floors on cold concrete slabs that have taken three days to set up, and others on plywood that are ready to grout three hours later. But on the average, it takes 24 hours before you can walk on the floor.

Setting the tile—Depending on the size of the section I'm about to set, I either pour the adhesive onto the floor or scoop it out of the bucket with my notched trowel. I spread out a skim coat using the flat side of the trowel, and then work it back in the other direction with the notched edge (photo top left). The depth of the notch should be about two-thirds the thickness of the tile. Spreading the mastic in several directions ensures good adhesion.

For this job, I started setting the tiles

From *Fine Homebuilding* magazine (October 1983) 17:70-75

against the wall beginning at the intersection of lines AB and CD. I pressed each tile down until it met solid resistance (photo facing page, bottom left), and if a tile corner stood a little proud, I tapped it down with the handle of my trowel.

Each tile should be completely embedded in the adhesive, and from time to time I pull up a freshly set tile to make sure the coverage was correct (photo facing page, bottom right). The bottom of the tile should be completely coated with adhesive, and the adhesive has to be wet enough to stick. If the epoxy mortar starts to set up, it has to be thrown out—its pot life can't be extended by adding water. If there isn't enough epoxy on the bottom of the tile I check, I use a trowel with a larger notch.

It's also important to make sure that there isn't too much adhesive because it will squeeze up between the tiles, and fill the gap that has to be occupied by the grout. Trenching out clogged grout lines is a wearisome task. If there's too much epoxy, I turn to a tool with a smaller notch. And if I get some mastic on top of a tile, I wipe it off right away with a wet sponge while it's still easy to remove.

On this job, I continued setting the trimmed tiles along the west wall, carefully aligning them with the layout, and then set in as many full-size tiles as possible around the toilet flange. This left some gaps, and I had to cut some tiles with curves to fit.

Cutting curves—This is where the biters come into play. With them I can shape a tile to fit almost any peculiar gap in the floor, but the tile has to be cut slowly and in the correct sequence (photos and drawing at right). To cut the curve in the tiles around the flange, I first drew the curve on the tiles. Because they will be covered by the toilet, these cuts don't have to be very precise. So I drew freehand guidelines. For radius cuts that are visible, I use a compass. Once the cutlines were drawn, I marked concentric lines about ¼ in. apart and extending to the edge of the tile. The drawing at right shows the sequence for removing the waste bit by bit. Start at the edge of the tile, and always work toward the middle, as shown. This is the best way to shape your cuts and avoid breaks.

Angular cuts—Seven rows in from the north wall of the bathroom, the shower stall takes a 45° jog across the floor, and this change of direction occurs in the center of a tile. To shape this five-sided piece (photos far right), I marked my cutlines with the aid of a sliding bevel and removed most of the waste with the snap cutter, nibbling from the corners toward the center. When I'd finally cut to the line, I smoothed the nibbled edges with my abrasive stone. The stone is also very useful for tile-shaping work that's too minute for the biters or snap cutter.

Trim tiles—The trim tiles where the wall and floor meet can be set as the job proceeds or after all the floor tiles have been placed and the adhesive has set. I used a bullnose base

Cutting curves. Concentric lines leading to the final line mark the sequence of cuts (drawing, below). To trim tiles to fit around the toilet flange, first mark the tiles with the outline of the curve, then nibble away the bits with the biters, starting from the edges and working in (photos below). Two tile shards used as shims under one of the tiles (bottom photo) compensate for an uneven subsurface. The long bolts allow for the thickness of the new floor.

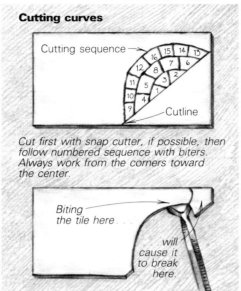

Cutting curves

Cut first with snap cutter, if possible, then follow numbered sequence with biters. Always work from the corners toward the center.

Cutting angles. The shower-stall angle is transferred to the tiles with a bevel gauge (top). To make a pair of angular cuts, begin by removing as much waste as possible with a snap cutter. Then work slowly with the biters from opposite corners to the middle (center). When you reach the line, smooth the raw edges with an abrasive stone (above).

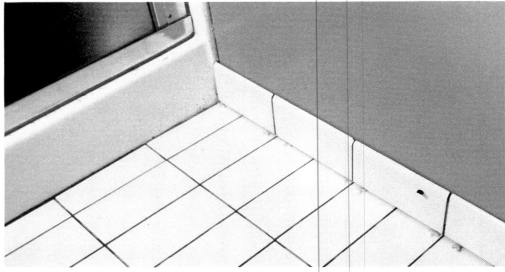

Trim tiles. It's easier to apply the epoxy to individual trim tiles, left, than it is to comb the mastic onto the wall. Trim tiles are temporarily held in place by plastic spacers, below, while the mastic sets up. Notice that the trim tile on the left has been shortened to match the width of the field tiles adjacent to the shower enclosure, so that the grout lines on floor and trim align.

Ceramic tiles

All tiles, even the most elegant, start out as the earthy ooze that lines the bottom of a streambed. As upstream mineral deposits slowly erode, particles are washed downriver where they mingle with organic materials to form sediments known as clay. This is the same soil that expands and contracts as it gets wet and dries out, and it's famous for giving builders fits. But if the mineral particles (primarily aluminum silicates) are removed from the soil, molded into flat pieces, dried and heated to high temperature, the resulting tile is as hard as flint.

Water absorption—The purity of the clay and the temperature at which it's fired determine how much water the tiles will absorb. This is a factor in choosing the right tile for a particular job. Impervious and fully vitrified (made glasslike) tiles are made from highly refined clay (the bisque), and have been fired at temperatures as high as 2,345°F. At this temperature the clay particles begin to fuse, becoming very dense and almost glasslike.

An impervious tile won't absorb more than 0.5% water. This rating means that a tile will absorb no more water than 0.5% of its dry weight after being boiled for five hours. Fully vitrified floor tiles won't absorb more than 3% water; a semivitreous floor tile won't take on more than 7% water while nonvitreous (soft-bodied) tiles absorb more than 7%.

As a rule, 5% and below is considered an acceptable absorption rating for tiles in wet locations; so impervious, vitreous and some semivitreous tiles make good countertops and bathroom floors. Other considerations are acid resistance, resistance to abrasion, slip resistance and glaze hardness. Nonvitreous tiles can also be used in wet places, but they should be secured to a mortar backing over a moisture barrier to prevent water from seeping through and damaging the framing. Never use nonvitreous tiles in wet locations where they might freeze—the moisture in them will expand and pop them loose.

Glazes—Many tiles have color built right into them—terra cotta is a good example. These unglazed tiles range in earth tones from yellow to deep red. Other tiles are finished with a baked-on surface of glass (a glaze) that can take on nearly any color and that's easy to clean.

When you're choosing a floor tile that's glazed, make sure its finish isn't so slick it's dangerous to walk on. And be sure the glazed tile is rated for floor use. Wall tiles are too soft to hold up to foot traffic, their glazes will scratch fairly easily, and they are very slippery.

Some glazed tiles are called "button backed" because of the little feet cast into their backs. These feet allow the tiles to be stacked in the kiln without the use of kiln furniture—tiny, high-fire shims that keep the tiles from fusing together. Integral button shims keep manufacturing costs down without affecting quality. Button-backed tiles must be embedded in a high-compression mastic so foot traffic won't snap off their unsupported corners and edges.

Types of tile—The various types of tile are manufactured in different ways and are suitable for different uses.

Quarry tiles are hard-bodied, with color throughout the clay. They are usually a deep red, but black and off-white are also available. They have a water-absorption rating of 5% or less.

Quarry tiles are made by an extrusion process that squeezes a moist body made from natural clay or shale through a die. This shapes a constant cross section, which is cut at intervals with a wire. Quarry tiles range from 3 in. by 3 in. up to 12 in. by 12 in., their dimensions are reasonably accurate, and they're modestly priced—around $2 to $3 per sq. ft.

Paver tiles can be glazed or unglazed, porcelain or natural clay. The unglazed varieties are less expensive, about $2 per sq. ft.

Most pavers are formed by a process called the dust-press method. Depending on the type or color desired, various clay bodies are mixed together, and the wet mix is squeezed through a filter to remove excess moisture. The resulting crumbly mix is allowed to dry almost completely,

then it's poured into steel molds mounted on hydraulic presses and compressed into tile shapes. This method is especially good for making precisely sized tiles.

Ceramic mosaic tiles are either porcelain or natural clay. They range from ¾ in. by ¾ in. up to 4 in. by 4 in. These tiles come arranged on fabric or paper sheets to make them easier to handle and set. Ceramic mosaics can be either glazed or unglazed, and some contain an abrasive additive to make them a better walking surface. They're made by the dust-press method or by plastic pressing, which uses a die to form wet clay body into tile shapes by direct pressure. Ceramic mosaics come in a mind-boggling variety of colors and designs, and usually cost more than quarry or paver tile—$3 per sq. ft. and up.

Mexican paver tiles are the fat handmade tiles from south of the border. They are rolled out like pastry with a rolling pin. Frequently they are formed directly on the ground, and their backs show the irregular imprint of some faraway courtyard. Their faces sometimes show the tracks of chickens and other barnyard creatures, giving them a quality called "distressed" in the trade. Mexican pavers readily absorb water, and their surfaces will dust with heavy use. They should be coated with a protective sealer (available at any tile store) to create a durable surface. They're not recommended for bathrooms.

Mexican pavers are cut out with big cookie cutters and the fresh tiles are set aside to dry in the sun. They are usually large (12 in. by 12 in.) square tiles, but interlocking shapes like octagons and ogees are also made. These pavers are made of a soft-bodied clay of varied earth tones that is fired at a low temperature and sometimes under primitive conditions. Some small outfits even use old cars as kilns. The sun-dried tiles are arranged inside the car and its trunk. To fire them, old tires are piled around and on top of the car and set ablaze.

For more on tile specifications and installation, see **The Ceramic Tile Manual.** It costs $21 plus $2 shipping (Calif. residents add 6%) from the Ceramic Tile Institute, 700 N. Virgil Ave., Los Angeles, Calif. 90029. **—Charles Miller**

tile for trim here, and made sure that the trim-tile grout lines lined up with the floor-tile grout lines. I back-buttered each tile and pressed it in place, then shimmed each one from below (photos facing page).

Grout—Grouting tiles is both an art and a science, and while there's no substitute for experience, knowing a little of the science can make the art happen a lot easier. Grout doesn't just fill the spaces between the tiles. It should be packed in from the setting bed to the surface of the tile. Sometimes a tile won't be completely supported by mastic, with a gap that may undercut its edge. These gaps have to be filled with grout, so the grout has to be viscous enough to flow into the voids.

Before I mix the grout, I dampen the entire floor with a sponge. This makes it easier to spread the grout, and it keeps water from being sucked out too quickly by a dry setting bed or highly absorbent tiles. Premature drying weakens the grout.

There are many grouts on the market, but for this floor I mixed my own with equal parts of standard portland cement and 30-mesh sand. A few years ago I started using latex additive in my grout, and I wouldn't do a job now without it. The latex makes the grout easier to spread, and it also speeds curing. Latex additives are made by Custom Building Materials (6511 Salt Lake Ave., Bell, Calif. 90201), Upco (3101 Euclid Ave., Cleveland, Ohio 44115) and by Laticrete International; these companies also make epoxy thinset.

Without a latex admix, a freshly grouted floor has to be kept moist and covered for at least 72 hours. With the latex, the floor is ready to use in 24 hours, and it doesn't have to be covered, unless it's especially hot and dry. I haven't had any problems with corner cracks or grout shrinkage. And when used full strength, the latex reduces mold and mildew growth on tiles in damp spots.

Follow the directions on the package if you use a latex admix. The procedure usually amounts to slow machine or hand mixing until the grout is smooth and lump free, and about the consistency of drywall joint compound. After letting it sit about five minutes, you mix the grout again, and it's ready to use.

I remove any standing water from the floor, and if any areas have dried out (a problem on hot days) I remoisten them with my sponge. Then I dump enough grout on the floor to cover about 10 sq. ft. With my rubber trowel at about a 30° angle, I force the grout into the voids (photo above center). I go over each area a few times with a side-to-side motion until the gaps are packed and then I scrape off the excess grout with the edge of the rubber trowel. Next I thoroughly wring out a sponge and I go over the freshly packed area to remove any grout that stands above the level of the tiles (photo top right). The pressure on the sponge determines how quickly the excess is removed.

I avoid bullying the grout, and if it seems a little too soft, I spread and pack another portion of the floor, and then come back. But it's

Grouting. After excess epoxy is removed from between the tiles, grout is forced into the spaces with the sharp edge of a rubber trowel, below. It takes several passes from different directions to fill the voids. Most of the excess grout is scraped away with the trowel. As the grout begins to set up, the grout lines are brought down and made slightly concave with a sponge, right. The sponge is worked in parallel strokes, and rinsed out frequently to remove the sand and cement that it picks up. The last cleaning, below right, is with a nearly dry sponge that is rinsed out after each pass.

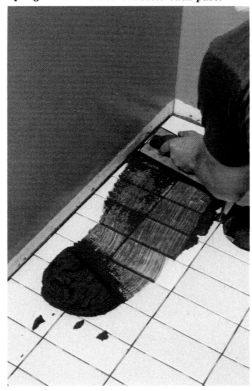

important not to get too far ahead of the cleaning process—it takes a lot longer than the spreading. During this stage of the job, I remix the grout about every 10 minutes to keep it from setting up in the bucket.

When the joints have been formed and all the sand is gone from the surface, I make parallel sweeps with the sponge to complete the wet cleaning (photo center right). I use one clean side of the sponge per wipe. The rest of the cleanup is done dry.

After about 10 or 15 minutes a cement haze begins to form on top of the tiles. I remove it with cheesecloth, making sure not to distort the grout lines by pressing too hard. If some of the haze won't come off, I rub the area with a moist sponge. Then I remove with a margin trowel any grout that may have found its way into the expansion gap between the plywood underlayment and the wall.

Once the grout has hardened (about 24 hours), I vacuum the dust and grit from the floor, and I apply a bead of silicone caulk to the tile where it abuts the tub or shower stall, and to the trim tiles at the margins of the floor (photo and drawing, right). The caulk keeps the water out and allows the floor to expand and contract without damaging itself. □

Michael Byrne lives in Walnut Creek, Calif.

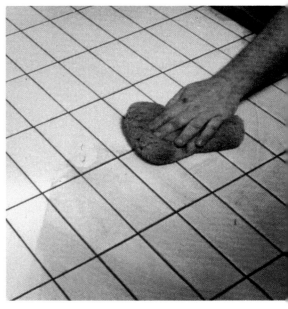

Caulking and finishing. Before the grout sets up, it is squared with a margin trowel along the edges of the shower (below), and excess grout is removed from expansion joints. Once it sets, a bead of silicone caulk is applied.

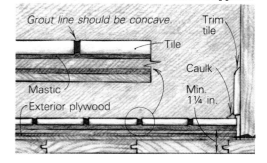

Grout line should be concave.   Trim tile

Tile

Mastic   Caulk

Exterior plywood   Min. 1¼ in.

A Mortar-Bed Shower

Building the critical parts— the pan, the wall membrane and the mortar bed

by Michael Byrne

More and more of my clients want a fancy bathroom, and the showpiece in nearly every one that I work on is a shower done in tile. Because it's easy to clean and impervious to water, tile is an ideal finish material in the bathroom. Even more compelling is the vast array of contemporary tile colors that are available. Some tiles are small enough to conform to almost any shower configuration, so I sometimes find myself building round or oval shower stalls. But regardless of the shape of the project, the three most important components of any first-class tile shower are the pan, the wall membrane and the mortar bed to which the tiles are affixed. This article is about the materials and methods that I use to build leak-free tile showers. The photos are of several different jobs.

The shower pan—When the water swirls down the drain in a mortar shower, it passes through a two-piece cast-iron or brass fitting called a sub-drain (drawing, below left). The upper half of the sub-drain is a hat-shaped casting with an open top that's fitted with a chrome screen. The lower half is similar, but it has a threaded opening in its center to secure it to a nipple extending from the shower's p-trap. Around the circumference of the top half are six small holes. Three of them accommodate the bolts that clamp the drain halves together, with the pan's membrane sandwiched between. The other three are weep holes to let any moisture that gets into the mortar bed escape into the drain. If this residual moisture is trapped, it can promote the growth of fungus and bacteria in the mortar bed.

A shower pan waterproofs the floor of a shower stall. Pans are often made of metal—usually copper, lead or galvanized sheet metal. Although metal is traditionally considered a superior pan material, my experience has taught me otherwise. I've found that a metal shower pan will usually disintegrate around the drain, a victim of electrolysis. I've seen this happen even when the metal has been given a protective coat of asphalt.

Hot-mopped pans, made of alternating layers of 15-lb. or 30-lb. felt paper and melted tar, have long been used for showers and carry the blessing of most building codes. Some localities may have air-quality control laws that prohibit open melting of tar, and some installers consider hot-mopped pans just plain dangerous to work with. Finding someone to install one may be a problem, because this is specialized work requiring experience, speed and precision.

About ten years ago, an accident that dumped about 4 gal. of hot tar onto a carpet convinced me to look for an alternative. I tried fiberglass cloth and resin pans, but quickly rejected them because they crack at the slightest movement of the framing.

Finally I discovered CPE (chlorinated polyethylene) pan membrane material. It is thick (40 mil), tough and flexible, and it carries a 50-year guar-

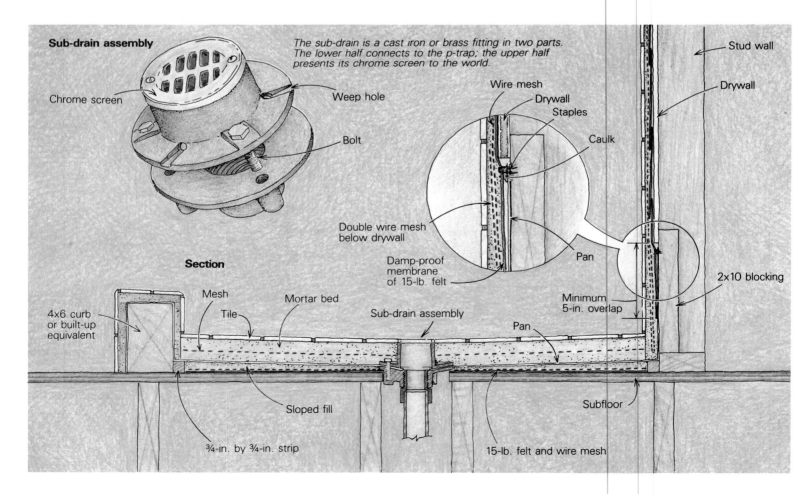

Sub-drain assembly

The sub-drain is a cast iron or brass fitting in two parts. The lower half connects to the p-trap; the upper half presents its chrome screen to the world.

Chrome screen

Weep hole

Wire mesh

Drywall

Staples

Bolt

Caulk

Double wire mesh below drywall

Damp-proof membrane of 15-lb. felt

Pan

Stud wall

Drywall

Section

Mesh

Mortar bed

4x6 curb or built-up equivalent

Tile

Sub-drain assembly

Pan

Minimum 5-in. overlap

2x10 blocking

Sloped fill

Subfloor

¾-in. by ¾-in. strip

15-lb. felt and wire mesh

antee. In addition, companion sealers, caulks and accessory patches (preformed corner pieces) enable me to create shower pans in any shape. Chloraloy 240 (The Noble Co., 614 Monroe St., Box 332, Grand Haven, Mich. 49417) is the brand I use, with no failures on over 600 pans. A similar product is called Composeal 40 (The Compotite Corporation, PO Box 26188, Los Angeles, Calif. 90026).

Sloping the sub-floor—To ensure that the sub-drain weep holes work properly, the shower floor must be sloped toward the drain at no less than ¼ in. to the foot (drawing, facing page, right). This involves a sloping mortar base over a level plywood subfloor.

First, I position the lower half of the sub-drain on the plywood subfloor. I cut a circular hole in the plywood that is about ½ in. smaller in diameter than the drain flange. This gives the flange ¼ in. of solid bearing, which prevents the drain casting from punching through the pan when someone steps on it. I check both halves of the casting for burrs, and if I find any, I file them off. With the lower drain half bearing on the plywood, its flange stands proud by about ¼ in.

To get the proper slope, I first lay ¾-in. by ¾-in. strips around the perimeter of the 3-ft. square shower and nail them to the subfloor next to the plate. If the floor is larger than 3 ft. square, I use thicker wood strips to maintain the slope. My calculations are made from the point on the floor farthest from the drain. Then I cover the plywood with a layer of 15-lb. felt and 20-ga. 1-in. wire mesh, stapled in place. Next I mix up a batch of mortar using Laticrete 3701 (a latex admix made by Laticrete International, 1 Laticrete Park North, Bethany, Conn. 06525) instead of water. This "deck mud" is on the crumbly, dry side of mortar mixes (for more on mixing mortars, see sidebar on p. 109). I pack the deck mud over the paper and wire, and float away the excess using the wood strips and drain flange as guides (photo bottom right). I let the mortar harden overnight before I fabricate the pan.

Installing a pan—In my area, the code requires the pan to extend at least 9 in. up the walls, and it must have a solid backing. Also, the lower edge of the drywall usually ends up about 9 in. above the floor, and it too must have a solid backing. Both of these needs are filled by nailing 2x10 blocking above the plate and between the studs (drawing, facing page, right).

Square shower pans are the easiest to make. First I measure the dimensions of the floor, and then add 9 in. for each wall and about 14 in. for the curb to determine the size of the CPE. The curb must be covered completely, inside face, top and outer face. The CPE will be cut to lap over the curb once the pan is in position. CPE

A tile shower can add a dazzling touch to any home (above right), but before the tiles can be applied, a careful sequence of work must be followed to prevent water damage. One way to get the necessary drainage to the center of the shower pan is to slope mortar fill over a flat subfloor (right). The thickness of the mortar is controlled by wooden strips placed around the perimeter of the pan. They needn't be removed.

From *Fine Homebuilding* magazine (April 1986) 32:46-52

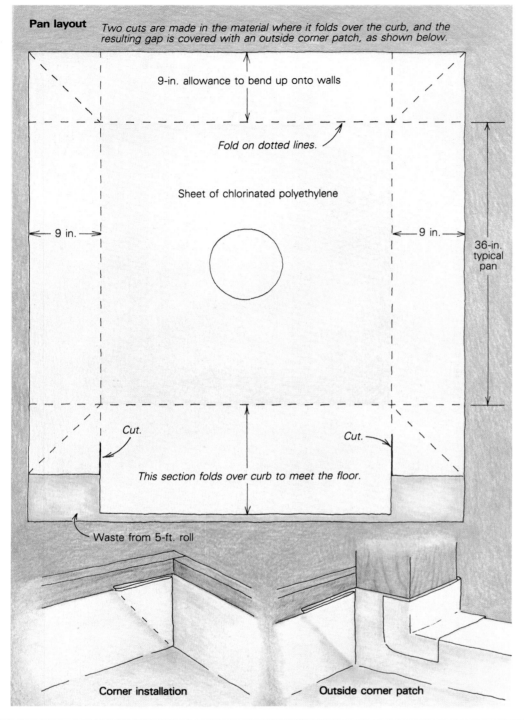

Pan layout *Two cuts are made in the material where it folds over the curb, and the resulting gap is covered with an outside corner patch, as shown below.*

9-in. allowance to bend up onto walls

Fold on dotted lines.

Sheet of chlorinated polyethylene

← 9 in. →   ← 9 in. →

36-in. typical pan

Cut.   Cut.

This section folds over curb to meet the floor.

Waste from 5-ft. roll

Corner installation   Outside corner patch

comes in 5-ft. wide rolls, so I cut off a piece that best matches one of my total dimensions. At $8 to $10 a linear foot, I don't want many scraps hanging around.

I draw the layout onto the CPE with a felt-tip marker or a pencil as shown in the drawing at left. The dotted lines show where the material laps up the walls, and how the corners are creased. At this point I glue a circle of pan material to the area that will end up between the drain halves. This makes a thicker gasket for the drain to grip at this potential point of abrasion.

To fold the pan, crease the material along the four lines that represent the perimeter of the pan. Then fold the diagonal corner creases away from the center of the pan (photo bottom left), so the triangular tabs end up between the pan and the blocking (detail drawing, far left).

During installation, this type of pan droops away from the wall, which slows down the job. To counter this tendency, I coat the blocking and the floor with asphalt roofing cement. I spread it around evenly with a ⅛-in. notched trowel. Roofing cement can be a fire hazard, so make sure the room is well ventilated and wear a mask with a charcoal filter for protection against the fumes. I also wear rubber gloves to keep the black goop off my hands.

Once I've spread the roofing cement, I screw the three bolts into the lower half of the sub-drain. This lets me feel where the bolt heads are so I know where to cut the pan for the bolts. For added insurance against leaks, I run two beads of butyl caulk around the lower drain half—one bead inside and one bead outside the bolt circle. I use either Bostik 2000 (Bostik Div., Emhart Corp., Boston St., Middleton, Mass. 01949) or Noblebond 150 (The Noble Co., address above).

Next, I roll the prefolded pan into a bundle and position it over the shower floor. Starting at the drain, I smooth the air bubbles out toward the wall and press the material into the corners, leaving no voids under or behind the pan. To flatten the folds in the corners, I drizzle some Nobleweld 100 liquid glue (also made by The Noble Co.) into the fold and hold it in place a few seconds until it sets. When I'm satisfied the pan is snug, I staple it to the blocking along the top (photo below right). Then I cover the staples

Installing the shower pan. The pan is made of a piece of chlorinated polyethylene (CPE) sheet. After the folds in the pan (dotted lines in the drawing, above left) have been laid out, the piece is spread out flat to make the necessary folds at the corners. In the photo at far left, a circle of CPE has been glued in place at the center of the pan to thicken it where it will be sandwiched by the halves of the sub-drain. The corners of the pan are folded so that the triangular-shaped tab ends up next to the blocking. Once the pan has been positioned on the sloped mortar base, it can be stapled to the blocking along the top inch of the material (left). These staples are then covered with a layer of compatible caulking compound.

with a glob of caulk. No staples should be located below the finished height of the curb, which is usually 6 in. At the threshold, the pan is cut and folded over the curb. The resulting gap in the pan is covered with a corner patch (detail drawing, facing page, right). These corners can be purchased from your tile supplier or made from scrap. They are glued in place with the recommended adhesive.

To put the drain halves together, feel around for the bolts, and press the CPE down over the head of each bolt with one hand. With the other hand, use a utility knife to cut out a ¼-in. dia. circle of pan material, using the bolt head as a cutting board. When all three holes are made, stretch the CPE over each bolt. Then unscrew the bolts, position the top half of the drain over its mate, reinsert the bolts and tighten them evenly with a socket wrench. Finally, remove the drain screen and cut away the disc of CPE locked in the drain.

Typical mortar-bed layout—Most showers are 3 ft. square, and the wall tiles extend one row above the shower head. The flanged elbow that accepts the shower-head gooseneck is usually 72 in. above the plywood subfloor. Another full row of wall tile extends beyond the curb on the bathroom side of the shower. The layout line marks the edge of the mortar bed, and it begins next to this row of tile (drawing, top right). Its placement depends on the trim you use. The drawing at bottom right shows two trim styles, and their relationship to the bed.

Wall membrane and wire mesh—The wall membrane is made of horizontal bands of 15-lb. felt, which are bedded in asphalt roofing cement, shingle fashion, over a substrate of water-resistant drywall. You can hang the drywall either before or after installing the pan, but be sure to protect the pan if you do the latter.

Because felt paper puckers slightly between staples when mortar is floated over it, some areas may be difficult to screed. My solution to this problem is to spread roofing cement with my ⅛-in. V-notched trowel over all the drywall, and bed the paper just like the pan (top photo, next page).

Laminating the paper to the drywall takes about 10 min. and costs about $12 to $15 for a 3-ft. by 3-ft. shower. But it's worth it. The only staple holes needed are those on the edge that laps the pan. The paper lies absolutely flat, and the roofing cement seals the paper where it usually frays and cracks in the corners—where most leaks start. The thin layer of asphalt seals around each staple as it enters the wall and is a bit of insurance against any breaks in the membrane that may go unnoticed. This step is well worth the time and effort.

The first wrapping of paper overlaps the pan by at least 5 in. (drawing, p. 118, right). After it is fastened with ½-in. staples 6 in. o. c. to the drywall, the portion overlapping the pan should be pressed into the bead of caulk, and stapled to the blocking through the caulk and the top edge of the pan. To get the felt snug in the corners and to eliminate any little coves, use a straightedge. The paper should be flat against

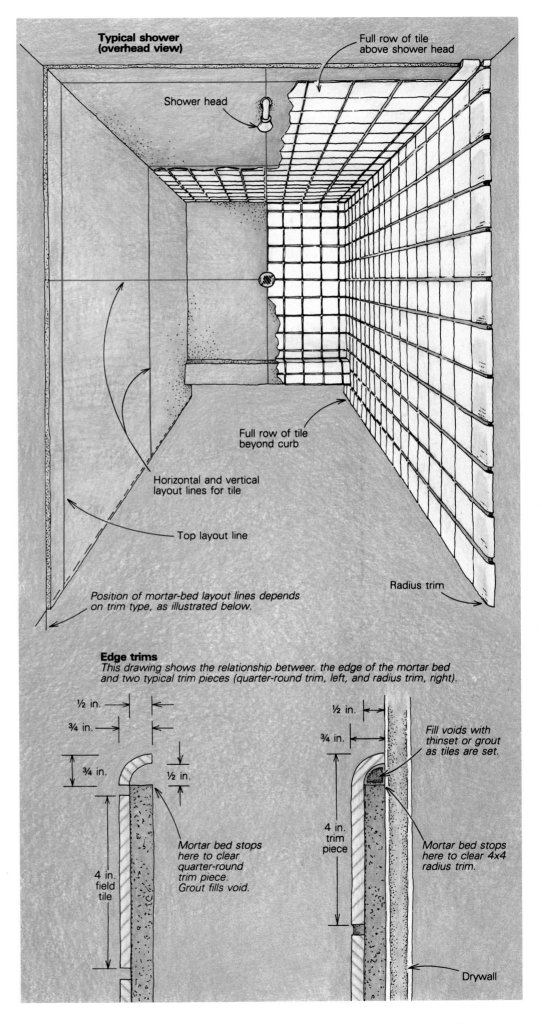

Typical shower (overhead view)

Full row of tile above shower head

Shower head

Full row of tile beyond curb

Horizontal and vertical layout lines for tile

Top layout line

Radius trim

Position of mortar-bed layout lines depends on trim type, as illustrated below.

Edge trims
This drawing shows the relationship between the edge of the mortar bed and two typical trim pieces (quarter-round trim, left, and radius trim, right).

½ in.
¾ in.
¾ in.
½ in.
4 in. field tile

Mortar bed stops here to clear quarter-round trim piece. Grout fills void.

½ in.
¾ in.
4 in. trim piece

Fill voids with thinset or grout as tiles are set.

Mortar bed stops here to clear 4x4 radius trim.

Drywall

the wall and make a sharp right-angled turn. Subsequent bands of paper should overlap.

Once the wall membrane is in place, the 20-ga., 1-in. wire mesh follows (photo below). The twists in the mesh should always be parallel to the floor. This way they provide the most support for the mud. The bands of mesh should be fastened with 9/16-in. staples every 6 in. so there are no bumps or bulges, and bands should overlap each other by 2 in. The wire should be neatly folded in the corners. I find that working the tips of the tinsnips along the corner keeps the bend sharp and crisp.

At the curb, I like to double up the wire and prefold it so that it hugs the curb tightly. This allows me to use staples on the outside face only, where leaks are less of a problem. Staples are not allowed below the top inch of the curb, so to keep the wire snug here, I sometimes glue the wire in place using small strips of CPE like little belt loops. I also double the wire below the junction of the pan and the drywall to reinforce the thicker mortar (drawing, p. 118, right).

Water test—Except for placing the screeds, the job is now ready for floating the mortar bed, but at this point, do a water test. Plug the lower drain and fill the pan with water right to the top of the curb and let it sit, undisturbed, for 24 hours. If possible, get under the floor with a flashlight and look for any sign of leaks.

If I spot a leak, I first check the drain. Did I tighten the bolts firmly and evenly? If the leak is behind one of the envelope folds, I peel back the wire and cover the corner with more glue, a scrap of CPE or an accessory piece made by Noble. Any punctures are easily repaired with a little square of CPE glued on like a tire patch.

Placing the float strips—I begin on the back wall by plumbing two 1/4-in. by 1 1/4-in. wood float strips that are bedded in vertical columns of mud (photo facing page, top). The strips are located 6 in. to 8 in. in from the corners. The flanged elbow for the shower head is usually on this wall, and at this point I thread a 6-in. pipe nipple into the elbow to keep mortar out of it as the walls are floated.

To form the mortar columns that secure the float strips, I press a thin layer of mud tight onto the wire to ensure a good grip. This layer need only be thick enough to cover the wire—no more. Additional layers can then be built up 1/4 in. at a time. I cut the float strip to run the full height of the mortar bed, and then I wet it on both sides to keep it from warping. I push each one into its column of mud. With a level held against it, each float strip is plumbed so the minimum wall thickness equals 1/2 in. Due to the vagaries of wood framing, the thickness of the float will vary on the wall. But the mud allows you to make up for these framing inaccuracies, and to create plumb walls and parallel rows of tiles that don't have to be tapered. This is one of the benefits of a mortar-bed shower.

Once plumbed, the strips guide a straightedge, which screeds off the excess mud floated between the strips. After the central part of the wall has been screeded off, the two areas at the sides are in turn floated and screeded. The side walls need a slightly different treatment.

The portion of side wall nearest the back wall should be plumbed so that when tiled, the corner does not appear tapered from top to bottom. Along the outside portion, where the trim tiles meet the drywall, the bed must be a consistent 1/2 in. thick—even if the wall is out of plumb. Otherwise the grout joint between trim tiles and drywall will be tapered and unsightly. In other words, when tile meets tile—make it

Top, Byrne spreads a layer of asphalt gum on the drywall backing before he applies the felt membrane. The asphalt will help to keep the felt tight to the wall, and it seals any holes made by driving staples into the drywall. With the pan, membrane and wire in place (left), the shower stands ready for its layer of mortar. This shower is fancier than most, with a bench and what will be a glass-block wall on the left. The wire hanging down is a thermostat to control a steam-bath attachment. At this stage be sure the nipple that goes to the shower head is in its fitting. Many a shower has gone to the tiled-and-grouted stage with the supply fitting entombed somewhere above the mixer valve.

plumb. When tile meets drywall—keep the bed thickness uniform. I do this by tacking a ½-in. thick float strip vertically along the margin of the paper and wire (photo bottom right).

Mixing mortar—The mud I use for walls is different from the mud that will be used for the curb top and floor of the shower. Both are made up of 3 parts clean, sharp sand to 1 part portland cement. For the wall mortar, I add extra liquid to the mix to make a thick, spreadable paste called fat mud.

Fat mud for walls always seems to behave better if mixing is kept to a minimum. The purpose of mixing is to homogenize all the ingredients. Proportions may allow a wide margin of error, but I prefer to play it safe and measure out the dry ingredients in 5-gal. buckets. The mixing process can be a messy one, so I try to work outdoors when I can.

Once measured, the sand and cement are layered evenly in a mixing box and combined using small bites of the mixing hoe. The dry stuff needs to be mixed about three times. That means gradually chopping the mix first to one side then the other, piling it up each time. Once the sand and cement have been combined, I pour in about three-quarters of the latex admix and chop the dry stuff into it, once again back and forth with small bites. Temperature and humidity will affect the consistency of the mix. I want to end up with mud that is wet enough to be sticky and spreadable without being runny. Excess moisture weakens the mortar bed, so I add the remaining liquid carefully. Once the mud is mixed, it's dumped onto a 3-ft. sq. plywood mud board that has been dampened so it doesn't suck any moisture out of the mix. The hawk is then loaded from the board by plowing mud onto it with the trowel.

Mortaring the walls, and screeding—The mud is applied to the walls in stages. With the float strips already in place, I press a thin coat of mud firmly into the rest of the exposed wire mesh (middle photo, right) to ensure that the entire bed will be keyed into the wire. Then I apply a fill coat, depositing a layer about ¼ in. thick with each pass. When troweling over the wire coat, I don't have to press so hard, and the face of the trowel is tilted at about 35° to the wall. This can be hard work, but when I'm working with a sweet batch of mud, it becomes a pleasure. When there's enough mud on the wall, I make a pass with my screed to check for depressions in the mortar bed that need to be filled in.

For screeding, I have a set of ten nesting aluminum straightedges, which range in length from 18 in. to 6 ft. They have an L-shaped cross section, which keeps them fairly rigid and true. When I'm screeding a wall float, I use a straightedge that's at least 6 in. longer than the distance between the two float strips. Facing the wall, I grip the straightedge with both hands and ease the long blade onto the float strips. Starting at the bottom, I move the straightedge back and forth against the strips, lifting upward at the same time. This removes the excess mud (photo bottom right). The pressure against the strips

should be fairly light—they should act as guides, not supports.

Where a lot of excess mortar must be removed, the straightedge may not even touch the strips. Screeding off too quickly usually tears chunks out of the mortar bed, leaving holes that have to be packed full and screeded again. Screeding too slowly may agitate the bed enough to loosen the setting particles of sand and cement and cause the bed to slump.

If the mortar is too wet, it may sag and slump away from the wall. This kind of mix must be allowed to sit a while before screeding. Mud that is too dry will take considerable effort to screed, and the float strips are often forced out of alignment.

When the straightedge is filled with mud, I remove it from the wall by continuing a sideways motion and gradually pulling it away from the surface. Good mud has a tenacious grip. If I simply pull the straightedge up and away from the wall, it may pull some mud off with it, leaving me with more holes to backfill.

Once the central portion of the back wall is screeded off, the two edge voids must be filled. I go through the floating and screeding routine first on one side, then the other.

Each individual plane is treated this way until all the vertical surfaces have been covered. After each is finished, I remove the embedded float strips and pack the channel with mud. To do this, I flatten the mud on the hawk until it's about 1 in. thick, and then I cut a strip of mud about 1 in. wide and about 1 ft. long and trowel it into the channel.

Finishing the mortar bed—The surface of an unfinished bed will be pockmarked with craters. Filling these voids increases the potential for adhesion between the tiles and the bed.

After about an hour, most of the walls have set up firmly enough for me to finish the bed with a wood float. Floats are sometimes confounding tools. My favorite is twisted all out of shape when it is dry, but after soaking in water for about five minutes the face is perfectly flat. The finish is noticeably coarser than a steel-troweled finish. I prefer the coarse finish because it leaves tiny crannies that help bond the tile to the wall.

The wooden float should literally "float" on the surface of the mud. The mortar bed is already flat from screeding, so the float is used to slice off the excess above the float-strip channels, and to pack the voids with mud. To be most effective, the float should be in constant motion, lightly carving away at any excess mortar with its edge. Whether the float is moving up or down, it must also be moving sideways as well, or the tool will begin gouging the surface. Inside corners are cleaned up by moving the float vertically, with the edge at about a 35° angle to the corner. I sometimes further sharpen an inside corner with a steel trowel to allow additional clearance for thin glass mosaics or tiny penny-round tiles.

Wall-tile installation—Once the mortar beds have been finished with the float, I let them sit overnight to get good and hard. The additive I

Floating a shower begins with the back wall—the one where two float strips have to be embedded in mortar. In the top photo, Byrne checks the strips for plumb, adjusting them inward with a tap of his hammer. The mortar, a sticky blend, is applied in thin layers with upward strokes of the trowel (above). The float strips on the back wall have been removed, and their cavities await backfill. Below, the excess mortar between the float strips is removed with a straightedge worked back and forth while it is simultaneously lifted slowly upward. On this wall, one ¼-in. thick float strip is embedded in a column of mud, while the other ½-in. strip is tacked to the drywall at the edge of the shower.

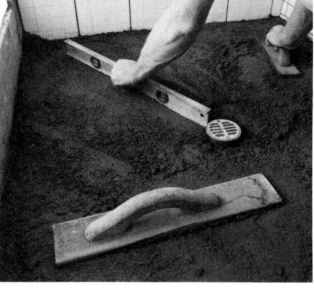

Crumbly deck mud is built up to half the thickness of the final depth over the pan (top left), and then a layer of wire mesh is laid upon it. Care must be taken not to clog the weep holes in the top half of the subdrain. A deposit of pea gravel or the tile spacers used here (top right) keep the mortar from plugging the holes. The last layer of deck mud is applied over the wire mesh and spread about with a wooden float. Byrne checks the slope of the mortar with a level (right), and brings its finished elevation to the edge of the drain so that the tile will be flush with the drain screen.

use frees me from having to keep the bed damp and covered.

Before I start setting the tile, I snap in some chalk lines to divide the walls into quadrants so I don't have to fuss with the level once the walls are covered with goo. On a typical shower, such as the one in the top drawing on p. 121, one vertical and one horizontal line are usually all I need on each wall. Most walls will need to have some tiles trimmed along the side to fit. Rather than just cut the tiles on one side of a wall, I take an equal amount off both sides.

I don't like to rely on shims or sand to help level the first course of tile. Instead, I use a high-quality thinset mortar that holds the tiles in position on the wall without sagging. This way I can start setting the tiles at the intersection of the plumb and level layout lines and move outward. For more detailed information on setting and grouting tile, refer to the articles on pp. 106-111 and pp. 112-117.

Floating the floor—After the wall tiles are set, the curb top and floor can be mortared. These areas both receive a layer of deck mud—the same mix used for the sloped fill under the pan.

The floor should be floated in two steps to allow a sheet of wire mesh to be placed in the center of the bed. First I spread out enough deck mud to build up half the thickness of the finished bed (top photo, far left). To allow the water to flow freely into the weep holes in the drain, I surround the bolting flange of the drain with a handful of either pea gravel or the little plastic spacers used to align tiles (top photo, near left). The sheet of chicken wire is then placed over the first layer of mud, and the remaining mud is troweled over it to bring the bed to its finished height (middle photo, left). I level the perimeter of the bed using the wall tiles as a guide. From this height, the floor should match the subfloor's slope as it makes its way to the drain. I could use float strips to regulate the float's thickness, but I've done enough of these to use only a wood float and level to check my progress; there must be no level spots where water can collect. I usually use two wood floats for this type of work: a 14-in. float for the bulk of the mud moving, and a 10-in. float for the final forming and finishing.

Setting the curb—If I'm using surface bullnose trim for the curb, I wait until the tiles on the inside of the curb have set up to float the top of the curb. This lets me use the tiles as a guide for the thickness of the mortar (drawing, left). The curb top is pitched inward at an angle of about ½ in. per foot so water sheds quickly.

When the last of the tiles is set, I allow the job to rest for a day so the thinset can harden. This lets me really force the grout into the tile work. As a final precaution against leaks, I wait until the grout has cured (three days with additives, twenty-eight days without) and then I run a bead of silicone caulk along all the inside corners to seal off any cracks that may appear once the shower is in use. □

Michael Byrne is president of Ceramic Tile Associates in Burlington, Vt.

Curb details
Once the vertical mortar beds are in place on the curb, the inside of the curb is tiled (section A, below). The top edge of the tile stands above the mortar, and along with a straightedge, becomes a guide for the curbtop mortar (B). Surface bullnose and field tiles are placed on the curbtop mortar (C), followed by bullnose and field tiles on the outside of the curb (D).

Mortar beds — Mortar — Straightedge — Surface bullnose — Surface bullnose

A   B   C   D

A Remodeled Bath

A better plan, a greenhouse window and some bold blue tile give a dingy bathroom a brand-new look

by Dennis Allen

My friend L. Dennis Thompson bought a small stucco house in one of Santa Barbara's older downtown neighborhoods. Dennis is an architect, and he immediately began to make lists of the remodeling jobs he wanted to do. They ranged from plumbing repairs to sky-lights, porches to second-story additions. But because he's working on a tight budget, the projects had to be assigned priorities, with some scheduled as more distant dreams.

Ironically, the job that got done first wasn't the highest on the list. He decided to tackle the bathroom right away because he was made an offer he couldn't refuse—free labor. I was teaching my annual tile-setting course at the local university extension program, and I was looking for a suitable site for hands-on in-

struction. Dennis assured me he could have plans and materials ready in two months.

Superficially, the bathroom looked fine. It had been hastily upgraded to help sell the house. A huge mirror covered one wall, and thin wood paneling had been applied around the tub. But there were gaps between the strips of paneling—a lousy wall covering for a damp location. A cheap carpet covered the old vinyl floor, and the toilet occupied the most prominent spot in the cramped room. Beyond it stood an antique vanity. The room had only one small window, and Dennis wanted a lot more light. So the challenge was to turn an adequate bathroom into a light-filled space, and to give a group of student tile-setters a range of experiences.

Planning with constraints—To reduce costs, Dennis wanted to keep plumbing modi-fications to a minimum. His new plan kept the supply and drain lines in nearly the same place, but switched the location of the vanity and the toilet (drawing, below). This made the vanity the center of attention and tucked the toilet behind a low privacy wall.

The room needed more floor space, but there wasn't any easy way to claim it. The adjacent rooms didn't have any extra square footage to give up, and the setback limitations of the local building code wouldn't allow any footings beyond the existing foundation. The solution was a room-wide bay window with a wide shelf supported by knee braces. Since this bay is defined by the building department

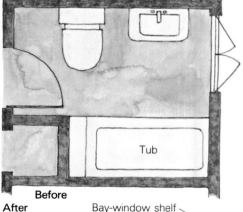

Before

After

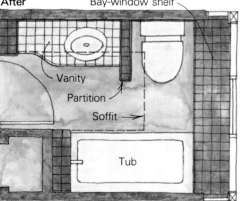

Bay-window shelf

Vanity

Partition

Soffit

Blue tile winds its way around the room in this view from the bay window. The soffits create a coffered ceiling, and mask the dropped header made necessary by the bay window. The old wall mirror was removed and trimmed to compensate for the lowered ceiling, and the scrap piece saved for the medicine-chest door.

From *Fine Homebuilding* magazine (August 1984) 22:65-67

Shower framing
A 2x framework under the blue tile, photo above, made room to run new plumbing supply lines without disturbing the wall behind it.

Rough framing—vanity and partition
Under the vanity's tile finish lies an armature built of standard framing lumber. The counter works as a box beam turned on its side, and it's bolted to the walls at each end to stiffen the entire assembly. The object of this remodel was to add light and the illusion of more space. The photo above shows the result.

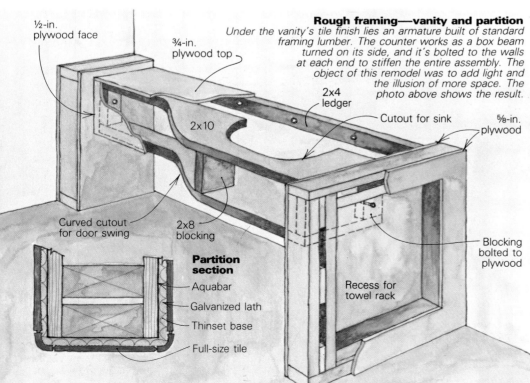

½-in. plywood face

¾-in. plywood top

2x4 ledger

Cutout for sink

⅝-in. plywood

2x10

Curved cutout for door swing

2x8 blocking

Partition section
- Aquabar
- Galvanized lath
- Thinset base
- Full-size tile

Recess for towel rack

Blocking bolted to plywood

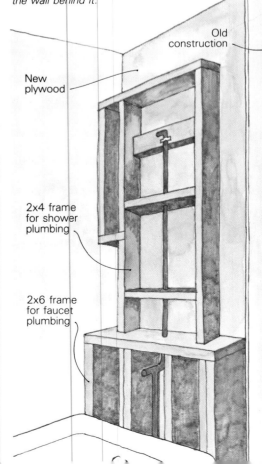

Old construction

New plywood

2x4 frame for shower plumbing

2x6 frame for faucet plumbing

as just another cantilever, it doesn't violate the setback code.

Dennis picked a cobalt-blue tile to establish the color in the room. He wanted it to march along the wall above the vanity, over the partition wall and then wrap around the corner and onto the bay window shelf. To balance this dazzling blue, he chose creamy white tile for the vanity itself and around the tub. He decided that both color tiles should be 4¼ in. square, which would create a strong, grid-like pattern in the room—if everything could be made square and plumb.

To keep from having to trim too many tiles, Dennis drew elevations of the room, at a scale of a half-inch to the foot, showing all the fixtures and every tile in place. The drawings were a lot of work, but they were worth it. They helped both of us to lay out the framing to accommodate the tiles, and to anticipate the detail problems before the place filled up with eager students of the tile trade.

Demolition and new framing—Only one piece of the existing bathroom survived the remodeling—the wall-size mirror over the vanity. We hired a glass company to remove it and cut it down to a size that would fit into the new space. We used the 1-ft. wide scrap that resulted to make a door for the medicine cabinet (photo, p. 125). With the mirror out for fitting, we gutted the bathroom down to the studs, and opened up the exterior wall for the bay window.

The horizontal members that support the bay window (photo right) are essentially floor joists, only at sill height, and they are supported by 2x4 knee braces. These braces are tied to the cripple studs by plywood gussets. The result is a rigid framework that may seem overbuilt, but with two rigid surfaces—stucco finish on the outside and tile on the inside—we didn't want the kind of movement that results in cracks.

The bay faces southeast and catches plenty of sun, so we gave its sill a 1½-in. mortar bed for a bit of thermal mass. The major opening in the bay is finished with three Pella windows. They have double-glazed, snap-in panels, with translucent glass on the inside. The shed roof and ends are fitted with custom-cut pieces of clear safety glass. When the landscaping grows enough to provide some privacy, Dennis plans to replace the translucent glazing with clear glass.

Shower solution—There is a closet between the tub and the hallway, and we didn't want to disrupt the existing framing. The problem was where to run the plumbing for the shower head. Dennis solved this one by detailing a furred-out frame that butts the existing wall, and holds the shower supply line and the tub faucet (photo and drawing, facing page, right). Its dimensions were worked out to allow full tiles wherever possible. This solution left the closet intact, and created a pleasing ceramic sculpture reminiscent of a high-tech office building. The nook near the wall is a good place to store shampoo bottles.

Vanity and partition—In a room this small, all of the parts are interdependent. The low partition wall not only screens the toilet, but also serves as a towel and magazine rack and holds up the end of the vanity top. The vanity, in turn, is a box-beam on its side, and it firmly anchors the partition (photo and drawing, facing page, left).

The thickness of the partition was determined by the width of one full tile plus two quarter-rounds. At its core is a 2x4 frame covered with ⅝-in. plywood. It's best to use kiln-dried lumber for this kind of framing because green lumber will shrink away from the outer layer of tile, creating voids between the two that at the very least will crack the grout. A layer of moisture-barrier paper covers the plywood, followed by a thinset mortar base about ¼ in. thick to bring the wall out to the right dimension for the tile.

I like to use Aquabar B paper (Forti-Fiber, 4489 Bandini Blvd., Los Angeles, Calif. 90023) for the moisture barrier in this kind of work. It's a sandwich of two layers of kraft paper with an asphalt-emulsion center, and it gets high marks for water resistance. It's more pliable than builder's felt, making it a lot easier to fold around angles and projections. Also, it doesn't bulk up at corners the way felt does.

The thinset base hangs on galvanized expanded metal lath. This stuff comes in several weights. I used 3.4 lb. per sq. yd. I specify galvanized lath for wet locations because in many of the bathrooms that I've remodeled, the non-galvanized lath behind the old tile is often close to total disintegration. Although it's nearly impossible to recognize visually, expanded metal lath has a right-side-up. On a vertical surface, the cups in the lath need to slope upward, away from the backing. You can check the lath's orientation by rubbing your hand over it—when you've got it right, the upstroke will feel relatively smooth, while the downstroke will grab at your fingers.

Like the partition, all the tiled surfaces in the room have a thinset bed on lath over plywood. We used bent-over 5d galvanized box nails to secure the lath, and we spaced the nails about every 8 in.—close enough to eliminate any springy spots.

Tiling tips—To begin setting the tile in this room, we marked a line one tile above the top lip of the tub. We carried this index line all around the room, and tacked 1x2 guide boards to the walls just below it. My ten students laid up most of the tile in one weekend. Some mixed thinset, some cut tiles and smoothed edges and some laid up the courses. It was chaotic but marvelous, and I was amazed how ten people could work harmoniously in such a small space.

The tiles that we used have tiny lugs built into their edges to ensure uniform spacing. The danger here is that they will occasionally overlap one another, producing a high tile in an otherwise smooth wall plane. A good way to prevent this problem is to cover the windows and hold a drop light directly above the tile. The raking light will create exaggerated

Virtually the entire exterior wall was removed and reframed to form a greenhouse bay window. To stiffen the structure, triangular gussets tie the horizontal members and their knee braces to the cripple-wall studs.

shadows next to the protrusions, allowing you to correct the position of the tiles before the mortar sets.

The most difficult part of the tiling was laying the curved section in the face of the vanity top. Dennis and I cut lots of little pieces, 1 in. wide, to lay like piano keys around the curve. We used a water-cooled, diamond-blade saw for this, but I wish we'd had a newer blade. The thicker the band of diamond chips on the blade, the cleaner the cut, and our blade left ragged edges that had to be smoothed down with a stone. We gave the tiles a day to set, and then grouted them (see p. 117).

The completed bath is now the most delightful room in the house. The bay window warms up the room at an early hour, and makes it a pleasant place to pry open your eyelids in the morning. Plants do well on the window shelf, and the room contributes a bit of solar heat to the rest of the house when the bathroom door is left open. The large mirror and the bay window team up to create a surprising increase in the amount of light and perceived space.

If Dennis were to do it again, he'd do a few things differently. First, the room needs a heat source other than the windows. It's warm during the day, but chilly at night. Also, he's had second thoughts about the flooring. He finished the floor with oak strips, stained to match the floors in the rest of the house. Hardwood floors in the kitchen and bath are okay for the fastidious, but guest bathers sometimes fail to mop up their splashes, and some of the strips are beginning to cup.

The total cost of the project was almost exactly $7,000, which included replacing some of the old galvanized water pipes under the house with copper ones. Besides getting the bathroom he wanted, Dennis saved about $800 by using student labor. □

Dennis Allen is a contractor who lives in Santa Barbara, Calif.

If you enjoyed this book, you're going to love our magazine.

A year's subscription to *Fine Homebuilding* brings you the kind of practical, hands-on information you found in this book and much more. In issue after issue—seven times a year—you'll find projects that teach new skills, demonstrations of tools and techniques, design ideas, and new materials and methods that will bring home building into the next decade. You'll also find articles about historically significant architects and designers and the contributions they've made to home building.

To subscribe, just fill out one of the attached subscription cards, or call us toll-free at **1-800-888-8286.** And as always, **we guarantee your satisfaction.**

Subscribe Today!

7 issues for just $26